Pragmatist Ethics

SUNY series in American Philosophy and Cultural Thought
―――――――――
Randall E. Auxier and John R. Shook, editors

Pragmatist Ethics

A Problem-Based Approach to What Matters

James Jakób Liszka

Published by State University of New York Press, Albany

© 2021 State University of New York

All rights reserved

Printed in the United States of America

No part of this book may be used or reproduced in any manner whatsoever without written permission. No part of this book may be stored in a retrieval system or transmitted in any form or by any means including electronic, electrostatic, magnetic tape, mechanical, photocopying, recording, or otherwise without the prior permission in writing of the publisher.

For information, contact State University of New York Press, Albany, NY
www.sunypress.edu

Library of Congress Cataloging-in-Publication Data

Name: Liszka, James Jakób, 1950– author.
Title: Pragmatist ethics : a problem-based approach to what matters / James Jakób Liszka.
Description: Albany : State University of New York Press, [2021] | Series: SUNY series in American philosophy and cultural thought | Includes bibliographical references and index.
Identifiers: LCCN 2021023967 | ISBN 9781438485874 (hardcover : alk. paper) | ISBN 9781438485881 (pbk. : alk. paper | ISBN 9781438485898 (ebook)
Subjects: LCSH: Ethics. | Pragmatism. | Ethical problems.
Classification: LCC BJ1031 .L57 2021 | DDC 170—dc23
LC record available at https://lccn.loc.gov/2021023967

10 9 8 7 6 5 4 3 2 1

For Genie Babb

How does one go from a God-ordered world to one of flesh and bone?
Is it like a veil lifted?
Or does it crumble like weather-worn mortar?
Gradually, the wall falls apart
And the cold truth comes through.
What's the exchange?
Heaven for earth, life for death, safety for risk, solace for none.
It's no bargain.
Yet truth has its soothing ways
When one sees the falseness of others.

Contents

Acknowledgments	ix
Notes on In-Text Citations	xi
Introduction	1
Chapter 1. What's the Good of Goodness?	**15**
Plato's Doubts	15
James's Doubts	19
The Tragic Sense of Life	21
Problem-Based Ethics	24
Chapter 2. Pragmatism and the Roots of Problem-Based Ethics	**29**
The Pragmatic Maxim: Theory to Practice	29
Truth and Goodness Reconceived	35
Communities of Inquiry	39
Democracy as a Community of Inquiry	43
Scientific Ethics and Experiments of Living	48
Meliorism: Convergence, Growth, Improvement, Progress	51
Chapter 3. Practical Life	**55**
Practices	55
Practices as Solutions to Problems	57
What Is a Problem?	58
The Normative Character of Practices	60
The Normative Governance of Practices	64

Chapter 4. Practical Reasoning — 69
- The Desire-Belief Model of Moral Motivation — 71
- From Practical Reasoning to Practical Knowledge — 84
- Problems as Moral Guidance — 87

Chapter 5. Normative Science — 91
- The General and the Particular in Practical Knowledge — 93
- Know-How and Know-That — 98
- Practical Hypotheses — 102
- Normative Naturalism — 104
- The Empirical Warrant for Prudential Norms — 107
- The Empirical Warrant for Good Ends and Righteous Means — 108

Chapter 6. Communities of Inquiry — 115
- The Ends and Means of Inquiry — 116
- The Problem of Epistemarchy — 126
- Problems and the Governance of Practices — 134

Chapter 7. Change for the Better — 139
- Progress as Preference for Ways of Life — 139
- The Cumulative Theory of Progress — 142
- Progress as a Function of Problem-Solving Effectiveness — 145
- Moral Progress — 147
- Has There Been Progress? — 154
- Generalizing Problem-Solving Effectiveness — 157

Conclusion — 165

References — 171

Index — 183

Acknowledgments

I would like to thank my colleagues whose comments helped to shape and refine this book. These included presentations at the Society for American Philosophy, the American Philosophy Association, the Charles S. Peirce Society, and the Center for Pragmatism Studies at the Pontifical Catholic University of São Paulo. In addition, I'm grateful to the reviewers of the manuscript whose careful reading improved the original. I would like to acknowledge the very helpful conversations, both written and spoken, with Nathan Houser, Vincent Colapietro, André De Tienne, Ivo Ibri, and Cornellis de Waal. I'm especially beholden to Genie Babb for many long talks that helped to work out some of the more difficult arguments of the book. This book is dedicated to her. I would also like to thank Dr. Michael Rinella, Senior Acquisitions Editor at SUNY Press, for being so helpful in shepherding the manuscript to its publication.

Parts of chapter 2 are extracts from "Peirce's Convergence Theory of Truth Redux," published in *Cognitio* 20(1), 91–112 (2019), and "Rethinking the Pragmatic Theory of Meaning," also published in *Cognitio* 10(1), 61–81. The introduction and chapter 1 use extracts from "New Directions in Pragmatic Ethics," published in *Cognitio* 14(1), 51–62 (2009). Thanks to the editor, Ivo Ibri, for permission to use these passages. Parts of chapter 5 are extracts from "Peirce's Idea of Ethics as a Normative Science," published in *Transactions of the Charles S. Peirce Society* 50(4), 459–79 (2014).

Notes on In-Text Citations

All in-text citations are in APA style, with the following exceptions:

Aristotle. (*title of work*, standard Bekker number).

John Dewey. (original date, *MW*, volume, page). Reference to Dewey, John (2008a). *John Dewey: The middle works, 1899–1924* (Jo Ann Boydson, Ed.). (15 vols.). Southern Illinois University Press.

(original date, *LW*, volume, page). Reference to Dewey, John (2008b). *John Dewey: The later works, 1925–1953* (Jo Ann Boydson, Ed.). (17 vols.). Southern Illinois University Press.

Charles Peirce. (original date, *CP* volume.paragraph). Reference to Peirce, Charles (1978). *The collected papers of Charles Sanders Peirce* (Charles Hartshorne, Paul Weiss & Arthur Burks, Eds.). (8 vols.). Harvard University Press.

(original date, *W* volume, page). Reference to Peirce, Charles (1982–). *Writings of Charles S. Peirce* (Max Fisch, et al., Eds.). (7 vols.). Indiana University Press.

(original date, NEM volume, page). Reference to Peirce, Charles (1976). *The new elements of mathematics* (Carolyn Eisele, Ed.). (4 vols.). Mouton.

(original date, R number, page). Reference to the manuscripts of Charles Peirce, as catalogued in Robin, Richard (1967). *Annotated catalogue of the papers of Charles S. Peirce*. University of Massachusetts Press.

Plato (*title of work*, standard Stephanus pagination).

Introduction

It has been the tradition in philosophy to develop a concept of the good with the hope that it might serve as a guide to solve the problems of practical life. What if the strategy were, instead, to forego a notion of the good in favor of looking to the problems themselves for such guidance? After all, problems tell us what needs fixing and solutions tell us what is better. In this way, they play a normative role comparable to any notion of the good. Serious problems have urgent clarity, but the good remains that obscure object of desire. Aristotle states the obvious ". . . [T]he removal of bad things must be good" (*Rhetoric*, 1362a30–35*)*. The case made here is for a pragmatist ethics, one that looks for moral guidance from the troubles in the works and days of practical life.

Advocates for various concepts of the good—such as pleasure, happiness, utility, flourishing, virtue—assume they can serve as a criterion to measure against the current state-of-affairs. Simply put, the more the difference between the outcomes of actions, and the outcomes envisioned by the particular concept of the good, the less morally satisfactory the current state of affairs. Problem-based ethics works on a different measure. It focuses on progress from previous states of affairs rather than progress toward an ideal good. In *The Ethical Project*, Philip Kitcher emphasizes that moral progress is not measured by decreasing the distance to a fixed goal of the good, but there is progress *from* as well as progress *to* (2011, p. 288). Progress can be measured in terms of the distance from a starting point—rather than progressing toward an ideal. *Pragmatic* progress, as he calls it, is a type of progress that focuses on overcoming problems in the current state (2015, p. 478). Colin Koopman echoes this thought: ". . . [I]nstead of talking about certain practices as true or good, we should instead talk about them as truer and better. Instead of focusing on . . . moral rightness, we should instead focus on . . . moral melioration, improvement, development, and growth" (2015, pp. 11–12). "For better or for worse? Isn't that the crucial thing?" (2015, p. 13).

In the pragmatist approach, problems act like the stones a traveler feels for when crossing the river. A problem makes it patently clear what is undesirable and, thereby, points to an improvement when solved. Thinkers in this tradition, such as John Dewey, are puzzled as to why people think a concept of the good is necessary in order for people to want to improve their lives when, as he writes in *Human Nature and Conduct*, problems confront them daily, motivating them to fix things (1922, *MW* 14, p. 195). After all, as Dewey notes, a doctor rarely attempts to bring a patient to an ideal state of health but focuses rather on improving a poor health condition. Does the medication stop the infection or not, does it reduce the fever?

Problems are strong motivators because people are directly affected by them and, if not directly, then affected by those who are. Serious problems are like a sharp stick in the foot and need addressing one way or another. Sidney Hook noted that "a problematic moral situation . . . expresses a special concern or urgency" and "has a quasi-imperative force" (1950, p. 198). Just as doubt is a subcutaneous irritation, so problems call for resolution. When things are working with a minimum of problems, there's no cry for change, as Dewey says in the *Theory of Valuation* (1939, *LW* 13, p. 220). If things are not working, there's obviously something lacking in the existing situation that drives a change, and hopefully a solution to the problem. Think of the manifold problems of the day: climate change, famine, the COVID-19 pandemic, abortion, war, racism, pollution, wealth distribution, mass killings, terrorism, discrimination, domestic violence, the opioid crisis, corruption, policing, immigration, sustainability, fracking, food insecurity, child labor, LBGTQ rights, genetic enhancement, consumerism, treatment of animals, ethical eating, the death penalty, sexism, euthanasia, health care access and affordability, vaping, suicide, media issues, privacy, mass incarceration, bullying—and the list goes on. The ill in these situations is not something general, but existent in the situation. It has to be discovered and repaired on the basis of the exact defect, something that a general notion of the good cannot do.

Every serious problem solved situates people and communities in a better place on their normative landscape. It may be a tautology, but the more adept a community is at solving its problems—the more effective its problem-solving ability—the more likely the community will become a better one. People want a just society as a goal, but justice is often nominally conceived and indeterminate. In the long run, justice attained is what remains when justice practices become minimally problematic. Kitcher argues that ethical progress is found in the ability to solve normative problems more thoroughly, reliably, and with less costly effort (2011, p. 221). Communities that are good at solving their problems will, perforce, tend to work better than those that do not. If problems are not solved, they tend to accumulate and intensify until a change is welcomed, demanded, or forced. Practices and institutions that work have a tendency to persist or, at least, adapt to changing conditions. The better solutions become indurated as habits, practices, and institutions that manage the problems to various degrees of effectiveness. Like it or not, things will continue to work themselves out until something works out. So long as there is substantial dissatisfaction with the human condition, there will be efforts to improve its lot. Under this view, it is not so much the desirability for the good that drives human effort, as the intolerability of serious problems widely felt and endured.

The effort here is to make a case for a pragmatism-inspired, problem-based ethics—to demonstrate its logic and normative force. It begins in the first chapter with a contrast between Plato's quest for the good, and James's reaction to 2300 years of philosophers following in his footsteps. Plato's failed projects with the elder and younger Dionysios at Syracuse demonstrate the futility of imposing a ready-made ethical ideal on an imperfect community. In "The Moral Philosopher and the Moral Life" (1891), James promotes two radically new theses. First, the role of moral philosophers is not to be the arbiter of what is good. This is a collective, ongoing project. It is worked out through the trial and error of living together over time. Dewey sees eye-to-eye with James. In "The Need for Recovery in Philosophy" (1917), he argues for a new role for the moral philosopher as facilitator, engaged in the moral problems of practical life, rather than an arbiter or law giver wrestling with abstract concepts of the good. Plato failed to prove that in knowing the good people would do the good. Instead, the pragmatists argued that in doing good, people come to know it. As people implement norms and rules in their communities to guide their lives, the lessons of practical life teach which norms are better and which are worse by means of the problems they solve or create. Over time, human condition progresses through experiments of life.

James's second thesis is that there is no one good "to rule them all," that there is a plurality of goods that people seek. But this creates a tragic sense of life, in that no political, social, and normative organization of practical life can in principle accommodate them all. This creates a pattern of disruption and accommodation, disequilibrium and equilibrium that characterizes human history in people's efforts to get their goods recognized and realized. The best that can be hoped for to solve this problem of sociality, of living well together, is by maximizing the number of goods while minimizing the number of problems in doing so. This sets the stage for a problem-solving ethic.

If the original pragmatists were not the first thinkers to see the matter of ethics in practical, functional, problem-solving terms, they were its strongest advocates. The second chapter explores five pragmatist themes that flow together to serve as a platform for problem-based ethics. The first, based on Charles Peirce's pragmatic maxim, is that concepts, including concepts of truth and goodness, can be best understood functionally. True beliefs and good things, as William James interprets the matter, can be understood in terms of what they *do* in practical life, rather than what they are. The second lesson of the pragmatic maxim is that theory can be transposed to practice, theoretical reasoning transposed into practical reasoning. Moreover, the truth of practical hypotheses depends on the truth of their corresponding theoretical or empirical hypotheses. Third, the road to the avoidance of error and true belief was through inquiry done rightly. Fourth, as both Peirce and Dewey argue, successful inquiries into matters of truth and goodness required a community of inquiry with certain norms, and practitioners with certain virtues. Fifth, progress in such inquiries was made through the detection of error in hypotheses, and through the solution to social problems. Progress was indicated by convergence to the truth for Peirce and by growth for Dewey. All-in-all, the triumvirate of Peirce, James, and Dewey provides the platforms for a pragmatist, problem-based ethics.

The goal of the remainder of the book is to show how this platform is built up by a number of thinkers who are sympathetic to the pragmatist tradition and to organize those efforts into a coherent account of a problem-based approach to ethics.

Since the pragmatists insist that ethics is a collective effort done in experiments of practical life, what are the key features of practical life? Chapter 3 begins with an analysis of James Wallace's account in *Norms and Practices* (2009). Practical life is constituted by practices. He argues that practices have three core features: they originate and continue as solutions to practical problems; they are inherently normative, and their principal mode of reasoning is practical reasoning or practical knowledge. Practices are established to solve certain problems. If they persist that is because they continue to solve those problems fairly well. They are normative in the sense that they prescribe the best ways to attain their ends. Practices integrate technical and ethical norms. To be a good carpenter is to be an honest one. Science cannot be done if data is falsified. They involve practical reasoning, which is essentially reasoning concerned with how to attain desirable ends.

Chapter 4 focuses on the matter of practical reasoning. Does it suffice as ethical reasoning? Practical reasoning is usually formulated as reasoning about the means most likely to attain desired ends. It is commonly based on David Hume's (1739) internalist, desire-belief model of human action: people are motivated to act on means that will attain what they desire. Such reasoning appears to be purely instrumental and, thus, ethically problematic. Practical reasoning, so understood, would prescribe the means likely to attain any end, good or bad; it would also prescribe any means that is likely to attain an end, whether those means are right or wrong. Moreover, it would seem subjective in that what is desirable is dependent on the desirer. Practical reasoning, so understood, could permit all sorts of villainy.

Can practical reasoning be reframed to solve these problems? Current debates in metaethics between internalists, such as Mark Schroeder (2013), and externalists, such as Christine Korsgaard (1999), Thomas Nagel (1970), T. M. Scanlon (1998), and Robert Brandom (2000) address that question. It would seem that internalists have to admit that the only reason to act ethically is if it is a means to something the agent desires, such as happiness, or that it is in one's best interest to do so. This, as the externalists claim, suggests that normative claims have very little normative force for people to do the right thing. Externalists argue that people can believe something is right to do and be motivated on the basis of that belief. This defines the divide in contemporary terms between consequentialists and deontologists. Since pragmatists favor practical reasoning, and consequentialism, generally speaking, is their ethical program in trouble?

Robert Brandom provides a way out of this situation by showing how practical reasoning is not necessarily based on a desire-belief model of motivation, but rather on an intention-belief basis. Brandom takes his theory of *normative pragmatics* (1994) and applies it to the matter of practical reasoning (2000). Normative pragmatics argues that speech practices contain norms concerning how it is correct to use speech, under what circumstance it is appropriate to perform those speech acts, and what appropriate consequences such performances entail (1994, p. xiii). When applied to the matter of practical reasoning, it has to be understood that desires are influencers of behavior, but intentions are the conduct-controlling aspect of action since they entail commitments to act. Desires for certain ends may, after all, be simply wishful thinking, but intentions to act imply commitment to do so. If this is combined with Wallace's account of practices, it becomes clear that intentions to act are almost always in the context of some practice, so intentions to act are commitments to the ways and means by which the practice prescribes the pursuit of ends. As Brandom notes, a bank employee may not desire to wear a tie to work, but the intention to go to work is a commitment to the norms of the banking practice which, in this case, prescribes the proper way to dress for work.

In this way there can be objective norms for means to ends that moral agents recognize that trump their subjective desires. Much of the contemporary discussion of practical reasoning treats it as an ahistorical, asocial process, based on what an individual would reason as if individuals were free of any consideration of the practice in which the reasoning is taking place. Since practices are collectively developed and governed, then, to that extent, they are not subjective ways of doing things. People cannot do whatever they wish to do in a community constituted by those practices.

Since practices are collective forms of practical reasoning, there is a collective affirmation that the ends they attain are good and the means righteous. Of course, that does not mean that the collective is right, only that it is not subjective. Practical reasoning in this sense is a collective version of what Aristotle calls *phronesis*, reasoning concerned with doing the right thing in the right way for the right reason (*Nicomachean Ethics*, 1140b 20–21). As such, practical reasoning contains three implicit norms that characterize the normative character of practices: a prudential norm that people ought to do what is likely to attain the ends they desire; a norm of good ends, and a norm of righteous means. Together, when properly ordered, they express an overarching norm of practical reasoning that is ethically conducive: *What ought to be done is what is right to do that is also likely to attain ends that are good to desire.* This makes explicit what Wallace claims to be the inherent normative character of practices, and it constitutes the core of what he calls practical knowledge.

However, this overarching norm is purely formal since it doesn't define what counts as good ends and righteous means. It is argued that problems can serve as a proxy for each variant of good in the overarching norm. Problems do not define what is good, but they indicate where it is present and where it is absent. Since practices are developed and sustained as solutions to problems, then practices that are relatively problem-free are an indication that their means are righteous and their ends good. If they are problematic, then solutions to those problems are indications of what ends to pursue and what means to correct. Both processes together help people converge toward the right sorts of practices. Since practical reasoning for Wallace is problem-solving, then practical reasoning is the means by which the formal aspects of its overarching norm can be specified.

The transposition of theory to practice, theoretical reasoning into practical reasoning is a principal theme of the pragmatists. It is part of the reason that Dewey in particular thought that ethics could be scientific and naturalistic. The pragmatic maxim, for example, argues that the meaning of the scratch-hardness of a diamond is whether it is scratched or scratches other materials, that is, the practical consequences that are observed from interventions in experience. But if the theoretical hypothesis is true, that diamonds scratch glass, then that can be transposed into a practical hypothesis; a hypothetical imperative, namely, if the end is to cut glass, then using diamonds is the best means. Theoretical reasoning can be transposed into practical reasoning, and the truth of a practical hypothesis or a hypothetical imperative gets its warrant from the truth of its corresponding theoretical or empirical hypothesis.

If practical reasoning gets its warrant from scientific reasoning, and if the reformulated version of practical reasoning is a viable form of ethical reasoning, then is it plausible to argue that ethics can be scientific and naturalistic? This is the subject of chapter 5.

Aristotle plainly said that phronesis could not be a science. He thought that, first, it dealt with particulars in varying situations, whereas science deals with generals that do not vary from situation to situation. Contemporary ethical particularists like Jonathan Dancy agree (2004). Second, he thought it was more of a skill than knowledge, requiring keen perception, good judgment, and experience. That was why young people could do science well but were not always good at ethical judgment. A third roadblock to a scientific ethics is the problem of normative naturalism, how are norms to be explained as natural properties.

Wallace addresses the particularist issue in a debate with Martha Nussbaum's work in *Love's Knowledge* (1990). Diana Heney (2016) debates with Jonathan Dancy (2004). Wallace thinks that moral situations always involve a kind of dialogue between generals and particulars. Good plumbers do not come to the job with a blank slate and muck around with the particulars of the situation until they figure out the problem. Heney argues the stronger point that, if the particularlists are right, neither moral learning, nor collective practices would be possible. This clearly flies in the face of what can be readily observed in practical life.

There is a third way to address the problem of particularism as brought out by Frederick Will (1997). Particular moral situations do not involve deductive reasoning in the form of the subsumption of a case under a general rule, but they are more like Peirce's sense of abduction, where surprises or novelties in the situation lead to modifications of practical hypotheses acquired over time. Detection is a good example, where detectives come to a crime with a set of practical hypotheses about murders, but the discovery of certain pieces of evidence may cause them to modify or even reject those hypotheses in this particular case but not reject them outright for other cases yet to come. Detectives may have learned as a general rule to suspect the husband if the wife has been murdered, but there can always be clues that dispose of that hypothesis in a particular situation. However, that does not necessarily cause them to dismiss the practical hypothesis since it is statistically true. Since, according to Peirce, abduction is part of scientific reasoning, then explaining surprises or anomalies in observations of particular situations is as much a part of scientific reasoning as inductive reasoning.

The issue of whether practical knowledge is more of a skill than knowledge can be articulated in terms of Gilbert Ryle's distinction between know-that and know-how (1949). The received view of expertise is the Dreyfus model (2005), which insists on a distinction in kind between know-that and know-how. This is reframed in psychology as a distinction between declarative knowledge and procedural knowledge. If that's the case, if practical knowledge is more about skill than knowledge, and science about knowledge, then it seems unlikely that ethics can be scientific.

There are two responses that could be made to this. One is to take the position of Jason Stanley (2011) that, contrary to the received view, know-how is really know-that; it is a specific form of what he calls *know-wh*, knowing when, where, why and how to do something. Knowing how to catch a fly ball must fit into a more general account of knowing when to catch a fly ball, where to position one's glove, and so forth, in order to catch the ball. But a second position takes the commonsense view that the practice of science like any practice requires skill. Doing science is not all about knowledge of facts and theories, but laboratory or field work, technical expertise, learning how to fix instruments. Scientists have to acquire skills in the lab, as much as the knowledge of chemistry in order to do chemistry right.

This leaves the bigger question of normative naturalism. It is thought that one of the strongest arguments against normative naturalism is the so-called naturalistic fallacy, the open question argument, proposed by G.

E. Moore. As he describes the fallacy, a claim that the good is a natural property, such as pleasure or happiness, still leaves an open question as to whether pleasure or happiness is a good end to pursue (1903: sect. 10). Non-naturalists such as Derek Parfit (2011) and Russ Shafer-Landau (2003) make variants of this argument.

Taking the lead from Larry Laudan (1987), it is argued that, whether or not normative properties can be reduced to natural ones, normative claims share the same epistemology as empirical ones. This by-passes the ontological question of whether norms are natural or non-natural entities and, so, avoids the naturalistic fallacy in that way. If the warrant for the three norms in practical reasoning lie in corresponding empirical claims, then this argues for the *plausibility* of a genuine normative science. Whether ethics can achieve the status of a science is another matter.

Consider the prudential norm that people ought to do what is likely to achieve the ends they desire. A prudential norm is a hypothetical imperative: If one desires X, then one ought to do Y. But that claim is true just in case doing X likely attains Y, which is an empirical claim. Although a reason for doing X is that the prudential norm commands people to do that which is likely to attain what they desire, that is only warranted if doing X likely attains Y. If doing X did not attain Y, then the prudential norm alone would not justify doing X. The normative force of the prudential norm lies in the truth of its corresponding empirical claim.

There is a somewhat more complicated case to be made for the norm of good ends. Good ends here have been characterized in terms of a proxy, that is, in terms of problems. The matter of good ends requires two interconnected arguments. The first concerns identifying something as a problem, which seems to be an evaluative, normative claim. Counting something as a problem seems to be counting something as bad, morally speaking, and, therefore, claiming that it is undesirable. The second concerns the norm of good ends translated to the matter of solving problems, namely, that people ought to pursue solutions to problems as good ends to pursue.

The first argument relies on the ethical supevenience thesis, which has wide support. It argues that normative properties supervene on natural ones. Something that is counted as good or bad supervenes on natural properties, such that a change in the natural properties results in a change in their evaluation, normatively speaking. If famine is bad, it is because it has certain natural properties and empirical markers, such as death or ill health as a result of starvation. If famine led to good health, and had no other ill effects, it would certainly not be counted as morally bad. Thus, the warrant for claiming something bad is that it has certain natural properties and, since problems are counted as bad things, it would also hold for identifying something as a problem.

If the empirical markers of a situation are what warrants counting them as a problem, there is still the question of what warrants the norm that people ought to seek solutions to problems. To the extent that something is identified as a problem, it is also identified as bad, an undesirable state of affairs. Consequently, to the extent that something is considered to be a likely solution to a problem, then that is identified as a desirable state of affairs. Since, by the norm of prudential reasoning, people ought to do what is likely to attain what they desire, then people ought to do what is likely to solve their problems. But since the warrant for any prudential norm is an empirical one, then the normative force for pursuing the solution to a particular problem is also empirical, to the extent that the proposed solution is likely to solve the problem.

There is, finally, the norm of righteous means to consider. What warrants that norm? Given Wallace's claim that practices are inherently normative since they prescribe and proscribe right ways to attain the ends of the practice, it would follow that, assuming the ends good, the ways prescribed are not right if they tend to make the practice problematic. Since problems have empirical markers, the warrant for counting something as a righteous means would be based on the empirical markers associated with problems that the means of the practice create. Since the prudential norm claims that people ought to do what is likely to attain what they desire, and it is desirable to have relatively problem-free practices, then people ought to retain those practices that work and fix those that cause problems.

A community that solves their problems is better for it. If communities are to be successful in solving their problems, they must engage in inquiries for that purpose and use practical reasoning in solving those problems. The pragmatists insist that such inquiries must be a collective endeavor over time and, so, involve the community in such inquiries. Peirce, Dewey, and contemporary pragmatists such as Cheryl Misak (2000), Robert Talisse (2005), and Diana Heney (2016) argue that in order to be successful, such communities of inquiry require certain norms of practice, and demand certain virtues of their inquirers. Peirce recognized that scientific inquiry involved methodological and logical norms, as well as ethical ones, the latter counted among the "most vital factors" in the practice of inquiry (1902, *CP* 7.87). This is the subject of chapter 6.

The practice of inquiry, like any practice, is claimed to have good ends and righteous means that prescribe the most likely way to achieve that end. The end of moral inquiry, these thinkers argue, is truth. Relative to problem solving, this boils down to discovering true practical hypotheses, hypotheses that, if translated as interventions, will likely ameliorate the problem. To the extent that such hypotheses do ameliorate problems, this is a measure of what Larry Laudan calls their "problem-solving effectiveness" (1977, p. 5).

As to means, they must be both righteous and effective to satisfy the overarching norm of noninstrumental practical reasoning. The most effective means for inquires known to human beings is scientific methodology, generally understood. Since, by the prudential norm, people should employ means that are most likely to achieve their ends, then, to the extent possible, science should be employed to develop and test such practical hypotheses. Short of that, inquirers must use the next best means of inquiry.

As to the righteous norms of inquiry, Misak follows Peirce in articulating these as openness to inquiry, commitments to provide reasons and justifications to others, and the equality of roles in the inquiry, allowing others to make criticisms and counterclaims, to ask questions, to seek clarifications, and the like. Misak argues, like Karl-Otto Apel (1980), Jürgen Habermas (1990), and Robert Brandom (1994) that these norms are implicit in making assertions or claims, as inspired by Peirce as well.

Robert Talisse raises Dewey's question of whether the norms of communities of inquiry should be the norms of communities as such. Since practices need practices of inquiry to right their wrongs, and communities are constituted by practices that have wider and narrower domains, then shouldn't the community as a whole adopt the norms of inquiry? Misak thinks that the norms of inquiry are more or less the norms of democracy, equality, and freedom of speech in particular. So, in effect, the norms of inquiry more or less validate the basic norms of a democracy.

However, Talisse points out that if inquiries aim at truth, then adopting the norms of inquiry for a community as a whole might be more consistent with what he calls an "epistemarchy" than a democracy. If truth is the end of inquiry, shouldn't those with expertise in inquiry, those who have the practical knowledge, have a greater share in the governance of the practices in which they have the expertise? After all, by analogy, why bother with amateurs when a cure for cancer is at stake. Yet this would seem to violate the basic norm of democracy, participation by the governed in their governance. Ironically, this calls up the position of Plato's republic, which the pragmatists had hoped to discredit. As David Estlund (1993) characterizes the problem, how can truth be a guiding factor in practices without privileging expertise?

Interestingly, John Dewey tackles this problem is his book *The Public and Its Problems* in 1927. It is a debate with Walter Lippmann who, in *The Phantom Public* (1927), argued for a rule by expertise as a way to cure some of the problems of modern democracy. Lippmann argued convincingly that it is an illusion to think that there is an omnicompetent public, who would have enough knowledge and information to meaningfully participate in the government agencies that govern it, as democratic principles dictate. This job must fall to experts in each of these areas. Thus, the role of the public is mostly to use whatever democratic means available to identify problems with expert governance and to use voting and other mechanisms to get rid of those who are causing the problems.

Dewey concedes Lippmann's account of the eclipse of the public in democracy but holds to the fundamental principle of a social democracy—the participation of the governed in the practices of governing. The remedy requires, so Dewey argues, more opportunities for dialogue, debate, and conversation, less political propaganda, and better dissemination of the results of scientific inquiries on matters of public concern. Most would say that's a tall order. The important point that can be garnered from this debate is that practices, both large and small, both wide-ranging and narrowly focused must devise the ways and means by which their problems can be remedied. They must be designed for self-correction. This involves the cooperation of expert practitioners and the publics that are affected by the problems. Practices must devise ways and means by which the publics affected can identify those problems and propose their remedies. Practices must establish the best scientific means to sort out the more plausible practical hypotheses for their solution, implement interventions, and use the best scientific methods to assess their effectiveness, particularly as gauged by the affected publics. Finally, practices must provide the ways and means by which failed practical hypotheses can be replaced or amended.

How do communities know that the solutions to their problems are making things better, that there is genuine progress? This is the subject of chapter 7. Philip Kitcher tackles this problem in his book *The Ethical Project* (2011). He argues that ethical progress is made to the extent that communities solve their altruism problems. He understands these, as James did, as problems of expanding the circle for the enjoyment of endorsable ends and goods, while minimizing the problems that emerge in doing so. To the extent that ethical norms persist and continue to solve these sorts of problems, then they can be counted as right and true.

How do communities know that these corrections, proposed solutions to their problems are making things better, that there is genuine progress? This is the subject of chapter 7. It is argued here that Larry Laudan's notion of problem-solving effectiveness can provide a good understanding of what constitutes progress. It is thought that science makes progress, but what makes it so? Laudan argues that it is science's ability to solve problems, to detect error in hypotheses and to make corrections, that accounts for progress in science. Laudan identifies two important features of problem-solving effectiveness: saliency and efficacy. Saliency involves ranking, so that the progressive theory is one that solves the more important problems that its predecessor could not solve. Efficacy, on the other hand, is a feature of a theory such that it is able to create scaffolds for more solutions and solves other problems that emerge at a good rate, so that problems do not outpace solutions.

Although Laudan provides a good account of *scientific* progress, Philip Kitcher addresses the problem of *moral* progress in his book, *The Ethical Project* (2011). To make moral progress, a community must be able to solve the problems of sociality. Problem-solving requires solidarity and must avoid polarization. It must maximize cooperation and minimize conflict as people pursue their various ends. Kitcher sees the problems of sociality as mainly altruism problems, that is, failures to recognize and act on the good of others. Kitcher argues that moral progress is made to the extent that communities correct or change norms that solve their altruism problems better than those norms previously held. Moral progress occurs when, as James argued, norms are adopted that expand the circle of those who can attain collectively endorsable ends and goods, while minimizing the problems that emerge in doing so. To the extent that ethical norms persist and continue to solve these sorts of altruism problems, then they can be counted as right and true.

Laudan's notion of problem-solving effectiveness can provide more definition to Kitcher's notion of moral progress. If practices are designed to solve certain problems, then progress happens when changes to those practices solves their more salient problems more efficaciously than what was previously adopted. Changes to means, ends or the norms that govern those means and ends are progressive to the extent that they solve the most critical, basic and common problems; and they do so in such a way so that more people enjoy more of the collectively endorsable goods that the community provides.

The human condition is rife with problems and is poorer for it. Rather than looking to a vague notion of the good for solutions, problem-based ethics focuses on solutions to problems as markers of moral progress. Although, certainly, people act on their concepts of the good, people are more motivated to solve problems directly, either because they are affected by them, or they are affected by those suffering the problems. Problems identify what is wrong in the world, and solutions to these problems tend to make the human condition better. The better solutions become indurated as habits, practices, and institutions that manage the problems to various degrees of effectiveness. On the other hand, when problems are not reasonably resolved or managed, things fall apart. Habits dissolve, and practices change as new problems arise, and old ways no longer work. To solve problems well, a community needs to strengthen its problem-solving effectiveness. The better the community is at solving its problems, the better the community.

Chapter 1

What's the Good of Goodness?

Plato's Doubts

Plato must have had his doubts. The deep Mediterranean blues of the Ionian Sea and the green and tawny-colored islands near the shores may have been calming, but Plato was surely reflecting on his third failed voyage to Syracuse. He had just escaped from Dionysius the Younger, the Tyrant of Syracuse, thanks to the intercession of Lamiscus, whose thirty-oared ship now bore him toward the Peloponnesus to meet Dion.

It was his disciple, Dion, uncle to the young Dionysius, who had begged him to return to Syracuse for the third time, despite the disaster with Dionysius the Elder and the first try with his son. But Dion believed that the young Dionysius had changed and was ready for the teachings of Plato. Dion's own position in the government was influential, and he had a number of kindred folk who also believed as he did. Plato remembered Dion's entreating words in his *Seventh Epistle*: "Now, if ever then will be realized any hope there is that the world will ever see the same man both philosopher and ruler of a great city" (*Seventh Letter*, 328a). Plato believed this too. If anyone were ever to attempt to realize his ideals in regard to laws and government, "now was the time for the trial." If he "were to convince but one man, that in itself would ensure complete success" (*Seventh Letter*, 328c). His greatest fear was to be, at last, "nothing but words," someone who would never "lay hand to any concrete task" and, thereby, to prove traitor to his own philosophy (*Seventh Letter*, 328c).

The doubts he had to have were not about politics as a means to the good and just society. He had already, long ago, given up that hope after witnessing the abuses of the Thirty Tyrants in Athens, their orgy of murder of many good Athenians. The Restored Democracy was not much better since they put to death the wisest and most just man in Athens, his great teacher, Socrates (*Seventh Letter*, 325b). In fact, he concluded that all states were beyond redemption (*Seventh Letter*, 326a). No, the doubts had to be about what he contrived as a remedy to the disappointment of political practice. He thought the only hope was the correct philosophy, an ideal of goodness and justice that could afford a vantage point from which all cases of what is just for communities and for individuals could be discerned. The human race "would not see better days until those who rightly and genuinely follow this philosophy acquire political authority." The only alternative would be if, through some disposition of providence and "much good luck," they lit upon the right way (*Seventh Letter*, 326a). For all his brilliance, Plato's remedy was simple: since the political world was an inferior copy of the ideal form of justice, use the ideal of goodness and justice to correct the copy (Vlastos, 1981, p. 217). Here, as Dion had urged, was the one chance to make a trial of his remedy. He needed only one man to heed it. Had Dionysius been won over, practically all of humankind "would have been brought deliverance by its spread" (*Seventh Letter*, 336a).

Its failure had to be a great blow. So thought the renowned Plato scholar, Gregory Vlastos, among others (Vlastos, 1981, p. 216; Morrow, 1954, p. 6; Gould, 1955, p. 163; Von Wilamowitz-Moellendorff, 1919). Vlastos reckons "Plato's early faith in enlightened absolutism . . . crashed" just after "Plato's final encounter with Dionysius the Younger." He thought ". . . the disillusionment came when he was more than 60—66 or 67, if my guess is right" (1981, p. 216).

So, why wasn't Dionysius won over? If goodness was so good, so beneficial, justice so great, why did he not grasp at the opportunity to know their ideal forms like a hungry man to a feast? How did Plato reconcile all of that? When Plato learned later that Dion, his disciple, had overthrown Dionysius and had become ruler of Syracuse, but in a short period had been assassinated by his own supporters, he still relied on his old ways of thinking. In the defense of his actions in an epistle written to the followers and kin of Dion, he still held onto the Socratic-inspired belief that to know the good was to do the good (*Protagoras*, 358c 6-d4; Xenophon, 371 BCE, III.9.5; Burnet, 1914, p, 170; Cornford, 1932, p. 51; Shorey, 1965, p. 21; Taylor, 1957, p. 27; Vlastos, 1956, p. xxxviii). Therefore, if Dionysius did wrong, it was because he was ignorant of the good, and he was ignorant of the good because he did not have the character nor the wherewithal to acquire such knowledge. The failure with Dionysius lies in Dionysius—not Plato's theory of the good.

To know the good is to do the good and its corollary—to do evil is to be ignorant of the good—is argued succinctly in *The Meno* (77–78a–b). Socrates asks Meno whether everyone desires the good. Meno says some do and some don't. Socrates asks whether it is possible that people who recognize evils as evils still desire them? Yes, Meno answers. Socrates responds: Do they desire them because they believe the evils will bring benefit, or because they believe they will bring harm to the possessor? Both, replies Meno. Of the first sort, Socrates, asks, do those who desire evils because they think they will benefit them, really think they are evil? Meno supposes not, so, Socrates concludes, they are simply mistaken in thinking that something is good, when in fact it is evil. Of the second sort, Socrates asks, do they really believe that something that harms them will bring them benefit? No, that can't be, replies Meno. So, Socrates concludes, nobody desires evil. People want what will benefit them. The good is always beneficial (*Meno*, 87e). Thus, if they believe something is good for them, they will want to do it, and if they know what is good, they will do it.

However, to know the good was not an easy task, he argued. Knowledge of these ideal forms "must come rather after a long period of attendance on instruction in the subject itself and of close companionship" (*Seventh Epistle*, 342d). To achieve enlightenment about the forms of justice and goodness, a supplicant must work through layers of appearances, first with names, then definitions, experience with its sensible shapes, but then on to knowledge and understanding, which is closest to the real forms of justice and goodness. But the apprehension of those forms—the "fifth" thing—occurs when "a flash of understanding blazes up" (*Seventh Epistle*, 344b). But if this account explained why it was difficult to achieve such knowledge, it also showed why it was difficult to verify that someone had achieved it.

Plato implicitly laid claim to this knowledge. Surely, if whoever achieves such enlightenment could communicate it to others, that would be the most useful thing in the world. As Aristotle understated the matter: "Will not the knowledge of it [the highest good], then, have a great influence on our way of life, and would we not be more likely to attain the desired end like archers who have a mark to aim at?" (*Nicomachean Ethics*, 1094a22–24). Yet, Plato insisted that it could not be communicated; it could not be written about. But even if it could, it should not. Plato believed that if there were to be such a treatise, he could do it best; but, even if he could, to spread it to the mass of people would only create contempt for these ideals. No, this was a matter for the very few, those who would be capable of discovering the truth for themselves (*Seventh Epistle,* 341d-e). For these reasons, "no serious man will ever think of writing about serious realities for the general public" (*Seventh Epistle,* 344c).

A thinker as good as Plato had to work through the logic of all of this. The forms of goodness and justice could only be apprehended by a few. They could only know them through a singular event, after an arduous course of study. The person would know it through a flash of understanding. That meant that only the person experiencing this singular event and the mentor would know they know it. But that meant the means by which such knowledge was acquired prevented it from being verified by others. Once acquired, it could not be communicated to others, nor should it be. Hence, it must be adopted by others solely on the faith and trust of someone's claim to know them through an event that cannot be replicated by others or, at most, a very few, nor verified except by the individual claiming to know it. As David Estlund says, "Who will know the knowers? No knower is knowable enough to be accepted by all reasonable citizens" (1993, p. 71).

If that were the case, Plato had to face the most radical question: *What then would be the good of goodness?* What would be the good of this ideal form of goodness? If Plato's remedy was to mold the imperfect, woe-begotten forms of government by an ideal form of justice and goodness known by a few and incommunicable to others, its logic had to be the road to despair (Gould, 1955, p. 163).

As it turns out, not only did Plato fail to persuade Dionysius to the good as he understood it, but he could not persuade a good number of those who followed him—including his student Aristotle. Many of these people—wise, scholarly, and well-intentioned—all with no mean intelligence and on the same quest as Plato, were all perfect supplicants. Yet, they did not hear their master's voice. The result has been a cacophony of claims about the good.

Although some scholars disagree, it seems that in the last work before his death, *The Laws,* Plato may have at last given up the remedy, the quest to correct imperfect communities by means of the ideal of goodness and justice (Gould, 1955; Von Wilamowitz-Moellendorff, 1919; Vlastos, 1981; Morrow, 1954). Perhaps Plato could see with the hardening of age that immorality is common enough, and even those averse to wrongdoing are not always attracted to what is right. *The Laws* clearly has a different character and tone than his other dialogues. It is without the voice of Socrates, and it foregoes drama in favor of the serious business of laying out a constitution for the new city of Magnesia, one that is constrained by the way people are, and so is "second best" compared to the city of the Republic (*The Laws,* 722b5–c2). In *The Laws,* Plato gives up the idea that to know the good is to do the good. He says this plainly: "There is no man whose natural endowments will ensure that he shall both discern what is good for human kind as a community and invariably be both able and willing to put the good into practice when he has perceived it" (*The Laws,* 875a). For this reason, in Magnesia, the focus is on cultivation of character rather than knowledge of the good, and establishing practices that can check and balance corruption and power. Plato also realizes that, contrary to *The Republic,* in Magnesia, there must be an effort to persuade people to what is best and just, rather than having such a matter imposed upon them (*The Laws,* 772b5–c2).

James's Doubts

Certainly 2300 years of effort at this quest for the good without consensus struck William James as problematic at the very least. In his reflection in 1891, "The Moral Philosopher and the Moral Life," he agreed that "if it were found that all goods *qua* goods contained a common essence, then the amount of this essence involved in any one good would show its rank in the scale of goodness, and order could be quickly made; for this essence would be *the* good upon which all thinkers were agreed, the relatively objective and universal good that the philosopher seeks. . . ." (1891, p. 606). But what stands out in history instead is the discordance of such claims: "A mean between two extremes; to be recognized by a special intuitive faculty; to make the agent happy for the moment; to make others as well as him happy in the long run; to add to his perfection or dignity; to harm no one; to follow from reason . . . from universal law; to be in accordance with the will of God; to promote the survival of the human species. . . ." The list concludes with a rather somber statement: "No one of the measures that have been actually proposed has, however, given general satisfaction" (1891, p. 607).

James traveled to Yale from his home in Boston, to deliver this—one of the most radical talks on ethics—to Yale's Philosophical Club. One could not have spoken at a more staid, traditional institution at that time. But it's interesting to note that, looking some years ahead, by 1905 three of the five papers delivered to the Philosophical Club had to do with James's pragmatism (Yale University 1905, pp. 174–175). Pragmatism had taken hold.

If Plato's thesis was to know the good is to do the good, James's thesis was to do the good was to know it. What is good gets sorted out in the trial and error of living experiments. Just as James claimed that "truth happens to an idea," so any claim to the truth becomes evident as it works in experience, so too with any norm, any notion of the good. The good cannot be preconceived then applied artificially to human practices. James states this theme directly: "the main purpose of this paper is to show that there is no such thing possible as an ethical philosophy dogmatically made up in advance. We all help to determine the content of ethical philosophy so far as we contribute to the race's moral life" (1891, p. 595).

James cringes at the thought of something like Plato's Syracuse experiment actually taking hold. He is afraid of "individual moralists . . . as pontiffs armed with the temporal power, and having authority in every concrete case of conflict to order which good shall be butchered and which shall be suffered to survive. . . ." "The notion," he says, "really turns one pale. . . ." James is afraid enough that he thinks, "Better chaos forever than an order based on any closet-philosopher's rule, even though he were the most enlightened possible member of his tribe" (1891, p. 610).

James juxtaposes the works and days, the problems of practical life, where people seek what they deem good and struggle to attain it, with the quest of philosophers for a single essence to the good, an "effort to substitute the content of their clean-shaven systems for that exuberant mass of goods with which all human nature is in travail, and groaning to bring to the light of day" (1891, p. 610). "On the whole," he says,

> we must conclude that no philosophy of ethics is possible in the old-fashioned absolute sense of the term. Everywhere the ethical philosopher must wait on facts. The thinkers who create the ideals come he knows not whence, their sensibilities are evolved he knows not how, and the question as to which of two conflicting ideals will give the best universe then and there, can be answered by him only through the aid of the experience of other men. (1891, p. 613)

Instead of archers with an ideal target, as Aristotle suggests, the situation is more like the Chinese proverb: "We must cross the river by feeling for the stones."

But all this striving for goods leads to a "tragic situation." Not all that people desire and believe to be desirable and hold right to have can be held together in the same order of things—either because they oppose one another, or because they tug at the curtain of delusion, or there is simply not the wherewithal to attain them. There is always some dissatisfaction with the way things are "some part" of someone's "ideal must be butchered" (1891, p. 609), and "the good which we have wounded returns to plague us with interminable crops of consequential damages, compunctions, and regrets" (1891, p. 615).

The Tragic Sense of Life

Many years later, in 1959, Sidney Hook—the student of John Dewey—gave a talk to philosophers at the American Philosophical Association and characterized this pragmatic vision of goodness as a "tragic sense of life," but perhaps better described as a fundamental *irony of life*. Irony in the narrative sense, like Orwell's *1984,* in which an oppressive order seems to prevail. By the tragic sense of life, Hook says, "I mean . . . a very simple thing which is rooted in the very nature of the moral experience and the phenomenon of moral choice. Every genuine experience of moral doubt and perplexity in which we ask: "What should I do?" takes place in a situation where good conflicts with good." It is a situation in which "Apparent good opposes apparent good. . . . No matter how we resolve the opposition some good will be sacrificed, some interest, whose immediate craving for satisfaction may be every whit as intense and authentic as its fellows . . ." (1959, p. 13).

Dewey, his mentor, had written that moral problems arise because of a struggle "between values each of which is an undoubtedly good in its place but which now get in each other's way" (1932, *LW* 7, p. 165). In "Three Independent Factors in Morality," Dewey explains this more systematically. Historically, there appears to be three different and incommensurate sources of morals. One is found in the desire for what is good in life, typically identified as pleasure or happiness. In time, this becomes elaborated teleologically as a system of goods, ending in an ultimate good (1930, *LW* 5, p. 282). The notions of duty and right emerge when it becomes clearly necessary to adjudicate among conflicts and demands from others in the pursuit of these goods. Dewey sees one other source of morality in the common practice of approbation and disapproval, which becomes manifested in the exercise of virtue and vice (1930, *LW* 5, p. 285). For Dewey, moral problems exist because these three sources of morality are intertwined in moral situations so as to cause conflict. The desire for a good may conflict with a duty and each, in turn, may conflict with what is socially approved. Dewey concludes:

> Each of these variables has a sound basis, but because each has a different origin and mode of operation, they can be at cross purposes and exercise divergent forces in the formation of judgment. (1930, *LW* 5, p. 280)

Hook argues that "the quest for the unique good of the situation, for what is to be done here and now, may point to what is better than anything else available but what it points to is also a lesser evil." (1959, p. 20). This is important to note. The pragmatists did not seek to realize an ideal, to perfect what is, but to improve on things by lessening what is imperfect. He continues,

> As I understand the pragmatic perspective on life, it is an attempt to make it possible for men to live in a world of inescapable tragedy, a tragedy which flows from the conflict of moral ideals—without lamentation, defiance or make-believe. According to this perspective even in the best of human worlds there will be tragedy—tragedy perhaps without bloodshed but certainly not without tears. (1959, p. 22)

When thought through, the upshot of pragmatism's tragic sense of life is that there cannot be an ultimate good, a good "to rule them all." If, in James's words, there are goods groaning to see the light of day, yet there are among them those that oppose one another, then there can be no order in which all of those goods worthy of consideration align with some ultimate good. If, in Aristotle's opening words of the *Nicomachean Ethics*, "every practical art, every inquiry, every action and decision, seems to aim at some good," his conclusion, that the "Good is that at which all things aim," does not necessarily follow (*Nicomachean Ethics*, 1049a3–4). Just because all things aim at some good does not infer that there is the same good at which all things ultimately aim. Aristotle notes this. True, he says, there are many types of arts, inquiries, and actions and, correspondingly, many kinds of ends (*Nicomachean Ethics*, 1049a1–2). Thus, there does not appear to be any unifying end—unless—Aristotle argues, all of these ends can be ordered through a chain of ends becoming means to other ends until, finally, there is some end which is a means to no other end (*Nicomachean Ethics*,

1094a20). Yes, if one could find that ultimate end for which everything is ultimately done then, as James argues, a moral order could be quickly made (1891, p. 606).

What else can that be, Aristotle asks, but flourishing? Yet as soon as it is named, Aristotle has to sort through the differing, contrary views of what it means. Some say it is wealth, some pleasure, others honor and fame. Many more definitions could be added. There are approximately 20,000 titles on Amazon with happiness in them. They don't all agree. Things do not appear to be settled. Perhaps this is why Schopenhauer claims that happiness "lies always in the future" (1818, vol. 2, p. 573).

But Aristotle argues that these people are mistaken because none of these fit the mold of a highest good. But—wait—wasn't the highest good something supposed, not proven? It's true that all these people say happiness is the goal—and they may be mistaken about what happiness is, so, like archers, they may miss the right target, hit the wrong one, or simply have no clue where to aim. How is the target known? Dewey remarks, "Men hoist the banner of the ideal, and then march in the direction that concrete conditions suggest and reward" (1909, *MW* 4, p. 224).

Hook understood the tragic, like James, as a conflict among goods that cannot be resolved in a manner that allows all of them to flourish. Some pragmatists, such as Raymond Boisvert, argue that Dewey and, by implication, Hook, seem to deny a deeper sense of the tragic that would challenge the whole ethic of meliorism. Boisvert argues that Dewey seems to ignore the common experience witnessed in history, the sense of "necessity" that constrains human progress, forces larger than what human beings can control by their intelligence (1999, p. 155). Despite Dewey's childhood experience of the Civil War, his witness of the horrors of the World Wars, and the Great Depression, Boisvert claims that Dewey seems to push on with the belief in an inevitable progress (1999, p. 153). As evidence, he claims Dewey's support of the Enlightenment's sense of progress.

But Dewey was certainly ambivalent about that period. In *Freedom and Culture,* written in 1939, just as the world was experiencing a confluence of three political movements that threatened the world order—fascism, Nazism, and Stalinism, he cautioned against a "simple faith" of the Enlightenment "that assured advance of science will produce free institutions . . ." (1939, *LW* 13, p. 156). As Donald Morse argues with goodly textual support, Dewey saw the world in terms of risk, the possibility of failure, danger, uncertainty and instability, with the possibility of complex and large-scale problems such as famine, plague, disease and war always just around the corner (2001,

p. 561). The ability of human beings to control this inexorable order of things is minimal. Even if science is able to secure "a degree of power of prediction and of control," still, ". . . the fundamentally hazardous character of the world is not seriously modified, much less eliminated" (1925, *LW* 1, p. 45). Dewey is hardly the naïve optimist, or the wistful utopian that Boisvert makes him out to be. Progress is neither inevitable, nor is it all-encompassing. Regress is just as likely as progress.

Dewey is a meliorist. It's a position that sits between the two poles of naïve optimism and jaded pessimism. Meliorism confronts evils head on, recognizes that they are real, and forces a humility in the effort to solve the evils, the problems of the day (1920, *MW* 12, p. 181). Optimism tends to think of the world as the best possible, and it is usually the viewpoint of those already privileged. As such, it conspires with pessimism to turn off sympathy for those who are enduring the problems of the world (1920, *MW* 12, pp. 181–182). As Morse puts Dewey's position in commonsense terms:

> This view does not deny tragedy; on the contrary, it admits the full force of evil and horror, of forces that may well crush us in certain circumstances, and simply asks us to respond to these and other circumstances as well as we can so that *maybe* we can make a difference somehow. More precisely, it asks us to determine first whether anything can be done *before* we accept that we are in a tragic and intractable situation. And it asks us to accept that, *after* a tragic situation, which will indeed be undeniably horrible, we *learn* from it. (2001, p. 564)

Problem-Based Ethics

So, if life is tragic both in the sense of an inevitable conflict of goods and an oppressive order to things that constrains human striving, can anything be done about it? Can things be made better? Is progress possible, granted that it is not inevitable? Both Hook's and Dewey's answers are clear: *To make things better is to resolve the problems of the day.* This is why pragmatism "focuses its analysis on problems . . . in order to reduce the costs of tragedy" (Hook, 1959, p. 22). Hilary Putnam calls Dewey a "hero" for ". . . emphasizing that the function of ethics is not, in the first instance to arrive at "universal principles." The primary aim of the ethicist, in Dewey's view . . . should not be to produce a "system" but to contribute to the solution of practical problems ..." (2004, p. 4). To use James Kennedy's handy phrase, the measure of goodness is the reciprocal of problems and error, so the index of improvement is a reduction of the kind and number of problems present in human communities (Kennedy & Eberhart, 2001, p. 50).

In his opening remarks of his address to the American Philosophical Association, Hook recounts his experience at a prestigious international conference, with the theme of what bearing philosophy had on social practice. As he recalls, the participants were told "to imagine that we had the ear of the statesmen of the world, and were challenged to give them counsel on how to put the world's affair in order." "No one," Hook said, "recalled Plato's experience at Syracuse."

In was his opinion that the task of the philosopher is not to offer ready-made solutions on the basis of principles or pronouncements about value, but to "immerse himself in the actual subject matters . . . out of which life's problems arise." "To enumerate the ends of the good life is not enough" (1959, p. 8). The philosopher must recognize that philosophy should "not start from a complete stock of philosophical wisdom which it dispenses to others with hortatory fervor but with an initial sense of concern to meet the challenge of the great unresolved problems of our time . . ." (1959, p. 9). "Problems . . . of morals in the broad sense—are the primary—not exclusive—subject matter of philosophy, and that reason or scientific intelligence can and should be used to resolve them" (1959, p. 10).

Hook echoes his teacher. John Dewey makes it clear that the more useful role for philosophy is to move away from solving abstractions to solving problems. Morality comes to the fore when a problem arises and something has to be done. "Philosophy recovers itself," Dewey writes, "when it ceases to be a device for dealing with the problems of philosophers and becomes a method, cultivated by philosophers, for dealing with the problems of men" (1917, *MW* 10, p. 46). Philosophical instruments get their trial and test through the "active use in dealing with the present problems of men" (1946, *LW* 15, p. 166). The good is not a vision independent of evils, solved by an appeal to some distant ideal or formulaic principle, but corrective of current evils (1922, *MW* 14, p. 195).

The evil in a current situation is usually something specific to that situation, so the solution has to be discovered on the basis of that evil (1938, *LW* 12, p. 176). As Richard Bernstein notes, for Dewey, "the primary situations of life are those where there is something to be done, where we manipulate the world in order to achieve desired ends, where we actively seek to transform the situations within which we find ourselves" (1971,

p. 207). As Hilary Putnam puts it simply, ethics for Dewey is concerned with "the solution of *practical* problems" (2004, p. 28). Richard Rorty says something similar. Pragmatists ask a "practical question":

> Are our ways of describing things, of relating them to other things so as to make them fulfill our needs more adequately, as good as possible? Or can we do better? Can our future be made better than our present? (1999, p. 72)

As Dewey emphasizes ". . . morals has to do with all activity into which alternative possibilities enter. For wherever they enter a difference between better and worse arises. . . . The better is the good" (1922, *MW* 14, p. 193). "Dewey," Hook thought, was "a man embattled in perpetual struggle for a *better* world" (1959, p. 10). The better *is* the good, meaning not that it is something "dogmatically made up in advance," as James said, but an alternative, less problematic than what is. Dewey is against those who see betterment as an "approximation to an exhaustive, immutable end or good." Instead, betterment is fixing "existing needs" (1922, *MW* 14, p. 198):

> Some methods of surgery, farming, road-making, navigating or what-not are better than others. It does not follow in any of these cases that the "better" methods are ideally perfect, or that they are regulative or "normative" because of conformity to some form. They are the methods which experience up to the present time shows to be the best methods available for achieving certain results, while abstraction of these methods does supply a (relative) norm or standard for further undertakings. (1938, *LW* 12, p. 108)

James sees the drama of improvement as a flow between disruption and equilibrium. Disruption follows from the fact that "pent in under every system of moral rules are innumerable persons whom it weighs upon, and goods which it repressed; and these are always rumbling and grumbling in the background, and ready for any issue by which they may get free" (1891, p. 611). So "the course of history is nothing but the story of men's struggles from generation to generation to find the more and more inclusive order" (1891, p. 610). In "following this path, society has shaken itself into one sort of relative equilibrium after another. . . . and though someone's ideals are unquestionably the worse off for each improvement, yet a vastly greater total number of them find shelter in our civilized society . . ." (1891, p. 611).

Dewey's larger picture of community is not, as Plato imagined in *The Republic*, a static utopian ideal that, once perfected, would not change. Instead, Dewey recognized that any community would always be facing problems; therefore, a community constituted by practices that could best address its problems would be, perforce, the better community. According to Gregory Pappas, the primary test of democracy in Dewey's sense is its ability to ameliorate experienced problems (2008, p. 219). "A community of inquiry that is not centered and guided by the unique problem at hand usually deteriorates into a mere conflict of ideologies without the fullness of interaction required for learning" (Pappas, 2008, p. 241). As Peirce would call it, such a community must be capable of "self-correction," which constitutes the core of reasonableness, something that is essential to growth (1898, *CP* 5.582; Liszka, 2021, pp. 203ff). In this way, Dewey avoids a reversion to the Platonic template of a preconceived ideal towards which communities should be directed, yet still is able to talk about a certain directedness in human affairs. The direction cannot be forecast. Its problems and their solutions guide development—and who knows how these will go. Nonetheless, it is those communities best equipped to provide good solutions to their problems that will lead the way.

A certain, unsurprising directedness emerges out of the pragmatists' tragic vision of life. If uncorrected, problems tend to break down practices and institutions—if in Aristotle's helpful turn of phrase, "the bad is that which falls apart," then things will tend not to work if their problems are not resolved, or tend to work if they are. If they work, they continue to work until they stop working. Like Hitler's Nazism, they enter the stage, destroy and disrupt but soon disappear. Communities that are good at solving their problems will, perforce, tend to work better than those that do not. If problems are not solved, they tend to accumulate and amplify until, like a cancer, they consume every working cell. Working practices and institutions have a tendency to persist or, at least, change adaptively to changing conditions. Like it or not, things will continue to work themselves out until something works out—or the opportunity to work out anything goes away. But, so long as there is substantial dissatisfaction with the human condition, there will be efforts to improve its lot. Under this view, it is not so much the desirability for the good that drives human effort, as the intolerability of serious problems widely felt.

Many would claim that the world without Plato's long-held assumptions is reasonably descriptive of the way the world is. There doesn't seem to be one definitive answer to the good. People may believe something good but not necessarily act on it. Some people may indeed desire what they believe to be evil and do it for that reason. Even if people knew what was good, it might be difficult to realize. Not everyone is rational in choosing what is beneficial. But this is not the argument of cynics for the hopelessness of the human condition. The world without Plato's assumptions is not necessarily the bleak landscape of Thomas Hobbes's "war of all against all." It is in fact the way it is experienced by most people—with some good, some bad, appalling atrocities and deeds of nobility, cooperation and competition, acts of altruism contrasted with greed and selfishness, but with many not interested in harming others. Dewey bemoans the fact that, on the one hand, "man's nature has been regarded with suspicion, with fear, with sour looks," with a sense of human nature as "bordering on depravity" (1922, *MW* 14, p. 4). On the other hand, there has been "a romantic glorification" of human nature, supposedly whittled down and oppressed by conventional morality (1922, *MW* 14, p. 7).

There has been for centuries a fight over whether someone's good is better than another's. That's a fruitless fight. Better to solve the problems that face the world than to worship some notion of the good. Doing good does not require a license from some abstract principle or ideal but stands upright in the problems the world faces and people endure every day. "Men have constructed a strange dream-world," Dewey says, "when they have supposed that without a fixed ideal of a remote good to inspire them, they have no inducement to get relief from present troubles, no desires for liberation from what oppresses, and for clearing-up what confuses present action. . . . Sufficient unto the day is the evil thereof" (1922, *MW* 14, p. 195). Solve problems, and good will follow. The measure of a good community is not how much it conforms to some ideal state, but how good it is at solving its own problems. The better the community is at solving its problems, the better the community.

Chapter 2

Pragmatism and the Roots of Problem-Based Ethics

The classic pragmatists developed a set of interrelated ideas that, collectively, form the framework for a problem-based approach to ethics. This is along five important themes. The pragmatic maxim, as formulated by Peirce, claimed that the way to get the clearest meaning of any concept was to articulate it in terms of what it does, rather than what it is. Second, as such, the maxim showed how theory could be translated to practice and theoretical reasoning to practical reasoning. As William James developed it, one could apply it to functional accounts of truth and goodness. Just as Peirce had shown that scientific, theoretical reasoning was primarily utilizing methods that detected problematic hypotheses and corrected then, correspondingly, John Dewey thought that the sort of reasoning that goes on in practical life had to centered on the detection of problems and their resolution and should employ science as far as possible. Peirce emphasized further that for the practice of science to be successful it had to adopt certain norms and inquirers had to have certain kinds of virtues. Dewey emphasized that the idea of social democracy and the norms of inquiry intersected at certain points. One could help the other in solving the problems of practical life and bettering communities. Peirce emphasized that the measure of the progress of scientific inquiries was a convergence of its claims toward consensus of opinion among inquirers. For Dewey, the measure of progress in communities was growth, the release of capacities for making things better.

The Pragmatic Maxim: Theory to Practice

Despite all the privileges and promise Charles Peirce had as a young man, his career as an undergraduate was rather lackluster. He was raised by America's greatest mathematician of the time, Benjamin Peirce, and lived in the Harvard environment, with its many opportunities to meet and mingle with the greatest minds of the time. However, when he entered the Lawrence Scientific School at Harvard University, something in him caught fire. In 1863, he graduated *summa cum laude,* with a bachelor's of science degree in chemistry from that institution (Brent, 1998, p. 55)

Founded in 1847, the Lawrence Scientific School was Harvard's first effort to provide a formal, advanced education in science and engineering. Neither was a particularly professional practice at the time, and engineering was hardly scientific. The school was named after Abbott Lawrence, an industrial entrepreneur, who had donated a generous amount of money to its founding. Lawrence's motivation for devoting a good portion of his fortune to this school is interesting. In a letter accompanying his gift, he wrote, "But where can we send those who intend to devote themselves to the practical applications of science? Our country abounds in men of action. Hard hands are ready to work upon our hard materials; and where shall sagacious heads be taught to direct those hands?" (Harvard University, 2015).

Peirce seems to have taken to experimental laboratory work at the school. One of its founding professors was Eben Norton Horsfeld, who had studied in Germany with the innovative experimental chemist Justus Von Liebig. Von Liebig developed a hands-on, problem-based pedagogy in the laboratory that emphasized team work. It's still the dominant laboratory pedagogy today. Horsfeld introduced the pedagogy to Lawrence. It was likely the study of rigorous laboratory testing that gave Peirce a brilliant idea that was later to become the hallmark of his most famous contribution to philosophy—the pragmatic maxim. Peirce undoubtedly wondered: Could the experimental method that had been key to the advance of science be applied to help with the philosophical task of clarifying the meanings of concepts? Could this improve upon the more subjective and intuitive Cartesian notions of clear and distinct ideas?

Peirce certainly thought so and says this plainly in his later years in an overview of his pragmatism: "All pragmatists will further agree that their method of ascertaining the meanings of words and concepts is no other than that experimental method by which all the successful sciences. . . have reached the degrees of certainty that are severally proper to them today; this experimental method being itself nothing but a particular application of an older logical rule, "By their fruits ye shall know them" (1906, *CP* 5.465).

In an article written for *The Monist* in 1905 explaining his version of pragmatism, Peirce begins with a manifesto of the laboratory scientist, identifies himself as this sort of "laboratory man," and links it to the pragmatic maxim (1905, *CP* 5.411–412). The manifesto proclaims in part that for any "typical experimentalist . . . whatever assertion you may make to him, he will either understand as meaning that if a given prescription for an experiment ever can be and ever is carried out in act, an experience of a given description will result, or else he will see no sense at all in what you say" (1905, *CP* 5.411). Indeed, one of his best illustrations of the pragmatic maxim, as it came to be called, is an example from chemistry. The *meaning* of lithium could be understood in terms of the observable effects of what can be done to it in practical operations:

> [I]f you search among minerals that are vitreous, translucent, grey or white, very hard, brittle, and insoluble, for one which imparts a crimson tinge to an unluminous flame, this mineral being triturated with lime or witherite rats-bane, and then fused, can be partly dissolved in muriatic acid; and if this solution be evaporated, and the residue be extracted with sulphuric acid, and duly purified, it can be converted by ordinary methods into a chloride, which being obtained in the solid state, fused, and electrolyzed with half a dozen powerful cells, will yield a globule of a pinkish silvery metal that will float on gasolene; and the material of that is a specimen of lithium. (1902, *CP* 2.330)

As Peirce explains, "the peculiarity of this definition . . . is that it tells you what the word lithium denotes by prescribing what you are to **do** in order to gain a perceptual acquaintance with the object of the word" (1902, *CP* 2.330). Reflecting the changing character of the university in the 19th century, he called such an approach "laboratory-philosophy" as opposed to "seminary-philosophy" (1905, *CP* 1.129).

In a letter in 1905 to his former student Christine Ladd-Franklin, he told her that the theory of meaning that was to be known as pragmatism was first delivered to his compatriots in the so-called Metaphysical Club in 1871 (1916, p. 716). It was a few years after, in 1878, that Peirce published a formulation of the pragmatic maxim in *The Popular Science Monthly*—but without that nomenclature and under the title "How to Make Our Ideas

Clear." The journal was intended for a broader audience, something comparable perhaps to *Scientific American* today—and Peirce wrote the piece in a style that laymen could easily understand. The maxim is formulated, somewhat clumsily, as the following:

> Consider what effects, which might conceivably have practical bearings, we conceive the object of our conception to have. Then, our concept of these effects is the whole of our conception of the object. (1878, *CP* 5.402)

The maxim argues that the best way to clarify the meaning of a concept—or the meaning of anything for that matter—was to determine what sorts of observable practical effects it entailed. If you wanted to know what something means, find out what it does when operated on in a practical way, the manner in which one goes about testing a hypothesis in chemistry in a laboratory experiment.

Peirce realized that this method could be applied to all manner of concepts, for example, "randomness." A random sample is one "taken according to a precept or method which, being applied over and over again indefinitely, would in the long run result in the drawing of any one of a set of instances as often as any other set of the same number" (1883, *W* 4, p. 427). The article contends that this sort of definition provides a "third grade of clearness" beyond the popular understanding of the term and its nominal definition. A third grade of clearness consists "in such a representation of the idea that fruitful reasoning can be made to turn upon it, and that it can be applied to the resolution of difficult practical problems" (1897, *CP* 3.457). In later reflections, Peirce considers even higher grades of clearness, most notably, how the meaning of a concept unfolds in the laboratory of history (1903, *CP* 8.176n.3).

But what is truly novel at the time about Peirce's account of meaning is what it reveals implicitly about scientific, laboratory reasoning. In using that sort of reasoning to clarify meaning, he presages what is to become the hallmark of the nineteenth century—the power of science for practical application (Liszka, 2021, p. 3). More broadly, he shows the implicit correlation between scientific, laboratory reasoning and *practical* reasoning.

As Peirce pointed out in the formulation of his maxim, each concept (or belief, hypothesis, and so forth) has "*practical bearings*," by which he means that *it could be transposed into a practical maxim*. For example, if the scratch-hardness of diamond means that it can cut glass rather than being cut by glass, then its corresponding practical maxim is that "if you want to solve the problem of how to cut glass, use a diamond cutter." "Every proposition has its practical aspect. If it means anything it will, on some possible occasion, determine the conduct of the person who accepts it" (1902, NEM 4, p. 291). As he states this more technically: "Pragmatism is the principle that every theoretical judgment expressible in a sentence in the indicative mood is a confused form of thought whose only meaning, if it has any, lies in its tendency to enforce a corresponding practical maxim expressible as a conditional sentence having its apodosis in the imperative mood" (1903, *CP* 5.18). In other words, the theoretical claim, if true, can be transposed into what Immanuel Kant calls a hypothetical imperative. Indeed, in *The Foundations of the Metaphysics of Morals*, Kant defines "pragmatic" imperatives as forms of hypothetical imperatives, essentially prudential rules of how best to attain ends (1785, pp. 31–32n4). He sees them as a form of prudence that "instructs the world how it could provide for its interest better than, or at least as well as has been done in the past" (1785, p. 34n6; Liszka, 2021, pp. 93-94).

These practical, pragmatic, or hypothetical maxims are the core of practical reasoning. Such reasoning is usually formulated in the following way: Given an end, and a practical hypothesis that claims what is likely to attain that end, then assuming that people desire, want or intend the end, then they ought to do the action prescribed. It's thought that practical reasoning rests on the desire-belief model of action (Davidson, 2006). Peirce develops a version based on Alexander Bain's theory of belief who, Peirce claims, inspired his pragmatism (1898, *CP* 1.635; Liszka, 2021, pp. 83-84). Peirce argues that a belief is "that upon which a man is prepared to act" (1906, *CP* 5.12). But Bain claimed more precisely that "belief is preparedness to act, for a given end, in a given way"—which articulates the core features of practical reasoning (Bain, 1889, p. 508). Peirce provides a rough outline of such practical reasoning:

> Now to say that a man believes anthracite to be a convenient fuel is to say no more nor less than that if he needs fuel, and no other seems particularly preferable, then, if he acts deliberately, bearing in mind his experiences, considering what he is doing, and exercising self-control, he will often use anthracite. A practical belief may, therefore, be described as a habit of deliberate behavior. (c. 1902, *CP* 5.538)

If, in Peirce's classic example, people desire to cut glass, then they ought to use a diamond cutter. However, as Peirce implies, *the validity of this practical reasoning is based on the truth of the empirical hypothesis* that diamonds are scratch-hard (and scratch harder than glass). As Peirce says, "For truth is neither more nor less than that character of a proposition which consists in this, that belief in the proposition would, with sufficient experience and reflection, lead us to such conduct as would tend to satisfy the desires we should then have. To say that truth means more than this is to say that it has no meaning at all" (1877, *CP* 5.375n2). The *meaning* of a true proposition, once transposed into practical reasoning, is how it would affect conduct, understood typically as goal-directed behavior. As Peirce insists, ". . . the rational purport of a word or other expression, lies exclusively in its conceivable bearing upon the conduct of life. . . ." "The most striking feature of the new theory," Peirce notes, "was its recognition of an inseparable connection between rational cognition and rational purpose." In direct reference to Kant's notion of the "pragmatic," it is ". . . that consideration . . . which determined the preference for the name *pragmatism*" (1905, *CP* 5.412). The fact that we can translate the meaning of something into a practical operation also means that we can use it for practical purposes as well—certainly for technical applications, but also more importantly as a practical guide to life.

"How to Make Our Ideas Clear" did not create a stir. This may have been because Peirce was so prescient about the impact of experimental science, that the significance of his maxim would have to wait until people could see the growing power of the application of science in the late nineteenth-century industrial revolution. As Bruce Hunt characterizes it, "the nineteenth century marked one of the great watersheds in human beings' power over the world around them." In many ways, he says, practical life in the eighteenth century differed little from the previous century. But moving forward a century later, "we find a very different world," one with "sweeping changes in the technologies of daily life." But it was one that also "witnessed striking advances in scientific understanding" (2010, p. 1). "By the opening decade of the twentieth century, science and technology had become in many ways defining features of modern life" (2010, p. 2).

There was a reason the two went together, according to Hunt. Even if science was primarily about knowing, and technology about doing, there was a significant overlap. There was an intermingling of the two in modern science, precisely because of its experimental methodologies. The great thermodynamic theories of physics had been developed in problems related to the steam engine, and the formulation of the electromagnetic theory of light from study of electrical currents and waves related to the development of the telegraph (2010, pp. 2–3).

Truth and Goodness Reconceived

The maxim lay dormant and unnamed for a number of years until William James revived the idea in a lecture delivered at Berkeley in 1898, a time when the practical impact of experimental science was being felt in industry, technology, and daily lives. James used the term "pragmatism" to describe the ideas presented in Peirce's "How to Make Our Ideas Clear." The title of the lecture was "Philosophical Conceptions and Practical Results," a title that appeared to emphasize the relation between theory and practice.

As James defines it in his entry on "pragmatic and pragmatism" for Baldwin's *Dictionary of Philosophy and Psychology*, it is "the doctrine that the whole 'meaning' of a conception expresses itself in practical consequences, consequences either in the shape of conduct to be recommended, *or* in that of experiences to be expected" (1902, *CP* 5.2). He was gracious enough to acknowledge Peirce as source and inventor of pragmatism, but it was certainly thanks to James that pragmatism eventually became as widely known as it was (1898, pp. 1078–1080).

As William James develops pragmatism after 1898, he uses Peirce's maxim not only as a way of clarifying meaning, but also as a theory of truth. James's thought goes along the following lines: In true pragmatic fashion, it should be asked what is it that true beliefs *do*? What are their practical effects? In other words, *what's the good of truth?* Supposedly true beliefs are better guides to navigating experience than false ones. As James emphasizes, they tend to "lead" us to the right place (1907, p. 202). Thus, the truth of a belief can be measured by how well it guides lives, particularly in terms of helping people to anticipate and predict events in experience (1907, p. 58).

However, Peirce disagreed with James on how the pragmatic maxim might assist in the matter of truth. There is an important difference in Peirce's mind between what a true belief does and, thereby, what it means, and, whether a belief *is* true. Peirce could not agree more with James that true beliefs are reliable guides to living. The *meaning* of truth is what true beliefs do and do *for believers*. As he says in "The Fixation of Beliefs," they assuage the subcutaneous irritation of doubt. And in "How to Make Our Ideas Clear," he makes it clear that they tend to bring inquiries to fruition and settle opinion (1877, *CP* 5.407). A false claim diverges opinion; a true one tends to converge belief.

All of this is true, Peirce says, but what is it that *makes* a belief *true*? It is not the fact that it is useful as a guide to experience, but that it has the ability to make consistent predictions about its content in the long run—and that requires sophisticated inductive tests. Being useful is the result of true beliefs and claims; that is, what it predicts is reliably so. It is not true because it is useful; it is useful because it is true.

But Peirce may have not been entirely fair in his criticism of James. Granted that hypotheses or beliefs are tested through rigorous inductive tests, the tests themselves are based on practical outcomes of the hypotheses that are predictable, per the pragmatic maxim. The hypothesis is either rejected or not rejected precisely by means of its practical translation—if not in the laboratory of life, at least in the scientific laboratory. A hypothesis almost always makes a prediction, and if it is not to be rejected, those predictions occur with some level of statistical significance; and if that is the case, then they can serve as fairly reliable, practical guides to whatever matter they're about. The fact that they are reliable guides in this sense is an indication of their truth. The problem with James's position is that usefulness is only an indicator: all true beliefs are good guides to the work of living, but not all beliefs that are good guides to practical life are true.

If the meaning of truth is what it does practically for us, and what it does practically for us is something good and beneficial, then "truth is *one species of good* . . ." (1907, p. 76). "The true, to put it very briefly, is only the expedient in the way of our thinking, just as 'the right' is only the expedient in the way of our behaving" (1907, p. 222). Colin Koopman emphasizes that "James's pragmatism . . . co-locates truth as simultaneously epistemological and axiological" (2015, p. 21). Cornel West thinks this claim is one of the more fundamental principles of pragmatism (West, 1999, p. 176). Later on, Peirce realized something similar. He thought all logical and scientific reasoning was normative since it lays out the best way to reason and, thus, depended on ethics. "Thinking is a kind of action, and reasoning is a kind of deliberate action; and to call an argument illogical, or a proposition false, is a special kind of moral judgment . . ." (c. 1904, *CP* 8.191).

If truth is a species of the good, then what James says about truth is also said of goodness. By proxy, if we were to substitute what he claims for truth in his more famous passages in the classic texts on pragmatism, as what he also claims for goodness, then among these claims are the following: Something is considered true (=good) in so far as it helps us "to get into a satisfactory relation with other parts of our experience" (1907, p. 58). The true (=good) is that which "will carry us prosperously from any one part of our experience to any other part, linking things satisfactorily, working securely, simplifying, saving labor . . ." (1907, p. 58). True (=good) things are measured by the "success with which they 'work' . . ." (1907, p. 67). The true (=good) is "what works best in the way of leading us, what fits every part of life best and combines with the collectivity of experience's demands, nothing being omitted" (1907, p. 80). It "gives us the maximum possible sum of satisfactions . . ." (1907, p. 217). If truth (=goodness) is traditionally thought to be that which is "in agreement with reality," then that should be understood in a certain way:

> To agree in the widest sense with reality can only mean to be guided either straight up to it . . . to be put into such working touch with it as to handle . . . it . . . better than if we disagreed. . . . Any idea that helps us to deal, whether practically or intellectually, with either the reality or its belongings, that doesn't entangle our progress in frustrations, that *fits* in facts, and adapts our life to the reality's whole setting will agree sufficiently to meet the requirement. It will be true of that reality. (1907, pp. 212–213)

True [=good] ideas "lead to consistency, stability and flowing human intercourse . . . The untrammeled flowing of the leading-process [is] its general freedom from clash and contradiction . . ." (1907, p. 215). Truth (=goodness) must "*work*" (1907, p. 216).

In his most developed reflection on morality, "The Moral Philosopher and the Moral Life," James says all of this more directly, although more succinctly. The philosopher "must vote for the richer universe, for the good which seems most organizable, most fit to enter into complex combinations, most apt to be a member of a more inclusive whole" (1891, p. 614). If this interpretation holds, *it creates a conceptual shift in an account of the good, away from what it is to what it does*. Put in the more prosaic language of pragmatism, any good action, practice, or belief that is to be counted as good is one that "works." If truth is measured by its "work-value," then that is also the measure of what is good (1907, p. 68).

Gathering these passages together, there are certain themes in describing the character of truth and goodness. These include how true and good beliefs cohere with experience and do not contradict it. They are fruitful, they lead to stability, and they do not block progress and the flow of human intercourse. What works and functions well may be the key terms. James seems to delineate three different aspects of how truth and goodness work. First, in terms of "success" (1907, p. 67). In its ordinary sense, something is successfully working when it accomplishes its goal or achieves the outcome that is intended. It is not successful if it fails to accomplish the goal or perform the function for which it was intended. Peirce says that "the question of the goodness of anything is whether that thing fulfills its end" (1903, *CP* 5.197). This aspect might be called *functionality*.

Second, when something works, it helps us "to get into a satisfactory relation with other parts of our experience" and ". . . fits every part of life best and combines with the collectivity of experience's demands, nothing being omitted." This might be characterized as *fit*, how well an optimally functioning part works with other parts of a whole; or, more broadly, how a practice works with other practices to which it is connected. Just as a flourishing species in evolutionary theory have fitness with their environments, so something works, when it works with other things of which it is a part. Peirce talks about ethics being, in part, the study of the "fitness" of ideals of conduct (1903, *CP* 1.600). How a practice works, and whatever ends or outcomes it produces, it needs to be consonant with other well-functioning practices. As Dewey says in regard to living organisms, "in life that is truly life, everything overlaps and merges. . . . Only when the past ceases to trouble and anticipation of the future are not perturbing is a being wholly united with his environment and therefore fully alive" (1934, *LW* 10, p. 24).

Something is working in a third sense when it "will carry us prosperously from any one part of our experience to any other part, linking things satisfactorily, working securely, simplifying, saving labor. . . ." It is those things that "lead to consistency, stability and flowing human intercourse . . ." This imagery calls up notions of growth, of flow, the power to thrive, flourish, and evolve positively, "a primordial element of the universe," according to Peirce (1892, *CP* 6.157). Peirce understood growth as not just increase, but diversification (1905, *CP* 1.174). Dewey too understood growth not simply as increase, but as something that creates the conditions for further growth. Indeed, in a rather remarkable claim, Dewey says that "growth itself is the only moral 'end'" (1938, *MW* 12, pp. 180–181).

These three aspects of what works also, at the same time, explain the different ways in which something *doesn't work*. Generally speaking, it is often said that problems occur when something is not working right. In this way, the three senses of what works also identify three different types of problems experienced in the practices of life. *Functional problems* are cases where something is not doing what it is meant to do; it is not achieving the end or the outcomes expected. *Systemic* problems are cases where, even if particular things are working as intended, they do not work well with other things of which they are a part. Finally, *growth or flow problems* are cases where, even if things are working as intended, and working well-together, the result does not seem to progress, to grow or flourish in its environment. It doesn't seem to go anywhere.

Communities of Inquiry

Peirce's pragmatic maxim pointed to a connection between theory and practice that was to be realized in the most dramatic ways in days yet to come. But he also showed that the truth of practical hypotheses was dependent upon the truth of their corresponding theoretical and empirical ones.

If truth had functional virtues in practical life, truth claims still had to be shown to be true or, better, shown not to be false and, therefore, reasonably reliable as a guide to conduct. But what Peirce realized perhaps more than other thinkers before him was that inquiries into the truth of claims involved a *community* of inquiry. This is ironic given that, at the height of his powers, Peirce himself was exiled from the academy and isolated in his inquiries in his last years on earth. It may have been all the more reason he appreciated the necessity of the communal aspect of inquiry.

The idea of a community of inquiry was not something he simply divined, nor a sentimental paean about fellow scientists, but he saw it as an inference from the various types of reasoning that he so assiduously studied. Peirce methodically demonstrates his claim that all logic and scientific reasoning is rooted in a "social principle." Peirce shows that the three fundamental reasoning processes employed by science—deduction, induction, and the logic of discovery, or abduction—rely on the possibility of an ongoing, indefinite *community* of inquiry.

Defined briefly, abduction is concerned with how a hypothesis is developed, based on surprising or anomalous observations that appear to conflict with received hypotheses (1903, *CP* 5.189). Deduction, in the scientific context, is concerned with inferring the testable consequences of those hypotheses (1901, *CP* 7.220), while induction is the logic of testing those hypotheses and assessing the results (1910, *CP* 7.115). Should induction reject the hypothesis, then the process begins anew until some modicum of stability or fixation of belief in a hypothesis over time is achieved. Peirce shows how these three types of reasoning are interconnected in a process that results in achieving better, less erroneous hypotheses (c. 1901, *CP* 7.220). Together they form a process of self-correction, sorting out the false from those not yet shown to be false (1898, *CP* 5.575). Scientific reasoning well-done was essentially a method for detecting error, detecting the problems in hypotheses. It could not guarantee the truth of hypotheses, only that, for now, they are error-free.

Each of these three fundamental reasoning processes has a leading principle, understood as a premise that, along with the standard forms of the various reasoning processes, contributes to the basic validity of that form of reasoning. The leading principle of abduction is that the human mind has so evolved as to guess at the truth *in the long run* (1903, *CP* 5.172). The ultimate leading principle of induction "*if steadily adhered to*, would at length lead to an indefinite approximation to the truth" (1901, *CP* 2.204). Finally, the ultimate leading principle of deduction is that no analogous case of a logically valid argument will lead to a false conclusion (1901, *CP* 2.204), something that must be shown *in the due course of reasoning*. All three leading principles, then, require an indefinite process of inquiry, generations of inquirers, bound together in a *community* of inquiry (1868, *CP* 5.311). Peirce sums this up in a famous passage:

> The very idea of probability and of reasoning rests on the assumption this number [of inferences] is indefinitely great. . . . [L]ogicality inexorably requires that our interests shall *not* be limited. They must not stop at our own fate, but must embrace the whole community. This community, again, must not be limited. . . . Logic is rooted in the social principle. (1878, *CP* 2.654)

But Peirce had a second great insight. A community of inquiry must itself be constituted in a certain way in order to inquire successfully. *Inquiry itself entails a certain sort of communal ethos* (Liszka, 2021, pp. 134–137). "The most vital factors in the method of modern science have not been the following of this or that logical prescription—although these have had their value too," says Peirce but, "moral factors." "The first of these has been the genuine love of truth and conviction that nothing else could long endure," such as the love of truth and, on the other, the recognition of science's social and public character, particularly in respect to the "solidarity of its efforts." "The next most vital factor of the method of modern science," he argues, "is that it has been made social." It is public in the sense that the investigations and their results "must be something open to anybody to observe. . . ." It is also marked by an inherent altruism among the investigators: "[I]n respect to the solidarity of its efforts. . . . the individual strives to produce that which he himself cannot hope to enjoy. One generation collects premises in order that a distant generation may discover what they mean." He continues,

> When a problem comes before the scientific world, a hundred men immediately set all their energies to work upon it. One contributes this, another that. Another company, standing upon the shoulders of the first, strike a little higher, until at last the parapet is attained. (1902, *CP* 7.87)

Another moral factor, Peirce argues is "self-confidence" in the method, that is, an enduring faith and hope in the scientific method to eventually light upon the truth (1902, *CP* 7.87). That is to say, scientists tend to believe that science will progress.

Whereas "How to Make Our Ideas Clear" had laid out the pragmatic maxim, the first article in the *Popular Science Monthly* series "The Fixation of Belief" emphasizes the virtues of a community modeled on science. Doubt is a subcutaneous irritation that must be fixed and prompts the need for inquiry. Doubt about widely held beliefs in a community causes instability, weakens solidarity, and foils cooperation. *It creates problems of sociality.* But there are several ways in which doubt can be assuaged. Which will be the most successful in the long run?

Historically, the most common way in which beliefs are fixated or stabilized is through the imposition of authority. Other ways are through dogmatism, tenaciously holding on to beliefs by refusing to consider any others; or through widely held beliefs that feel natural and intuitive to their believers, but prove to be enculturated conventions (1877, *CP* 5.377). In earlier drafts of this well-known article, Peirce also talks about the indoctrination of public opinion as another method, of fixing belief, "to cultivate a public opinion by oratory and preaching and by fostering certain sentiments and passions in the minds of the young. This method is the most generally successful in our day" (1872, *W* 3, p. 15).

Peirce argues that although these methods of fixing belief may work in the short term, history shows that they eventually fall apart. False beliefs tend to fall away because they are found not to work in making predictions needed to accomplish communal goals. Authority engenders an *ethos* that favors strong hierarchies, emphasizes the virtues of obedience and loyalty, discourages curiosity, cultivates a blind trust of authority, and stresses top-down, asymmetrical communicative practices (1877, *CP* 5.381–382). All of these communities must be highly censorious and manipulative in order to maintain solidarity and stability of belief (1877, *CP* 5.378).

The only method that guarantees the fixation and stability of beliefs in the long run is a method based on experimental inquiry since that method is more likely than others to sort out false beliefs from those that have not been shown to be false. It's the only method that does not rely on what people do in fact happen to believe, but on something external to believers that can verify those beliefs based precisely on the ability of beliefs to predict (1877, *CP* 5.384). Science requires a community that is open to inquiry, and opportunities to criticize and evaluate beliefs, and requires evidence and justification among those who make assertions and claims (1877, *CP* 5.384; c. 1899, *CP* 1.136). The "first rule of reason" according to Peirce is "do not block the way of inquiry" (c. 1899, *CP* 1.135). "To set up a philosophy which barricades the road of further advance toward the truth is the one unpardonable offence in reasoning . . ." (c. 1899, *CP* 1.136). Peirce had developed a nascent speech act theory of assertion that argued that making assertions committed those who made such assertions to providing evidence and justification for those claims. Peirce argued that "assertion consists in the furnishing of evidence by the speaker to the listener that the speaker believes something . . ." (c. 1895, *CP* 2.335), and likened it to going before a notary and making an affidavit, so that "one voluntarily puts oneself into a situation in which penalties will be incurred unless some proposition is true" (1905, *CP* 8.313).

Not only do communities of inquiry have norms, but inquirers also must have certain virtues to be successful. They cooperate with other inquirers and exhibit a certain sort of intergenerational altruism, the idea that one is making a contribution toward something larger than self, the benefit of which may not accrue to the inquirers in their lifetime (1902, *CP* 7.87; 1901, *CP* 7.185). Inquirers build on the work of their predecessors and at the same time lay the groundwork for their successors. Above all, inquirers must be honest in the observation, collection, and reasoning about the data of inquiry. Imagine if that were not so. The results of scientific fraud are patent enough to show how dishonesty could never advance inquiry in the long run. "A scientific man must be single-minded and sincere with himself. Otherwise, his love of truth will melt away, at once. He can, therefore, hardly be otherwise than an honest fair-minded man" (1903, *CP* 1.49). The scientist must have humility: "[H]e is keenly aware of his own ignorance, and knows that personally he can make but small steps in discovery . . ." (*CP* 8.136). Corruption is a related matter. Inquiry should be done for the sake of sorting out true and false claims, not for money or fame. Objectivity is a key virtue of inquirers (1898, *CP* 1.619; 1898, *CP* 1.642; 1900, *CP* 8.136).

Democracy as a Community of Inquiry

Whereas Peirce was born into a distinguished academic family with all the advantages and privileges that could afford, Dewey entered this world in 1859 by means of a grocer father and a mother who was a farmer's daughter. Dewey lived in the backwater of Burlington, Vermont, as opposed to the center of American intellectual life in Boston. Whereas Peirce had managed to avoid the draft in the Civil War, Dewey's father volunteered. Dewey was born in the year that Peirce had graduated from Harvard. At the age of 15, Dewey attended the university in Burlington. In his studies at the University of Vermont, Dewey had taken well to philosophy. However, once he graduated, he started out as a teacher in a small town in Pennsylvania, and he later worked in another school south of Burlington.

Thanks to the intercession of W. T. Harris, editor of *The Journal of Speculative Philosophy*, Dewey got admitted to Johns Hopkins University. Dewey had sent a paper on philosophy that Harris thought showed great promise. There Dewey took two classes with Peirce. The one on logic had students who were to distinguish themselves in the subject with publications based on the class. Dewey withdrew from that class, claiming that it was "very mathematical." He complained that Peirce didn't "think there is any philosophy outside the generalization of physical science" (Dykhuizen, 1961, p. 106). But he stuck with the other one on "Great Men." Instead of Peirce, he became attracted to the philosophies of G. Stanley Hall and George Morris at Johns Hopkins, thinkers who were on the other side of the philosophical spectrum from Peirce. As Jay Martin notes, "Thus casually, Dewey consigned Peirce to the dustbin of outmoded philosophers. It took him thirty years to begin to appreciate Peirce, and then Peirce became the philosopher who influenced him most" (2002, p. 73).

Dewey and Josiah Royce were perhaps the only early interpreters of Peirce to recognize the importance and fruitfulness of his notion of the community of inquiry (1916, *MW* 10, p. 78; 1938, *LW* 12, p. 484n3; Royce, 1913, pp. 285–286). Contrary to what James Feibleman thought, Dewey saw Peirce's theory of inquiry as something that completes the more formal aspects of his logic and embeds it into a larger picture of a community-based methodology that would more likely lead to truth than other approaches (Feibleman, 1969, p. 476). Dewey builds on the core insight of Peirce's thoughts on inquiry as a socially and community-based way of life. As Richard Bernstein interprets the matter, "Peirce supplied the intellectual backbone to pragmatism, but Dewey perceived the ways in which Peirce's ideal of a self-critical community of inquirers had important consequences for education, social reconstruction, and a revitalization of democracy" (1971, p. 201).

Having lived well into the twentieth century, Dewey had the advantage over Peirce of seeing more clearly the consequences divined in the pragmatic maxim, concerning the transposition of scientific theory to practice. There was good, but there was a great deal of ill. Peirce sensed this as well. In 1898, he gave a series of lectures in Cambridge at the invitation of William James that are thought to be perplexing by many Peirce scholars. It seemed to contradict the basic thesis of his pragmatism--the transposition of theoretical into practical reasoning (Liszka, 2021, pp. 40–42). In it he condemns "with the whole strength of conviction" the mingling of theory and practice (1898, *CP* 1.618). "The two masters, *theory* and *practice*, you cannot serve" (1898, *CP* 1.640). "The investigator who does not stand aloof from all intent to make practical applications will not only obstruct the advance of the pure science, but, what is infinitely worse, he will endanger his own moral integrity . . ." (1898, *CP* 1.619).

By the end of the nineteenth century, Peirce witnessed how science was being used instrumentally for all sorts of practical applications and, he worried, that it was at the cost of the goals of theory—the goal of truth. How was science to be saved from such instrumentalism? Peirce sets an interesting course to the solution of this problem. He realizes that logic, understood as the methodology of science, is also a normative science, since it prescribes a way of thinking. As such, it must come under the umbrella of ethics (1902, *CP* 8.255). If practical reasoning is at the basis of pragmatism, then practical reasoning must be made ethical. Ethics has two theoretical goals in this respect. One with the aid of esthetics—understood as a science of ends--was to determine what ends ought to be pursued; and, second, the righteous ways in which those ends are to be pursued (1903, *CP* 5.35-36; 1903, R 311, p. 9). In the end, Peirce thinks that the highest end is "reasonableness," understood as the willingness to self-correct from erroneous beliefs (1902, *CP* 5.4; Aydin, 2009, p. 431; Liszka, 2021, pp. 205-207). It is only in this way that truth could prevail.

By the mid-twentieth century, Dewey affirms what is obvious, that technologies "are the practical correlates of scientific theories" (1939, *LW* 13, p. 164). If, as Peirce says, the highest grade of clarity is how a concept unfolds in the laboratory of history in experiments of living with those concepts (1903, *CP* 8.176n.3), then the meaning of the pragmatic maxim was unfolding with some troubling consequences. The effects of the wedding of science and technology were for both good and ill. Dewey thought that the worry about the ills might be greater than the welcome of the goods.

In 1939, Dewey wrote *Freedom and Culture* as a response to this problem. It was an urgent matter for Dewey because it was at a time where the ideologies of fascism, Nazism, communism, democracy and capitalism came to loggerheads, and the order of the world was once again threatened after just a few short decades from the First World War. It was an existential crisis for democracy, not only from without, but also from within. What worried him most was that he could see that science was being used instrumentally by these various ideologies to promote their political ends—power mostly in the form of greater war-making technologies and the bolstering of economies. He saw how the seeming benefits that scientific technology had brought in terms of communication and dissemination of information could easily be turned into propaganda and ways to control large populations by dictatorships and totalitarian regimes (1939, *LW* 13, p. 156). Nazi Germany was using the name of science to promote racial purity, and democracies were finding social science helpful in rationalizing racism. Marxism was touted as a science, so its political manifestation was scientifically proven to be the best form of government (1939, *LW* 13, p. 158). Science could be used instrumentally for the ends of big business and, on the consumer side, for the individual consumer's wants or desires. Science had come under the control of the interests of states and the desires of individual consumers, who made scientific thinking purely instrumental to those ends. It could be used for good and ill purposes, but its ill purposes were strikingly frightening. In reference to Bacon's adage that "knowledge is power," Dewey concludes that "the power over nature which he expected to follow the advance of science has come to pass. But in contradiction to his expectations, it has been largely used to increase, instead of reduce, the power of Man over Man" (1939, *LW* 13, p. 163).

There was something amiss about the sort of practical reasoning that was going on. One of the problems with such practical reasoning centered on Hume's account of the role of belief and desire in human motivation.

Reason, according to Hume, was a "slave to the passions." In reference to the ethical emotivist theories of the positivists and analytic philosophers of his time, Dewey bemoans the fact that Hume's voice "was a lonely one," but now an "idea . . . echoed and re-echoed from almost every quarter," where desire is the synonym for passion (1939, *LW* 13, p. 161). It led to the view that "there are no such things as moral facts because desires control the formation of ends . . ." (1939, *LW* 13, p. 172). When this was combined with the ideology of capitalism and laissez-faire individualism, it reinforced the instrumentalist view of science. "The popular esteem of science," Dewey thought, "is largely due to the aid it has given to men for attainment of the thing they wanted, independently of what they had learned from science . . ." (1939, *LW* 13, p. 160).

The second problem of the practical reasoning of the day was the common belief that science was purely instrumental and "completely neutral and indifferent as to the ends and values which move men to act: that at most it only provides more efficient means for realization of ends that are and must be due to wants and desires completely independent of science" (1939, *LW* 13, p. 160). Dewey asks "the question as to whether scientific knowledge has power to modify the ends which men prize and strive to attain," or does it "add only to our power to realize desires already in existence?" (1939, *LW* 13, p. 161). "Is it possible for the scientific attitude to become such a weighty and widespread constituent of culture that, through the medium of culture, it may shape human desires and purposes?" (1939, *LW* 13, p. 163).

The question of whether science is capable of influencing the formation of ends "is the question whether science has intrinsic moral potentiality" (1939, *LW* 13, p. 171). Dewey affirms that it does, pointing to many of the virtues and norms that Peirce had articulated. Among this "morale" of science is included "fairmindedness, intellectual integrity, of will to subordinate personal preference to ascertained facts and to share with others what is found out, instead of using it for personal gain . . ." (1939, *LW* 13, pp. 167–168). Dewey warns that "if control of conduct amounts to conflict of desires with no possibility of determination of desire and purpose by scientifically warranted beliefs, then the practical alternative is competition and conflict between unintelligent forces for control of desire" (1939, *LW* 13, p. 171). "If it is possible for persons to have their beliefs formed on the ground of evidence, procured by systematic and competent inquiry," then nothing could be more disastrous than to have it formed instead by "propaganda and personal and class interest" (1939, *LW* 13, p. 167).

In order to achieve this, there must be an alliance between science and democracy: ". . . the future of democracy is allied with the spread of the scientific attitude" (1939, *LW* 13, pp. 135, 168). About a dozen years earlier, Dewey pointed to where that alliance meets. There was an important distinction between political democracy and democracy as a social idea. The core norm of a social democracy is for individuals to take a responsible share in their own governance, engaged in the solution of their own problems. In fact, this constituted the very idea of a community: ". . . it is not an alternative to other principles of associated life. It is the idea of community life itself" (1927, *LW* 2, p. 325.) Hilary Putnam thought that democracy in Dewey's sense "is not just one form of social life among other workable forms of social life; it is the precondition for the full application of intelligence to the solution of social problems" (Putnam 1992, p. 180). "If this is right, then an ethical community—a community which wants to know what is right and good—should organize itself in accordance with democratic standards and ideals . . . because they are prerequisites for the application of intelligence to the inquiry" (Putnam, 1995, p. 223). Political democracy implements mechanisms such as voting or majority rule, rights and so forth to implement that participation. Effective participation in the affairs of governing requires debate, open inquiry, free and open communication. In that sense, "we can borrow that much from the spirit and method of science . . ." (1927, *LW* 2, p. 339). Dewey concludes,

> I would not claim that any existing democracy has ever made complete or adequate use of scientific method in deciding upon its policies. But freedom of inquiry, toleration of diverse views, freedom of communication, the distribution of what is found out to every individual as the ultimate intellectual consumer, are involved in the democratic as in the scientific method. (1939, *LW* 13, p. 135)

This was a way not only to revitalize democracy but also to save it. For Dewey, the problem of sociality—how to live together in a way that maximizes people's good and minimizes the problems associated with them—is made likely through the collective, scientific inquiry of social problems. Bernstein says of Dewey that his persistent complaint was that traditional epistemology had failed to focus on knowledge claims "as they function within the process of inquiry itself." Dewey argued that "the lesson to be learned from experimental science" is that knowledge is gained in "the procedures within inquiry by which we discover, test and warrant our knowledge claims" (1971, p. 218). John Shook agrees: ". . . [A]s pragmatism has long insisted, agreement on what is real and valuable and justifiable must be forged within the social processes of scientific deliberation on human problems" (2003, p. 9). As Bernstein sees it, Dewey believes that "the norms of inquiry are not supplied from some source "outside" of inquiry, but are arrived at, refined and modified in the course of the process of inquiry" (1971, p. 218).

Scientific Ethics and Experiments of Living

Truth and goodness emerge through experiments of living. Experiments of living determine what is true and right by finding practices that work in the sense of minimizing problems as it seeks to maximize the attainment of people's ends and goods. The pragmatists recommend that communities need to be communities of inquiry to sort this out, communities equipped with the right norms and methods for solving such problems. Since the best methodologies of inquiries are scientific, could there be something like a scientific ethics?

James thought that experiments of living ". . . are to be judged, not *a priori*, but by actually finding, after the fact of their making, how much more outcry or how much appeasement comes about" (1891, p. 612). A philosophy of ethics cannot be done in an "old-fashioned" way. "Everywhere the ethical philosopher must wait on facts" (1891, p. 613). "All this amounts to saying that, so far as the casuistic question goes, ethical science is just like physical science, and instead of being deducible all at once from abstract principles, must simply bide its time, and be ready to revise its conclusions from day to day" (1891, p. 612).

Peirce had envisioned a normative science, but it was not empirical so much as formal, and he was worried about Dewey's more naturalistic approach to ethical questions (Liszka, 2014). It was Dewey, more than the other pragmatists who envisioned a naturalistic ethics, supported as far as possible by the empirical sciences. Commenting on Dewey, Jennifer Welchman thought that, in his view, the single greatest obstacle to the advance of ethical theory, was its failure to model scientific inquiry (1995, p. 143). It was a position consistently made throughout his writing in the twentieth century.

In one of his earliest papers on this subject, "The Logical Conditions of a Scientific Treatment of Morality," written in 1909, Dewey claims that what is distinctive about science is how it justifies its claims. To model the scientific method is not to reduce the normative to the empirical, but to strengthen the basis of normative claims. Pragmatism, "as an attitude represents what Mr. Peirce has happily termed the "laboratory habit of mind" extended into every area where inquiry may fruitfully be carried on" (1909, *MW* 4, p. 10).

In 1915, in "The Logic of Judgments of Practise," Dewey characterizes practical reasoning scientifically by showing, in accord with the pragmatic maxim, the similarity between practical and theoretical judgments (Welchman, 1995, p. 143). Practical judgments are about hypotheses about means to overcome obstacles to a certain end (1915, p. 507); they are about what to do in a certain situation (1915, p. 508). "The decision as to its validity must rest on empirical evidence" (1915, p. 508). As he elaborates, "the truth of practical judgments"

> [i]s constituted by the issue. The determination of ends-means which constitutes the content of the practical proposition is hypothetical until the course of action indicated has been tried. The event or issue of such action *is* the truth or falsity of the judgment. (1915, p. 510)

In other words, the truth of the practical judgment is whether it brings about the end for which it aims, and that is an empirical matter. In Bernstein's interpretation, just as the pragmatic maxim argues, practical judgments share the same sort of method of validation as theoretical judgments, "they are essentially hypothetical and prescribe courses of action to be followed to test and validate these judgments; and they can be confirmed or disconfirmed by the consequences which issues from these judgments" (1971, p. 217).

In *Human Nature and Conduct*, written in the early 1920s, Dewey argues, "A morality based on study of human nature instead of upon disregard for it would find that facts of man continuous with those of the rest of nature and would thereby ally ethics with physics and biology." It would also "link ethics with the study of history, sociology, law and economics." Such a scientifically and experimentally conceived ethics would not solve every problem, but "it would enable us to state problems in such forms that action could be courageously and intelligently directed to their solution." It would not protect against failure, but it would be certain to learn from failure. It would not protect against emergent problems, but it would be able "to approach the always recurring troubles with a fund of growing knowledge. . . ." (1922, *MW* 14, p. 11).

Five years later, in *The Public and Its Problems,* Dewey writes about the need for democracies to adopt scientific methods, results and norms in order to stop the decline of the public's participation in its own governing processes. People "have gotten used to an experimental method in physical and technical matters. They are still afraid of it in human concerns" (1927, *LW* 2, p. 341). Two years later in *The Quest for Certainty,* Dewey complains that ". . . we make so little use of the experimental method of forming our ideas and beliefs about the concerns of man in his characteristic social relations" (1929, *LW* 4, p. 216). "What is needed," he continues,

> . . . is intelligent examination of the consequences that are actually effected by inherited institutions and customs, in order that there may be intelligent consideration of the ways in which they are to be intentionally modified in behalf of generation of different consequences. This is the significant meaning of transfer of experimental method from the technical field of physical experience to the wider field of human life." (1929, *LW* 4, p. 218)

In his *Ethics* of 1932, he proclaims that ". . . the great need of the present time is that the traditional barriers between scientific and moral knowledge be broken down, so that there will be organized and consecutive endeavor to use all available scientific knowledge for humane and social ends" (*LW* 7, p. 283). As Abraham Edel and Elizabeth Flower write in their introduction to the book, it "needs no elaboration"

> that the 1932 *Ethics* assumes the input of scientific knowledge in an ethical theory and its relevant to every step of the way from the original perception of what a problem is, the clarification of ideas used by the theory, to the assessment of what resources can be invoked and where applied, as well as understanding where the possibilities of growth lie. (1985, p. xxxiv)

As noted, *Freedom and Culture*, written in the 1940s, expressly links ethics and science. Not only are the norms of scientific inquiry and democracy linked, but the methodologies as well, so that the solutions to problems are "but hypotheses" and demonstrate an "alignment of philosophy with the attitude and spirit of the inquiries which have won the victories of scientific inquiry in other fields (1946, *LW* 15, p. 166).

Hilary Putnam sums up the matter nicely. Dewey reconceptualized ethics as a "project of inquiry" (Putnam, 2004, p. 108). As he elaborates elsewhere:

> . . . *if* there are ethical facts to be discovered, *then* we ought to apply to ethical inquiry just the rules we have learned to apply to inquiry in general. For what applies to inquiry in general apply to ethical inquiry in particular. (Putnam, 1995, p. 223)

Meliorism: Convergence, Growth, Improvement, Progress

Said in different ways at different times, Peirce believes the aim of inquiry is truth (1901, *CP* 7.186). But truth is understood functionally. Truth tends to settle opinion, to converge beliefs (1908, *CP* 6.485). Scientific inquiry, in its general sense, both in terms of its methodologies and norms is the best method for converging beliefs. The result of a convergence of belief is stability of belief, which, on the side of practice, allows conduct based on those beliefs to be reliable and to guide the best means for human ends. "As regard human life," Peirce argues, "it is needful to get beliefs that the believer will take satisfaction in acting upon" (c. 1905, *CP* 2.763). The result over time is a growing concrete reasonableness, an embodiment of reason in the practices and habits of life (1903, *CP* 1.615). It is the ". . . Self-controlled growth of man's conduct of life" (1908, *CP* 6.480). Reasonableness was self-correction away from erroneous belief which, thereby, led to those less prone to error. This meant that reasonableness was something in process, something progressive: ". . . [A]gainst attempts to bind down human reason to any prescriptions fixed in advance . . . I say . . . ideas of progress and growth have themselves grown up so as to occupy our minds as they now do, [so] how can we be expected to allow the assumption to pass that the admirable in itself is any stationary result?" (1903, *CP* 1.614).

Peirce's convergence theory of truth was grounded in the Law of Large Numbers, which mathematically proved the intuition that the greater number of confirming observations in an experiment the surer the hypothesis (Liszka, 2019). Peirce claimed that there were three different indicators of convergence toward the truth: approximation as the cumulative results of inductive tests on a hypothesis (1901, *CP* 7.216); a growing consensus among inquirers about the matter (1893, *CP* 6.610), and the fact that different inquirers, independently of one another, came to similar conclusions (1871, *CP* 8.12).

Since convergence is approximation, a growing consensus over time, it is progressive. Inquiry progresses by detecting error and correcting it. "The Inductive Method springs directly out of dissatisfaction with existing knowledge" (1903, *CP* 5.84). Reason, Peirce says "always looks forward to an endless future and expects endlessly to improve its results" (c. 1905, *CP* 1.614). Peirce writes ". . . that inquiry of every type, fully carried out, has the vital power of self-correction and of growth. "The Rational mind is the Progressive mind . . ." (1902, *CP* 7.380).

Peirce argued that self-correction in science was a matter of using inductive reasoning to detect error in hypotheses, and abduction in devising new hypotheses that overcome the anomalies and problems of existing ones. These reasoning processes worked in a cycle to sort out the false from the not-yet-false hypotheses like the manner in which a geometric passenger might travel from the base of a conical helix to its apex, arriving at fewer and fewer errors in existing hypotheses.

This notion of convergence puts together the bones of meliorism. Hook argued that because of the tragic sense of life, pragmatism's outlook is "therefore melioristic, not optimistic" (1959, p. 22). As Peirce defines meliorism in the *Century Dictionary* (1889–1891), it is "the doctrine that the world is neither the worst nor the best possible, but that it is capable of improvement: a mean between theoretical pessimism and optimism" (cited in Bergman 2012, p. 127). In the same vein, Dewey writes:

> Pessimism is a paralyzing doctrine. In declaring that the world is evil wholesale, it makes futile all efforts to discover the remediable causes of specific evils and thereby destroys at the root every attempt to make the world better and happier. Wholesale optimism, which has been the consequence of the attempt to explain evil away, is, however, equally an incubus. After all, the optimism that says that the world is already the best possible of all worlds might be regarded as the most cynical of pessimisms. If this is the best possible, what would a world which was fundamentally bad be like? Meliorism is the belief that the specific conditions which exist at one moment,

be they comparatively bad or comparatively good, in any event may be bettered. It encourages intelligence to study the positive means of good and the obstructions to their realization, and to put forth endeavor for the improvement of conditions." (1920, *MW* 12, pp. 181–182)

Following Dewey, Colin Koopman argues that meliorism has two sides: "[T]he first side is that we humans really can improve the world in which we live; the second side is that the only way our world is going to be improved is through our actions" (2015, p. 148). Just as there is progress in science through the elimination of error, Dewey thought there could be progress in the human condition through the elimination of its problems. Improvement of the human condition occurs when what is working well continues and what is not is changed for the better. Progress is related to the solution of problems. Inspired by Darwin's theory of evolution, Dewey sees cultural evolution as a matter of fixing these problems, just as organisms develop adaptations to their environment. "Philosophy must in time become a method of locating and interpreting the more serious of the conflicts that occur in life," Dewey says, and must find a method for dealing with them, "a method of moral and political diagnosis and prognosis" (1909, *MW* 4, p. 13). A philosophy that "humbles its pretensions" from the cosmical to the practical, and engages in the work of fixing education or a number of other things, also becomes more responsible and meaningful (1909, *MW* 4, p. 14). Also, thereby, its ideas get tested by the way they "work out in practice" (1909, *MW* 4, p. 13).

James sees the narrative of history, of cultural evolution, as having a certain pattern: a movement from stability to disruption, sometimes leading to growth into a more inclusive equilibrium—all of this wrought through assuaging the dissatisfactions of the older regime. As James explains it, progress comes through a clash of the old with the new (1907, p. 59) and, if the new is worthy, it tends to settle into an adjustment of the new with the old (1907, p. 59). This adjustment preserves what is best in the older stock of beliefs and practices "with a minimum of modification; stretching them just enough to make them admit the novelty, but conceiving that in ways as familiar as the case leaves possible" (1907, p. 60). "It marries old opinion to new fact so as ever to show a minimum of jolt, a maximum of continuity." Something is good "just in proportion to its success in solving this 'problem of maxima and minima' " (1907, p. 61).

But growth is not a smooth, linear process for James:

> Following this path, society has shaken itself into one sort of relative equilibrium after another by a series of social discoveries quite analogous to those of science. Polyandry and polygamy and slavery, private warfare and liberty to kill, judicial torture and arbitrary royal power have slowly succumbed to actually aroused complaints; and though someone's ideals are unquestionably the worse off for each improvement, yet a vastly greater total number of them find shelter in our civilized society. . . . [T]here is nothing final in any actually given equilibrium of human ideals, but that, as our present laws and customs have fought and conquered other past ones, so they will in their turn be overthrown by any newly discovered order which will hush up the complaints that they still give rise to, without producing others louder still. (1891, p. 611)

Growth for Peirce is "not mere increase" but "diversification" (c. 1905, *CP* 1.174; 1892, *CP* 6.64). But it is not just more variety. As varieties emerge, they tend toward more complex organizations (1892, *CP* 6.58) and involve a "growth from difformity to uniformity," "an organized heterogeneity" (1903, *CP* 6.101). Growth is connected to progress (c. 1905, *CP* 6.585). Growth is connected to "evolutionary love," the impulse to take what has been received from the past and improve upon it, to take even what is hateful and make it into something better (1893, *CP* 6.289). Indeed, Dewey sees the basis of growth in Peirce's principle of continuity which, as Dewey interprets it, is that "every experience both takes up something from those which have gone before and modifies in some way the quality of those which come after" (1902, *CP* 1.171; 1892, *CP* 6.112; 1906, *CP* 6.179; 1939, *LW* 13, p. 19). Growth adds a positive dimension to continuity by picking up what is best from the past and making it better (Boyer, 2010, p. 29). Growth is "moving to become better" (1920, *MW* 12, pp. 180–181). "Growth itself," Dewey says, "is the only moral 'end'" (1920, *MW* 12, pp. 180–181). The basis of morality for James, Dewey, and Peirce rests on the desire to improve on the past.

Chapter 3

Practical Life

The pragmatists argued that morality is a collective, evolving, and on-going experiment in living. The *ethical project*, as Philip Kitcher calls it, is characterized by attempts to solve problems associated with the pursuit of a plethora of goods, some of which conflict, and not all of which can be accommodated in the same organization of practical life (2011, p. 2). Kitcher sees this as a matter of *altruism failures*, problems of recognizing and acting on the interests and goods of others (2011, p. 6). As he argues in accord with Dewey's thinking, such a position lends itself to a *pragmatic naturalism*, that ethics emerges out of the human social situation, out of practical life (2011, p. 3). If that is the case, what are the features of practical life that make up this ethical project?

Practices

The work of being human is practical work, work done in practices. As James Wallace argues, "human life consists in participating in practices" (2009, p. 11). From waking to sleeping and everything in between, practices constrain human work since they provide an organization for claims about how something is best done in order to attain the ends that are pursued by people in all walks of life. This comes close to Immanuel Kant's definition of practice: "An activity seeking a goal which is conceived as a result of following certain general principles of procedure" (1793, p. 412). Alasdair MacIntyre has a similar definition: a cooperative activity that generates some internal good (1981, p. 175). Because practices aim at some end, they are obviously goal-directed, and the people who practice in practices are also goal-directed since the practice, they hope, affords them ends that they seek.

Two pragmatists, James Wallace and Frederick Will, have interesting things to say about practices. James Wallace wrote *Norms and Practices* and comes out of the pragmatic tradition of John Dewey. Frederick Will wrote a collection of essays on practices and their governance. One can see the influence of Peirce in his writings. Wallace notes that his notion of practice "derives from the American pragmatists" (2009, p. 11) and defines it in a way consistent with Kant and MacIntyre:

> A practice, regarded as a complex norm, is a social phenomenon, a shared body of practical knowledge in a community. It is, at the same time, a psychological phenomenon, a complex shared habit of individuals in Dewey's terminology, a shared, structured set of skills, know-how, understandings, tendencies of thought and action, and appreciations. . . ." (2009, p. 16)

Wallace attempts to take the pragmatists' notion of habit and translate it into the more current notion of practice. Dewey struggled with defining what is now commonly called practices, but settled on the notion of habit, inherited from both Peirce and James:

> . . . [W]e need a word to express that kind of human activity which is influenced by prior activity and in that sense acquired; which contains within itself a certain ordering or systematization of minor elements of action; which is projective, dynamic in quality, ready for overt manifestation; and which is operative in some subdued subordinate form even when not obviously dominating activity. Habit even in its ordinary usage comes nearer to denoting these facts than any other word. (1922, *MW* 14, p. 31)

As Wallace notes, the relation between habits and practices is such that an individual "expresses this 'habit' by participating in the practice . . ." (2009, p. 16), so they are correlative to some degree. This is perhaps why practices are often viewed as tacit rather than explicit and deliberate. Consequently, people share certain presuppositions and expectations about practices (Bourdieu 1990; Turner, 1994, pp. 28ff). In general, taking Wallace's sense of it, it's reasonable to define a practice as work directed to a certain end on the basis of shared practical knowledge about how best to achieve that end.

In any case, Wallace makes three important points about practices: First, they evolve historically as solutions to a problem and persist if they continue to solve those problems; second, they are inherently normative; third, they are essentially forms of practical reasoning and knowledge.

Practices as Solutions to Problems

Wallace argues that practices are set up to solve the problem of how best to get the goods it is designed to get. Imagine if people had to reinvent ways of getting and preparing food each time they were hungry, how to build a house, how to relate to others, or how to educate or care for children. Practices develop as solutions to problems and persist, with some inevitable change, if they are good solutions to those problems. They are wrought through a collective wisdom over time. "The practices and their component practical norms . . . are the result of the experience over time of many people in dealing with the problems they encounter in living together and doing things" (Wallace 2009, p. 3). Frederick Will agrees: practices are ". . . complex social processes through which over time—sometimes slowly and sometimes rapidly, sometimes reflectively and sometimes with remarkably little conscious thought . . . undergo revision" (1997, p. 146). "Practical knowledge, knowledge of better and worse ways to do things, arises from people's encounters with the world and their sharing with others what they learn on these occasions" (1997, p. 83). Practices also change over time in order to address novel or changing circumstances or eventually fall apart if they fail in continuing to solve those problems. This is why practices have histories (Wallace, 2009, p. 1). Frederick Will notes that

> . . . not only do the conditions under which life is lived and practices engaged in change, generating inadequacies in previously achieved arrangements; so that present inadequacies may be attributed simply to failure of old governance to meet intervening new conditions. It is also the case that the success of previous arrangements may alter life in such a way as to lead to the modification or rejection of some of the very arrangements of practices . . . that have made this state of life possible. . . ." (1997, p. 74)

A full understanding of practices requires an understanding of their historical and cultural genealogy. Some pragmatists, such as Colin Koopman, see a failure in Dewey for not taking a more genealogical approach to current problematic processes and urges a correction using the model of Michel Foucault's work (2015, p. 200). Others, such as Vincent Colapietro, see more similarity between the reconstructionist approach of Dewey and the genealogy of Foucault. He claims both are sophisticated meliorists, pointing to where change in practices is needed by understanding their genealogies. "For both Foucault and Dewey, all we have are our own experiments and the histories in which they are rooted and out of which they are growing" (1998, p. 345). The caution with genealogical approaches is that they tend to problematize more than offer solutions to the problems with practices. Although understanding the historicity of a practice can certainly help solve current problems with the practice, the problem is in the present, as Dewey argues, and needs to be addressed in that context.

Practices are common since they are thought to be efficient ways of doing things. Dewey argues that habits (*cum* practices) form precisely because they successfully work relative to their environment, and allow individuals to operate with "ease, deftness, and accuracy" and "an economical and effective control of the environment which they secure" (1916, *MW* 9, p. 51). The psychologist, Daniel Kahenman notes that, "in the economy of action, effort is a cost . . ." and "as you become skilled in a task, its demand for energy diminishes" He argues for a "law of least effort" that applies to both cognitive and physical exertion, namely "that if there are several ways of achieving the same goal, people will eventually gravitate to the least demanding course of action" (2011, p. 35).

What Is a Problem?

If practices are proposed as solutions to problems, what is a problem? This may sound like a strange question, but it needs to be answered to get a better understanding of what practices do. The scholarly and research literature often characterizes problems as the inability to complete goals—which fits nicely with the character of practices. Witness the classic definition by E. L. Thorndike:

> A problem exists when the goal that is sought is not directly attainable by the performance of a simple act available in the animal's repertory. . . . (cited in Frensch & Funke, 1995, p. 6)

In *The Concept of a Problem*, Gene Agre defines a problem as "the gap between the current state of affairs and the desired state of affairs" (1982, p. 122). Philip Kitcher uses a similar definition: "Something is only a problem," he writes, "if it is felt as interfering with the satisfaction of desires" (2011, p. 251). Same with John Hayes, who says it is "the gap which separates where you are from where you want to be" (1979, p. 77).

Other definitions seem to focus on the relationship of problem to problem-solver, as in B. F. Skinner's definition as "a question for which there is at the moment no answer. . . ." (Skinner, 1966, p. 225; Frensch & Funke, 1995, p. 6), in which case a problem arises when the agent does not know how to resolve the problem. Consider Davis's definition: "a problem is a stimulus situation for which an organism does not have a ready response" (Davis, 1973, p. 12; Frensch & Funke, 1995, p. 6). D'Zurilla, Nezu and Mayeu-Olivares define a problem as "any life situation or task . . . that demands a response for adaptive functioning but no effective response is immediately apparent or available . . . because of the presence of one or more obstacles" (2004, p. 12). Similarly, Alvin Goldman characterizes a problem as something that occurs when a person wants an answer to a question but does not readily have that answer (1983, p. 23).

Combining these two general features of problems, Frisch and Funke's analysis suggests that the most critical feature of problems can be expressed by the metaphor of obstacle, either an obstacle between the actual situation and the goal state or an obstacle between the problem and its solution by some agent (1995, p. 7; Agre, 1982, p. 132). In other words, a problem is created by a constraint on reaching goals, as also expressed by Mayer (1977, pp. 4–5) and Nickles (1981) or in G. Chadwick's simple formula: "Problem= Goal +Impediment to the Goal" (1971, p. 124). Norbert Seel concurs: a problem is described by three components: (1) a given initial state; (2) a desired final state; and (3) a barrier which hinders the solution of the problem, that is, to come from the initial to the final state (2012, pp. 2690–2691). As Agre points out, the obstacle between initial and goal state and the obstacle between problem-solver and solution are correlative.

Walter Lippmann has an interesting way to characterize problems that translates this notion in terms of means and ends. "To create a problem," he says, "there must be at least two dependent but separated variables: wants and the means of satisfaction; and these two variables must have a disposition to alter so that an antecedent equilibrium is disturbed" (1927, p. 83).

The pragmatists' account of a problem certainly aligns with this view. Murray Murphey claimed that the theory of evolution provided Peirce

> with a new definition of the nature of a problem—a definition subsequently developed by Dewey. A problem situation exists whenever we find our established habits of conduct inadequate to attain a desired end, regardless of how the inadequacy comes about, and the effect of a problem situation upon us in the production of a doubt. . . . the theory provides a clarification of the nature of an answer. An answer is any rule of action which enables us to attain our desired ends. Accordingly, our objective is to find a rule which will always lead us to that which we desire. (1961, p. 163)

Dewey notes that practical hypotheses are formulated to "get around or surmount obstacles." For example, the need of a physician "implies the existence of hindrances in the pursuit of the normal occupations of life, but it equally implies the existence of positive factors which may be set in motion to surmount the hindrances and reinstate normal pursuits" (1915, p. 507).

The Normative Character of Practices

The second important aspect of practices according to Wallace is that they are inherently normative. "A practice *consists* in a structured body of norms. Norms are its constituents" (2009, p. 11). They are normative precisely because they prescribe and proscribe "good ways or right ways to do certain things" (2009, p. 1). There are better and worse ways to do things, and whatever is the current version of a practice typically proclaims it to be the better way (Wallace 2009, p. 11). But practices not only prescribe good and right ways to do things; they also implicitly suppose that what they aim at are also good, in some sense of that notion. A further proof of their inherent normativity is that cultures tend to educate their members in its ways. On the other hand, failure to follow the prescribed ways and means, or to engage in proscribed ways and means of practices, often involves sanctions or disapprobation of various kinds and degrees. They also serve as the basis for criticizing other practices (2009, p. 73).

Although practices are normative in this sense, many would say there's an essential difference between technical and ethical aspects of practices.

Wallace disagrees. Technical and ethical norms are interconnected (2009, p. 122). For example, if the practice of carpentry is to figure out how to build things in the best way, carpenters would not use flawed material deceptively or put it together in a manner they would knowingly cause it to malfunction. To do so would be to corrupt the practice, which means that the practice is not the best way to do things. Making a chair honestly and making a quality chair are of a piece. A scientist who fakes data does very bad science (2009, p. 27). Conversely, ethical norms have an implicit technical aspect to them. If the golden rule says "do unto others as you would have them do unto you," it also prescribes a procedure for attaining the presumed end of doing good things: "Here's how to go about doing good things." If good is to be done, then act to create the greatest happiness for the greatest number, so the utilitarians would say. It lays out a procedure for attaining the good of the practice.

As Wallace points out, philosophers and psychologists have tended to distinguish ethical norms in kind from practical ones. For example, based in part on the work of the psychologist Paul Rozin, Steven Pinker argues that there is a psychological "toggle switch" that turns on when people consider moral versus practical matters, in the sense of something non-normative (2008). Rozin (2007) studied the practice of vegetarianism and noted the behavior of two classes of vegetarians. The first were vegetarians primarily for reasons of their own health: to reduce cholesterol or avoid toxins. The latter were vegetarians in order to avoid what they considered to be the needless suffering of animals. Rozin showed that the attitudes and opinions of the latter have a significant difference. They tend to switch to moral emotions such as purity. Meat is treated as a contaminant. They tend to think that others ought also to be vegetarians, and they think that their diet tends to make people virtuous in other ways. The dietary vegetarians do not seem to have these habits and attitudes (2007).

Wallace argues that such categorical distinctions between moral attitudes and "practical" ones are misleading. They are both normative and integrated in any practice as forms of practical knowledge (2009, p. 3). Claiming to be inspired by Dewey, Wallace argues that one result of this division is that ". . . ethical norms are viewed as being fundamentally different in their origin, nature, and authority from the norms that practices comprise" (2009, p. 3). He doesn't provide much empirical evidence for the claim—and Pinker does.

Wallace's claims might still be defensible. For example, although Rozin's findings are consistent with Pinker's "moral toggle switch" hypothesis, they are also consistent with another hypothesis. It could be argued that Pinker's claim might not be the result of a difference between practical matters and ethical norms so much as differences in *moral intensity*. T. M. Jones argues that people will have different moral attitudes toward a situation depending on its intensity (1991). Intensity is a result of several factors, including the magnitude of the consequences of acting or not acting on something; how likely those consequences will occur. Also, it depends on whether the deleterious consequences will affect a few or many. Additionally, the moral intensity may be greater depending on whether the consequences affect people's own lives or their proximate community, as opposed to some distant group with whom they have no relation.

Consider a reconstruction of the practical reasoning of the two groups of vegetarians The way it is framed by Pinker is that the moral vegetarians believe that vegetarianism is a means to achieve the end of not harming innocent others. The diet vegetarians believe that vegetarianism is a means to achieve a higher level of health. Two different ends, but the same means. Certainly, harming or killing innocent others has a higher moral intensity than harming one's health, but is the first a moral attitude and the other only a practical, amoral one? One could reasonably argue that protecting one's health is a moral obligation, particularly for parents and spouses, who have children dependent on them for economic and emotional well-being. Kant, for example, emphasizes duties to self, and staying healthy is certainly a duty to self. The effects on a family of a member with a chronic illness or debilitation can be devastating and heart wrenching.

To this point, a recent study by E. Melanie DuPuis on the history of dietary advice in America shows another dimension to this issue. She argues that the history of dietary advice, starting with physician and civic leader Benjamin Rush was infused with moral meaning as to what is good to eat, morally speaking, and what is not. She argues that "dietary advice, in determining how Americans should eat, also propounded a particular and fixed vision of how they should live" (2015, p. 5). Certainly, much of the language of dietary proscriptions was couched in the language of purity. She sees in the Enlightenment values of the earlier American founders, a linkage between autonomy as self-control and liberty (2015, p. 20). Diet was a form of self-control and defined the difference between wanton pleasure-seeking and purity by means of such self-control. Indeed, the link between spiritual and moral purity and food purity is well-known by any follower of most any religion.

Surely, most would agree that killing innocent others has more moral intensity than managing what one eats for health reasons, but the health vegetarians, right or wrong, do not see the matter of killing animals for food as morally intense as the animal advocates do. By analogy, prochoice advocates do not believe that aborting zygotes and fetuses at certain stages of development is killing innocent human beings, as opposed to prolife advocates, who do. That does not make the prochoice position amoral and the other moral. The beliefs about the moral status of zygotes, embryos, and fetuses changes the moral intensity of abortion in each case. It's not so much that there is a moral toggle switch that turns on when the intensity of something reaches a certain threshold. It is also plausible to say that there is moral concern all the way up and down the intensity of situations, proportionate to that intensity. If, for example, it were found out that vegetarianism is actually unhealthy and leads to early death, the moral intensity of the health issue now increases, so that even the vegetarians concerned about animal suffering would see it as something wrong to do.

Thinking of ethical norms as a special additive to purely technical practices results in an artificial division that often leaves practitioners with the sense that doing work ethically is something over and above doing the normal work of the practice. When that happens, ethical norms often get codified as a layer placed on top of the practice for window dressing. Here's what the organization values—here's the code of ethics—check that box. The codifications usually happen precisely because there has been a breakdown of the ethical norms of the practice. Enron had a very lovely code of ethics prominently displayed, but that didn't stop its management from cheating its employees, shareholders and the general public and ruining many lives in the process.

In a practice that is working well, ethical norms are considered as much a part of the practice as any norm. In good plumbing, good teaching, or good anything, technical skill and ethical behavior work to reinforce each other. The very idea of teaching the practice to others, its transmission, the desire to do it right, and desire to improve it—what Will calls its governance structure—is part and parcel of any practice. The very idea of doing one's best in a practice that is doing well is already an ethical stance.

The norms may target certain functions in the practice. Some may be concerned with the means to the ends or products of the practice. Others may be concerned with how practitioners ought to cooperate in doing so, and still others may be concerned with how to cooperate or manage conflict with other practices (2009, p. 123). There is also the matter of the ethical consideration of the ends themselves. There is, additionally, the normative governance of the practice, which is concerned with making all of these work together and managing and correcting the problems that arise (Wallace, 2009, p. 14). Burning fossil fuels can be an efficient means of steel production, but it conflicts with the ends of a number of other practices by causing pollution (Wallace, 2009, p. 15). Not only may the goods of practices conflict with one another, but since practitioners are usually engaged simultaneously in several practices, this may also generate conflicts. People are parents, spouses, neighbors, employees, professionals, friends, citizens, all of which take place within practices, and all of which have the potential for conflict (Wallace, 2009, pp. 17–18).

The Normative Governance of Practices

Precisely because problems can arise both internally and externally to the practice, there is usually an interest in the governance of the practice. Practices have to work at making sure good work continues to go well—and there can always be better ways of doing things. No matter how well practices are good at producing their outcomes, they may still conflict with other practices, so there is the job of minimizing those conflicts. Also, things change in the larger environment of the practice, and that may require changes in practices. As Will notes:

> the collective body of practices is in widespread ways, in various degrees at various places, subject to change, revision, and reconstruction, results characteristically produced in it by discrepancies arising *internally* between component practices, or *externally* between various practices and the conditions of their application. (Will, 1997, p. 140)

For these reasons, Will claims that almost all practices have normative governance. By governance, Will means "all the processes by which, in both individuals and groups, social practices are developed and regulated; strengthened or weakened; changed or preserved against change; and sometime extinguished. These processes may be gradual and slow, or rapid and abrupt . . ." (1997, p. 64). As Matthias Kettner summarizes Will's notion: ". . . all good governance starts from more or less unsatisfactory practice and ends in more or less satisfactory practice" (1998, p. 309). Good governance leads to improvement and progress.

Will emphasizes that the governance of practice is inherent in the practice itself (1997, p. 66). One cannot be trained in these practices without being in some degree infused with rational governance since part and parcel of learning practices are also learning their coordination and adjustment (1997, p. 70). He makes a distinction in this corrective process between "governance *in* practice" and "governance *of* practice." The former is involved in the ability to apply and coordinate the better processes in practices to the various situations that it is intended to govern. The latter is the case where the standard processes of practices are themselves instituted, changed, or altered (1997, p. 71). They are coordinate concerns in that, often, the appeal to the governance *of* a practice arises from a problem that occurs with governance *in* a practice (1997, p. 71).

The legitimacy of governance norms derives from their ability to work in minimizing a practice's problems, rather than any abstract justification of rules or principles (Frega, 2012, p. 493). As Will notes, "Dewey repeatedly stressed that the authority of acts of governance lies in their capacity of these to meet the needs of the problematic situation in which the governance occurs and to which it ministers" (1997, p. 187). For Will, norms are "concrete ways of doing, and questions about their value—their validation, justification, legitimacy, and so on—are questions about . . . the products that are realized in and through them" (Will, 1997, p. 166). "The grounds of governance is in their performance, actual and promissory, in the lives of those who follow them" (1997, p. 178). As he points out, "two giant figures in American pragmatism, Peirce and Dewey," are part of a "newer tradition" that worked against the "divorcement of reason from practice" and "conceived of reason" as "fundamentally social" (1997, pp. 67–68).

The primary purpose of normative or rational governance is to prevent a practice from becoming problematic. David Copp, following J. L. Mackie, also developed a similar notion of the normative governance of practices, and recognizes its basis in problem solving (2009, p. 27). Normativity, Copp argues, is to be understood in relation to "generic problems faced by human beings in the circumstances they face in their ordinary lives" (2012, p. 38). He calls them "problems of normative governance because they are problems that we can better cope with when we subscribe to appropriate systems of norms" (Copp, 2012, p. 38). Coping with these problems is obviously better "when people are governed by appropriate systems of standards that they subscribe to than would otherwise be the case" (Copp,

2009, p. 29). "Our subscription to these systems enables us to deal with the relevant problems. This is the basic fact that underlies all normativity" (Copp, 2009, p. 26). Governance processes are often in play attempting to find the optimal solution to a problem, relative to alternatives (2009, p. 32).

Any community—and it can be argued, any practice—must settle on normative solutions to certain fundamental problems in order to pursue whatever ends they wish to pursue (2009, pp. 27–28). Copp argues that "sociality" is one of these fundamental problems. First, since no one is self-sufficient, then people have to rely on the cooperation of others in order to achieve any goal. Second, in order to induce cooperation, people have to accept certain limitations on their behavior and exercise self-control, as well as signal to others through their behavior that they are willing to cooperate. Finally, since the pursuit of goals requires beliefs about what constitutes those goals and how to attain them, there must be some successful epistemic standards for inquiries into these matters:

> [T]o achieve what we value and to meet our needs, we need information, at least some of which is provided by others. We need to be able to assess evidence and form beliefs that are reliably at least approximately accurate. So we need our processes of belief formation to be regulated by appropriate epistemic standards, standards conformity with which will help assure that our beliefs are justified and that our overall system of belief is one in which, very roughly, the ratio of true to false beliefs is as high as feasible. (Copp, 2009, p. 28)

In other words, in order to have reliable practices, that is, practices that reliably produce the outcomes they aim at, they will need to meet certain epistemological as well as behavioral norms.

Where does this all lead? Wallace claims that practices are inherently normative since they prescribe the best way to do things. But clearly there are good and bad practices. Thievery is a practice that can be done better or worse, in the sense that those ways make it more successful in accomplishing its ends. In order for practices to be *good* practices, it has to be supposed that they prescribe *righteous means that are also successful in attaining good ends*. In order for a practice to be counted as good, formally speaking, it must serve a good end and prescribe morally right means that will successfully attain that end. This overarching norm of good practices could be expressed in the following way: *practices ought to do what is likely to attain a good end in the right way.* But, of course, this norm is merely formal and does not supply any content as to what is right or good, so, it does not provide specific guidance. As Wallace argues, the latent norms of practices in their abstract form provide insufficient guidance for particular problems the practice might face since their very abstractness makes possible many incompatible solutions consistent with those norms (2009, pp. 41–42). The task is how to get to that guidance. Wallace relies on the notion of practical reasoning and practical knowledge as providing that guidance.

Chapter 4

Practical Reasoning

Wallace's third thesis is that practices involve practical reasoning. Practices form as solutions to problems, and Wallace emphasizes that practical reasoning is "a form of problem-solving" (2009, p. 18). Practical reasoning might then serve as guide to good practices. However, practical reasoning, as it is usually considered, is thought to be a purely instrumental form of reasoning—reasoning about means to ends, regardless of what those ends might be. It is considered to be problematic as *ethical* reasoning for that reason. Most agree with Robert Brandom that "according to this common approach," of characterizing practical reasoning, "the norms governing practical reasoning and definitional rational action are essentially *instrumental* norms, which derive their authority from intrinsically motivating preferences or desires" (Brandom, 2000, pp. 30–31). But because practical reasoning can be instrumental in this sense, it is fraught with problems from a moral point of view. It does not determine which, among alternative means, are morally right to do, only which means are likely to attain the end; nor does it provide guidance as to which ends are good to pursue. This can lead to all sorts of villainy. It fosters a Machiavellian world, and sits on the side of Thrasymachus in the debate with Socrates. It deliberates about what can be done, not what ought to be done. If a dictator wants to eradicate a certain ethnic minority, here's the best way to do genocide. For this reason, it does not appear to provide the needed normative guidance for practices of good ends and righteous means. Since the pragmatists promote practical reasoning as the sort of reasoning in practical life, then their ethical project appears problematic.

There are two obvious remedies to this problem. One of course is to abandon practical reasoning in favor of some other model of ethical reasoning. Another is to defend an interpretation of it that avoids the problems of instrumentalism. Wallace contends with the latter strategy, specifying the sort of practical reasoning that is most conducive to forming good practices. *Practical knowledge*, as he often calls it, is "knowledge of how to pursue the activity." As he explains, "knowledge of how to do something is normative; it is knowledge of how to do it *properly*, knowledge of better rather than worse ways of doing things" (2009, p. 11). He also emphasizes that practical reasoning involves knowledge of what is valuable to pursue (2009, p. 14). Thinkers such as Henry Richardson agree. He argues that it is a misconception to think that practical reasoning is restricted to deliberation only about means to ends, but also there can be a practical reasoning about ends as well (1997, p. 3). Practical reasoning, properly comprehended, could be a good candidate for the specific guidance needed about the means and ends of practices. It would be best at this point to review these various strategies.

There have been a number of formulations of practical reasoning. However, in its most generic form, the first premise is usually about a certain pro-attitude toward an end—either it is desired, wanted, needed, or intended. People want, need, desire and intend to have a rewarding, good-paying career. The second premise usually involves belief in what amounts to a practical hypothesis, a belief that a set of actions that, if executed competently, are likely means to attain the desired end (Audi, 2005, p. 86). Many people believe that the key to a good career is a college education and, to the extent that they desire good careers, they tend to act on that belief and attend college.

Practical reasoning can be helpful in explaining why people did what they did, it can also be helpful in predicting human behavior, although weakly. It also functions normatively by claiming, prudentially, the best means for attaining an end. Robert Brandom's language for each of these functions might be useful here: People can use practical reasoning to predict what people *will* do, and it can explain what they intended to do, that is, what they *shall* do, and also what they *ought* to do (2000, p. 85).

Because the second premise is a practical hypothesis, practical reasoning makes predictions about the practical reasoner. If Jake has a bear encounter and believes that climbing a tree will allow him to escape, then it would be a reasonable prediction that Jake will climb a tree should he encounter a bear. Of course, the predictive ability of practical reasoning is weak since there are so many factors that could intervene to prevent that action. A tree might not be available to climb. Jake might freeze and not climb the tree; the bear might attack before he can reach the tree. He might panic and just run; the tree might not support his weight.

Practical reasoning is very good at explaining an action that has already occurred. Jake climbed the tree because he wanted to escape the bear and believed that by climbing the tree he could do so. Practical reasoning provides an explanation, thereby, an understanding of why Jake did what he did. As such practical reasoning also provides a reason for actions. The desire to avoid the bear could be a good reason to climb the tree.

Practical reasoning has a normative function in the sense that it tells what ought or what ought not to be done. It turns out that black bears can climb trees, so Jake *ought not* to climb the tree, if he wanted to escape the black bear. As Bernard Williams notes, whether or not the second premise in practical reasoning—the belief that climbing the tree will provide an escape from the bear—is true or not does not alter the explanation of the action, but it does alter the normative prescription (1993, p. 102). The norm governing practical reasoning in this sense is what Bernard Williams calls a *prudential norm,* namely that *people ought to do what is likely to best attain what they desire* (1993, p. 114). It is essentially what Kant called a hypothetical or pragmatic imperative, or what Peirce calls a practical or pragmatic maxim. Practical reasoning can function like prudential advice to anyone who has certain ends or goals they would like to attain. But, as noted, in-and-of-itself, this makes it a purely instrumental form of reasoning.

The Desire-Belief Model of Moral Motivation

Many argue that practical reasoning rests on some variant of the so-called desire-belief model of human action (Anscombe, 1963; Goldman, 1970; Williams, 1993, p. 102; Davidson, 2006, p. 23). In its general outlines, it takes the position that human action is goal-directed, and people tend to act on what they believe will attain the ends they desire. Reasons for an action motivate people to act, and desires for an end serve as the reasons for such actions. David Hume is thought to have developed the standard model (1739). Hume's theses are the following: (1) desire alone drives the determination of the ends of action, ends are picked out by desires not reasoned beliefs (1739, p. 413; Korsgaard, 1999, p. 312); (2) desire is the only motivation of action, and belief can motivate only when conjoined with desire (1739, p. 413); (3) desire has no representational quality (1739,

p. 415); and (4) reason in the form of beliefs cannot prevent or produce any action by contradicting or opposing desire (1739, pp. 413, 458). In general reason "is and ought to be slave to the passions" (1739, p. 413). Updated, this would argue that the reasons for doing some action "is and ought to be slave to desires."

Bernard Williams calls this position *internalism,* that reasons for doing something are inherently connected to a "subjective motivational set," characterized predominantly by desire (Williams, 1993, p. 102). As Robert Brandom explains it, "the empiricist tradition seeks to trace back talk of reasons for action and norms governing action to underlying preferences and desires, which are understood both as intrinsically motivating and as the only sorts of things that can be intrinsically motivating. Thus, any complete expression of a reason for action must include a specification of what it is that the agent wants, in virtue of which the reasons functions (motivationally) as a reason for that agent" (2000, p. 38). As Thomas Nagel characterizes it, "since all motivated action must result from the operation of some motivating factor within the agent, and since belief cannot by itself produce action, it follows that a desire of the agent must always be operative . . ." (1970, p. 27).

Although Mark Schroeder is a defender of the Humean model, he also makes its problems very clear (2013). Internalism not only reinforces the instrumentalism in practical reasoning, but also promotes subjectivism in ethics. First, since the motivation to act morally depends on desires, if people do not desire to do what is right, there appears to be no recourse to a moral appeal. Either they desire to do the right thing or not. If, as in Schroeder's example, Jill's father, having divorced Jill's mother some time ago, has no desire to have anything to do with his daughter, then there is no reason for him to do that. There can be no appeal to an objective, agent-neutral norm, such as parents should support their children (2013, p. 103). Motivation always has to be tied to the internal motivational set of the individual, and for that reason whether to act morally is purely subjective, dependent on what a person desires. The choice to do the right thing would be like deciding which suit to wear today. As such, the model lacks what Schroeder calls *strong modal status,* namely, that people would have a reason, for example, to come to the aid of another person, even if they did not have the desire to do so. Under this model, ethical claims would have very little normative force (2013, p. 108).

Another problem that Schroeder points out with Hume's model is that it could support the eccentricity, irrationality or immorality of desired ends.

Since desires picks out ends, anything that anyone desires would seem to be a good reason for acting on whatever brings it about. In his example, if Aunt Margaret wants to reconstruct a scene from *Martha Stewart Living* on Mars, then she has a good reason to do so, simply on the basis of desiring it (2013, p. 84). In other words, the Humean model does not put any reasonable, yet alone ethical brakes on what is desired, the ends of actions. There's no way to judge the moral difference between Aunt Margaret's desires and Aunt Sue's desires for famine relief. Yet, intuitively, people would say that the first is crazy, and the second good to pursue.

Finally, a third problem Schroeder notes is that Hume's model seems to permit irrationality of means. Since beliefs cannot influence desires, then a desire, for example, to have iron in one's diet would motivate that person to eat cars, given that cars are made of iron. Since beliefs cannot oppose desires, as Hume argues, then the belief that cars are inedible shouldn't influence the desire (2013, pp. 95–96).

Schroeder comes to the defense of the Humean model, and tries to show how each of these major problems might be remedied. If this were science, most scientists would move on, given the number of anomalies. But Schroeder makes a clever stab at trying to show that the Humean model is still feasible. Of course, even if it is feasible, it may not be the better model, relative to alternatives.

Of the three problems, the first concerning the agent-neutrality and strong modal status of ethical claims is the most salient to the issues here. One obvious way to solve it, that Schroeder does not mention, is to argue that acting morally is a means to something that is universally desired. For example, David Gauthier argues that people would place moral constraints, such as promise-keeping, on their behavior because it maximizes their self-interest, assuming that the maximization of self-interest is a desire everyone would have. Keeping promises fosters cooperation with others, and cooperation maximizes self-interest, generally speaking (1986, pp. 2–3). Oddly, virtue ethicists, such as Julia Annas, would also fall into this line of thinking. She reiterates Aristotle's claim that virtuous behavior is constitutive of flourishing, and flourishing is inherently desirable. The implication is that the desire for flourishing is a reason to be virtuous (2006, p. 516). Of course, these rely on empirical claims that the desires are universal, and the means will attain those desires. Believe it or not, not everyone acts out of self-interest, and not everyone who acts virtuously, flourishes, nor does everyone act virtuously out of a desire to flourish. Bernard Williams, for example, argues the obvious that, even though there are certainly people who are not flourishing because of their viciousness, and there are those who are vicious because they are not flourishing, there are those who are miserable precisely because they are virtuous (1985, pp. 45–46).

Schroeder also seems skeptical about claims about universal desires. For example, he doubts J. David Velleman's thesis that desire for autonomy is constitutive of agency, and so is universal because it is a necessary for any agent as agent (2000). Schroeder thinks it's difficult to show there are such universal and necessary desires, but it also doesn't satisfy the condition of strong modal status, since if the agent doesn't desire autonomy, there is no reason to act morally (2013, p. 107). The point could be made somewhat differently. It could be supposed that autonomous agents could desire to be heteronomous, in Kant's language, and choose to be controlled by whatever moral rules dominate the agent's culture. Even though autonomy is necessary to choose heteronomy, it is not desired. So there are cases where autonomy is not desired. This is known to happen.

Schroeder's solution may not be any more successful. He bases his solution on a certain interpretation of Hume's standard model, which he calls *hypotheticalism*. Essentially, he argues that a reason for people to do some action is that they have a desire for some end, and the truth of the reason explains why the agent's doing that action promotes that end (2013, p. 59). The desire explains the reason, and serves in the explanation of every reason (2013, p. 60) He then argues something like the following. There may be several different desires that serve as reasons for the same end. People may choose to come to the aid of another because they feel distress over seeing suffering, or they may want to create a certain image of neighborliness to others, or they may want to impress their significant other. But whatever people desire, they will also desire what will truly attain the end. What will truly attain an end is agent-neutral for that reason since it rests on the truth that it will attain that end, rather than what an agent happens to believe (2013, p. 115). Although this voids the subjectivism of means, it does not void the instrumentalism, since it doesn't address the norm of righteous means, the goodness of the means to that end. Certain means may indeed attain the ends desired, but those ends may also be morally reprehensible. Hume seems to argue that desires for the ends are where the spade turns in grounding motivation and they are just what they are, with no representational content, nor moral evaluation. But this permits any actions in the pursuit of any desires, so long as they attain what is desired.

This leaves open the field for externalists, the view something like Derek Parfit's position, namely, that the reason for desiring some end is that there are certain factual properties of the thing desired that would give people strong reasons for desiring it (2011, vol. 1, p. 38). Desires can be informed by beliefs. Externalists argue that the internalist position is inconsistent with our intuitions about moral claims—that they have an authority, a normative force, a strong modal status, that is agent-neutral and extends beyond the individual agent's desires, and can in some cases oppose them. The internalist position doesn't account for the common experience of duty, where people feel compelled to do something, despite the lack of desire to do it. Some Humeans claim that the sense of duty requires a desire to do one's duty but, again, doing one's duty is often undesirable.

Externalists argue that desires are not the sole motivators, but beliefs, particularly moral beliefs, alone can motivate action. Externalists include Christine Korsgaard (1999), Thomas Nagel (1970), T. M. Scanlon (2000), Robert Brandom (2000), among others. People who believe that lying is wrong are motivated not to lie even if they desire to avoid some outcome that telling the truth would involve. The mere fact of believing something is right to do is sufficient motivation and provides a good reason for doing it. This obviously captures the sense of deontological ethics and Kant's notion of the categorical imperative.

Each of these thinkers takes a different tack in dismissing the principal theses of Hume's standard model. Among other claims, Korsgaard points to an internal contradiction in the model that goes something like the following. There is a tacit prudential norm in the desire-belief model as noted, namely that people ought to pursue what is most likely to attain what they desire. However, since the Humeans claim that desires are the only motivators and not beliefs in certain norms, people would have to first desire to abide by the norm: Whatever they desire, people would have to desire the desire to attain what they desire, which is rather circular (1999, p. 215). This same point could be made somewhat differently. Suppose the prudential norm is not believed, would it still be desirable to act on it? It's quite reasonable to suppose that people believe that it is not right for everyone, including themselves, to act on anything that will attain their desires, precisely because some desires and some means are morally reprehensible. It would seem odd to desire to do something that is not believed desirable. Belief in the prudential norm seems more fundamentally motivating than the desire to act on it.

Thomas Nagel's approach is somewhat different. He wants to hold to the primary thesis of the desire-belief model—that desires must be present for an action to be motivating—but he argues that some desires are the results of beliefs. He makes a distinction between *unmotivated* and *motivated* desires in this regard (1970, p. 29). Unmotivated desires would be cases of physiological desires based on hunger, thirst, and so forth. Motivated desires are desires informed by beliefs. Believing that something is right could cause the desire to do what is right. This distinction would explain how it is possible to have a causal arrow from belief to desire. Believing that something is right or wrong would cause the desire to either do or not do what is right or wrong. In this way belief and desire are always conjoined, as Hume suggests, but still allows beliefs to be motivational.

T. M. Scanlon makes a more radical claim that desires are not motivational at all. He agrees with Nagel that there are motivated desires, but he also argues that unmotivated desires are also not motivating. Instead, these desires, such as the desire for food or sex involve ". . . having a tendency to see something as a reason." Scanlon characterizes these sorts of desires as simply directed-attention: "A person has a desire in the directed-attention sense that P if the thought of P keeps occurring to him or her in a favorable light, that is to say, if the person's attention is directed insistently toward considerations that present themselves as counting in favor of P" (1998, p. 39). Scanlon would be hard-pressed to find support for his position among most research psychologists that desires are merely forms of attention and do not motivate people to act. Standard accounts in psychology identify desire as a psychological state of motivation (Papies & Barsalou, 2015, p. 37). "Desires are key motivators in our lives. . . ." (Hofmann & Nordgren, 2015, p. 1). The question, as Nagel notes, is whether the motivation comes from the bottom up as purely physiological states, or bottom down from beliefs and cognitions, and to what degree that inhibits or amplifies desires.

Peirce actually has a theory of desire that is similar to Nagel's position (Liszka, 2021, pp. 80–82). It is often the case that desires are obscure—an end is an obscure object of desire. For Peirce, desires are indeterminate along three dimensions (1902, *CP* 1.205). First, desires are *general* in the sense that what people desire is "always some *kind* of thing or event" (1902, *CP* 1.205; 1894, *CP* 1.341). For example, people want happiness, but typically what is meant by happiness is ill-defined (1903, *CP* 5.158). Dewey calls ends built on desires, *ends-in-view* (1939, *LW* 13. p. 220). These are to be distinguished from the ends understood as the result of deliberations about the means to attain the end-in-view (1939, *LW* 13, p. 216).

Peirce argues that "desires become more specific in the pursuit of them" (1902, *CP* 1.205). Dewey claims further that the significance of ends is constituted by their means, in a way that is consistent with the pragmatic maxim. If an end-in-view is something general generated by some desire, then its meaning is found in the effects of its implementation in practical life (1939, *LW* 13, p. 228). For Peirce, something is general in the sense that its properties cannot be specified below a certain scale. A triangle is a general term, but in order to be general, it can neither be said to be scalene nor equilateral. For example, if people desire lighting, it is not clear what type is meant by that: Incandescent versus LED, overhead versus floor lamp, and so forth (1902, *CP* 1.205). If people desire apple pie, it's not clear which sort of apples they want in the pie, which sort of crust, whether it should be mixed with other fruit or nuts, and so forth—all they know is that they want the sort of general pleasure associated with an apple pie.

A second source of indeterminacy in desires is their *vagueness*, meaning that the desire has a certain *latitude* depending on circumstances. If people want *economical* heating, people in more rural areas might find it more economical to use a wood furnace than a gas source; whereas in denser populations with sources of natural gas nearby, a gas furnace might fit the bill (1902, *CP* 1.206).

The third source of indeterminacy is what Peirce calls its *longitude*. "By this I mean that while a certain ideal state of things might most perfectly satisfy a desire, yet a situation somewhat differing from that will be far better than nothing . . ." (1902, *CP* 1.207). For example, a brighter lamp might be better for reading, but the cost would hurt the pocketbook, thus some compromise between these two ends—an economical lamp and a bright lamp—is made (1902, *CP* 1.207). One might call the longitude the local optimum, relative to alternative choices. Using a different model for this concept of desire, one might think of it as a process mapped by a conical helix. The diameter of the base is its generality, its height its vagueness, and the volume its longitude. The apex would represent the most determinate version of the desire. Starting at the base, the desire has the greatest generality, vagueness and lowest optimality. As one pursues the desire, one climbs up the helix toward the apex, the diameter of the base shrinks, making the desire more specific, its altitude shrinks, bringing it closer to the apex, and the volume shrinks, bringing its pursuit to a more optimal result.

This position would argue against Hume's claim that desires have no representational content—and if they do, it has important ramifications for this theory (1739, p. 415). Psychological research shows that desires become strengthened and amplified by cognitive imagery. For example, "hunger might lead to an initial image of a meal, but then to elaborated imagery of appetizing foods, and lead to a goal to eat the specific imagined food."

As further evidence of this, desires for certain things decline when they compete with unrelated, difficult cognitive tasks. Given people's limited cognitive capacity, they cannot gin up the imagery needed to reinforce the desire, if it is competing with other cognitive tasks (Andrade et al., 2015, p. 22). There is well-established empirical support for the common experience in which people can create a desire for eating something even if they are not hungry. Creating mental simulations of past consumption of a delicious meal can gin up the desire to have that meal again (Papies & Barsalou, 2015, p. 38).

There certainly appears to be representational content at least in the case of higher-order desires, and it could be reasonably argued that the belief in the representational content affects the desires. Desires as intentional states are directed to something, and that something is represented in the beliefs about it. For example, according to a fairly recent Harris poll (November 13, 2013), about 68% of Americans believe in heaven. Within the Christian religion alone, there have been many positive representations of heaven over the centuries, a place that would fulfil a number of desires (Holmes, 1915, pp. 285–286). But if people believed that heaven was a place of eternal boredom, or mindless existence, that belief would certainly deflate the desire for heaven.

Hume's exceptions to cases where beliefs influence the passions contravene his claim that cognitive beliefs do not influence the passions. These exceptions are cases when it is believed that the object of desire does not exist, for example, the nonexistence of an afterlife, or when it is believed that the end desired is not attainable (Hume, 1739, p. 416). As Hume notes,

> the moment we perceive the falsehood of any supposition, or when it chuses means insufficient for the design'd end, 'tis impossible, that reason and passion can ever oppose each other, or dispute for the government of the will and actions. The moment we perceive the falsehood of any supposition, or the insufficiency of any means our passions yield to our reason without any position. (1739, pp. 416–417)

If the Harris poll is correct and 13% fewer Americans believe in the existence of heaven than in the previous decade, it also has to be assumed that they also no longer desire it.

In regard to the second exception, Alexander Bain's account of belief may be helpful. Peirce argued that it was Bain's account of belief that inspired his pragmatism (1898, *CP* 1.635; Liszka, 2021, pp. 83–85). For Peirce, a belief is "that upon which a man is prepared to act" (1906, *CP* 5.12). However, Bain argued more carefully that "belief is preparedness to act, for a given end, in a given way"—which articulates a version of practical reasoning that lessens the import of desire in motivation, and includes what appears to be an element of intention to act in the analysis of practical reasoning (Bain, 1889, p. 508). Bain holds that desires alone are not always motivating unless there is a belief that they can be attained. Bain notes, even if relief of pain and attainment of pleasure are motives, belief is key in acting on those two goals. There is nothing in the pain of thirst that provokes a person to lift a cup of liquid water to the mouth, or run to a brook. It is the belief that doing these actions will result in the relief of thirst that motivates one to act (1865, p. 525). It is, as he says, the presentation to the mind of the belief in the solution to relieving the pain that brings the person to act, not just the pain alone (1865, p. 525). For example, if a person stuck in the middle of the desert has the belief that no water is accessible within a life-saving radius, although it would not dampen the desire to quench his thirst, it could be demotivating since the situation is believed to be hopeless. Nagel seems to agree. It is not thirst alone that motivates someone to put money in a vending machine to get a drink; belief in the effectiveness of quenching thirst by extracting a drink from the machine does (1970, p. 33).

Current psychological theory supports Bain and Nagel. Expectancy-value theory claims that motivation to do something is not only based on the desire or the value of the goal, but the belief that a certain set of actions will likely lead to the goal (Atkinson, 1957; Wigfield & Eccles, 1992). Attribution theory argues that people are more motivated to achieve a goal if they perceive a beneficial goal as more likely to be achieved (Eccles, et al. 1983). Elaborated intrusion theory also comes to the same conclusion: ". . . [D]esire to purse a future goal requires vivid, detailed, and positively affectively charged imagery of goal success and the behavioral path toward that success" (Andrade, et al., 2015, p. 29). Albert Bandura's concept of self-efficacy makes a distinction between the objective assessment that doing something will likely accomplish an end and the belief by actors that they are competent to do those things (1977, p. 247). Based on Bandura's work, Allan Wigfield and Jacquelynn Eccles (2000) concluded that people tend to value less, activities for which they show less competence. These studies infer that desires can be affected by beliefs about means to ends, and attenuates Hume's characterization of the relation between belief and desire.

Robert Brandom develops an interesting approach to the matter of practical reasoning, called *normative pragmatics*. It aligns somewhat with Peirce, Bain, and Nagel's more complex account of the relation between belief and desire and, as will be shown, connects with Wallace's account of practices. It's an account that shows how practical reasoning might avoid its instrumentalism and subjectivism.

Normative pragmatics is the position that "the practices that confer propositional and other sorts of conceptual content implicitly contain norms concerning how it is *correct* to use expressions, under what circumstances it is *appropriate* to perform various speech acts, and what the *appropriate* consequences of such performances are" (1994, p. xiii). This aligns with Wallace's thesis that practices, including speech practices are inherently normative. As will be discussed later, Peirce also holds to a theory of assertion that anticipates some of Brandom's claims about the normativity of such speech acts (1905, *CP* 8.313).

Brandom applies this notion of normative pragmatics to the matter of practical reasoning. Not only do people learn to do things with words, they also learn to do things. First, Brandom would appear to agree with Michael Bratman that practical reasoning involves intention, and the intention cannot be reduced to some relation between belief and desire, as Humeans such as Donald Davidson propose (Bratman, 1999, p. 18; Davidson, 2006; Brandom, 2000, p. 82). Bratman makes an important point about the distinction between desire and intention. Desires are more than directed attention as Scanlon proposes. They can *influence* behavior. But intentions, on the other hand, are *conduct-controlling* pro-attitudes toward an action. They involve, as he says, "a special commitment" to action that desires do not exhibit. They do not wane or wax, but resist reconsideration and have an inertia (1999, p. 16). Interestingly, Peirce makes a similar claim, using the notion of resolution as an aspect of self-control (1906, *CP* 8.320; Liszka, 2021, pp. 85–86). Similarly, Brandom defines intentions as commitments to act (2000, p. 83). Like Bratman, Brandom wants to account for the motivation to act in practical reasoning not because of desires, but in terms of beliefs and intentions (2000, p. 83). After all, since many people may wish or day-dream about certain ends, but have no intention to act on them, desire alone may not be sufficient to motivate action. Accounting for the motivation to act on the basis of intentions is a more reliable account of motivation for that reason.

The intention to act is a commitment to a certain set of actions. Brandom argues that intention in this sense is similar to the sort of commitments that are entailed in making an assertion. In claiming something to be the case, one is also *committed* to all its inferential implications. On the other hand, one is *entitled* to these commitments if one has good reasons for the commitments (2000, p. 43). This applies to intentions to act. The intention, for example, to make a promise infers commitments to other sorts of acts, presumably on the basis of the understanding and expectations of the practice of making promises. For example, making promises infers keeping promises when the time comes, not denying that one made a promise, making at the same time another promise that is incompatible with this one, and so forth. In the last case people are not entitled to make incompatible promises, because of the inferential anomalies (2000, p. 44).

This approach requires thinking about practical reasoning somewhat differently than versions based on Hume's desire-belief model. Brandom recognizes at least three different types of practical reasoning: *prudential, institutional,* and *unconditional* (2000, p. 91). Practical reasoning, such as the intention to use an umbrella to stay dry during a rainstorm, illustrates the first type. The intention by a bank employee to wear a tie to work is an example of the second type. The intention to refrain from malicious gossip is an example of the third sort (2000, p. 84).

The desire or preference in such cases to remain dry can be accounted for in terms of the practical inferential commitments made, for example, the intention to open an umbrella, remain in the car, or to seek shelter under an awning. In turn, institutional types of practical reasoning, the banker's intention for wearing a tie, are accounted for by inferential commitments related to the banker's status as an employee of the bank. The banker may not desire to wear ties but has committed to wearing one because of the commitments in adopting that status. For the same reason, the banker does not intend to wear a clown suit to work. As Brandom explains:

> Here the norm implicitly underwriting the inference is associated with having a certain status, as employee of a bank, rather than with exhibiting a certain desire or preference. Whether one has a good reason to wear a necktie just depends on whether or not one occupies the status in question. This pattern. . . . corresponds to an *objective* sense of "good reason for action. . . ." In this sense, that A is preparing to go to work can be a good reason for A to wear a necktie, even though A is not in a position to appreciate it as such. (2000, p. 91)

Brandom makes an important point here. Commitments from the status can, therefore, oppose individual desires contrary to that status. To link this idea with Wallace, there's no reason the notion of practice could not be substituted for one of status. *The fact that the banker has committed to the practice* makes the banker acknowledge the commitment to wear a tie and is the reason for the intention to wear the tie, regardless of the desire to wear the tie or not.

Finally, unconditional practical reasoning—what Kant would call a categorical imperative—is a commitment made by people regardless of their status and across practices. If people believe that it is wrong to engage in malicious gossip, then regardless of their statuses, they are committed to a number of actions that follow from that norm. Perhaps a better way to state this is that certain norms are relevant and implicit in almost all if not all practices.

Brandom's position can be elaborated in a way that should be clear and obvious. All three types of practical reasoning are *in the context of practices* (1994, p. 623). Much of the analysis of practical reasoning that has been discussed so far is ahistorical and asocial, based on what an individual would reason as if individuals were free of any consideration of the practice in which the reasoning is taking place. As Wallace argues,

> We are born into a life structured by a great number of practices; our education begins with induction into practices that are taught to us by other people. What is learned was and is shared, shaped by the cumulative discoveries of earlier practitioners of what conduces to achieving the purposes of the practices in a variety of circumstances. (2009, p. 12)

Practices prescribe or proscribe ways of doing things. Practices have formed, evolved, and changed to prescribe or proscribe better ways of doing things and for that reason are inherently normative. Even in the case of such mundane activity as staying dry in rainy weather, umbrellas or raincoats are used as one of the better means to stay dry. That is why on a rainy day, one sees almost everyone walking with an umbrella. Consider just about any end that people desire, from waking to sleeping, and the means for their attainment are prescribed or proscribed. Think of all the norms that apply to even the most mundane activities, such as the practice of eating. The practice prescribes what to eat, how to grow it, how to prepare it, how to serve it, and how to eat it with what utensils and in what manner.

Since practices are prescribed ways of doing things that have been collectively formed and evolved over time to solve certain problems of practical life, they are not subjective. They are collectively approved to the point of their institutionalization or count as standard or best practices. If people intend to attain certain ends, they almost always are pursuing those ends within a practice that aims at those ends. Aristotle comes to the same conclusion: "[F]or people seek their own good, and suppose that it is right to do so. . . . Yet . . . as a matter of fact a man cannot pursue his own welfare without domestic economy and even politics" (*Nicomachean Ethics*, 1142a10). In Brandom's terms, the intention to attain the end involves a commitment to the norms of the practice related to that end. Failure to follow on those commitments is often met with disapproval, advice, correction, disapprobation, and sanctions of various sorts and degrees. If, in Mark Schroeder's example, a father doesn't desire to financially support his daughter, there are legal and other sorts of practices that will enforce the expectations and norms of parenthood. So that even if the father doesn't desire to do so, the collectivity thinks he should.

The desire for the ends that practices will likely bring about may, in Bratman's language, influence practitioners to participate in the practice; but it is the intention to do so that is conduct-controlling, and that commits people to the norms, the ways and means of the practice. As such, these commitments may oppose desires to do or not do certain things to attain those ends that are in accord with the relevant practices.

This voids the subjectivism of the Humean desire-belief model. It also addresses its problems with the irrationality of means. If people want a supplement of iron in their diet, best practices would not prescribe eating cars. It also addresses the problem of the eccentricity of ends since existing practices delimit ends. As Wallace notes, "often, the purposes of the practices, their fruits, are socially important to the community" (2009, p. 13). As a result, practices center around ends that are counted as important or valuable. Practices are "shared bodies of moving, changing practical knowledge about what is valuable in a certain domain and how these valuable things are properly fostered and protected" (2009, p. 14). One should not expect to find, it is supposed, practices that encourage Aunt Martha's end of recreating a scene from *Martha Stewart Living* on Mars. Practices have a normative force that compels people toward what collectively counts as righteous means, and delimits those ends worthy of pursuit.

This does not mean that any community's practices are inherently good or right because they are collectively warranted—only that they are not subjective. Practices can be both morally and technically wrong about means and about ends, and the collective will can drive the community toward immoral directions. This also does not mean that practitioners are mindless robots that do the bidding of the practices since the application of the norms and ways and means to changing particular situations often requires experience, skills, insight, and know-how that modify the practices (Wallace, 2009, p. 12). Corruption, novel situations, atavistic or moribund practices also call for such modifications and changes to practices, and these are typically initiated by practitioners. Every generation experiences individuals such as Rosa Parks or Greta Thunberg whose actions initiate collective, radical changes in existing practices. In Wallace's language, if the rationale for a practice is that it solves a certain problem, then, if it is no longer solving that problem, or its solution causes more problems, this calls for change to the practice. However, because such practices are indurated, this is not to say that they are easy to change, only that change is warranted.

From Practical Reasoning to Practical Knowledge

To serve as ethical reasoning, practical reasoning has to not only calculate what is likely to attain an end, but the righteous way to attain good ends. For this reason, practical reasoning for Wallace takes the form of what he calls *practical knowledge*, not only "knowledge of how to pursue the activity" (2009, p. 14), knowledge of "better rather than worse ways of doing things" (2009, p. 11), but also determining what is valuable to pursue (2009, p. 13).

This is more or less how Aristotle characterizes *phronesis:* ". . . the disposition with true reason and ability for *actions* concerning human goods" (*Nicomachean Ethics*, 1140b 20–21). People who have phronesis ". . . can aim well at the things which are attainable by action and are best for man" (*Nicomachean Ethics*, 1141b1 2). Aristotle characterizes phronesis as a matter of both means *and* ends (Richardson, 1997, pp. 14, 54–55). Phronesis and virtue go hand in hand in this respect, since good ends only appear to good people, and vice corrupts such aims (*Nicomachean Ethics*, 1144a35). As Julia Annas describes it, phronesis is a version of practical reasoning that involves "doing the right thing for the right reason, in the appropriate way—honestly, courageously, and so on" (2006, p. 516). Good practices, then, are practices that, formerly speaking, use practical reasoning to successfully attain good ends by the right means.

This points to three implicit norms of practical knowledge (at this point the term "practical knowledge" will be used interchangeably with *phronesis* to distinguish it from purely instrumental or prudential forms of reasoning). First, there is a prudential norm of doing what is likely to attain what is pursued; second, a norm of righteous means, determining among those means likely to attain the end, which is right to do; and, finally, a norm concerning which among ends are good to pursue. "A good deliberator," Aristotle says, "[i]s a man who can arrive by calculation at the best of the goods attainable by man" (*Nicomachean Ethics*, 1141b12).

As noted, the first norm is what Bernard Williams calls a *prudential norm* (1993, p. 114), it is a norm of rationality: *people ought to do what is likely to attain their ends.* It is the implicit norm of all forms of practical reasoning. It's more or less Kant's notion of the *hypothetical imperative* or Peirce's notion of the pragmatic maxim: If people want to attain X, Y is the best way to do so. It often takes the form of advice. So used, "this ought also reveals itself to be *relative*, in a broad sense, to the projects, motives, and so on of the agent in question" (Williams, 1993, p. 125). As Williams notes, this sort of ought "has nothing specially to do with moral obligation. . . . and when moral obligation does come into the question, what I am under an obligation to do may not be what, all things considered, I ought to do . . ." (1993, pp. 124–125). Aristotle illustrates this through his classic example of the practical syllogism: light meat is wholesome, chicken is a light meat, therefore, people ought to eat chicken (*Nicomachean Ethics*, 1141b 18–22). This can be reformulated as a hypothetical imperative: If you want to be healthy, eat wholesome foods, and chicken is a wholesome food. Aristotle argues that such reasoning involves a kind of intelligence he calls cleverness (*deinoteta*), deliberating well about what will likely achieve the end.

If the first norm of practical knowledge is that people ought to do what is likely to attain their ends, the second norm of righteous means has to do with placing moral constraints on those means. Aristotle mentions that cleverness (*deinoteta*), which is the sort of intelligence needed to figure out the means to an end, can devolve into cunning and ruthlessness (*panourgous*), simply using any means to attain those ends (*Nicomachean Ethics*, 1144a25). Cunning and ruthless people are prone to deceive, cheat, and lie if they can get away with it, so long as it accomplishes their ends.

The second norm of righteous means is a counter to this Machiavellian form of prudence, which is often characterized as the end justifies the means. Although Machiavelli never directly made such a claim, it is implied in several statements related to prudential advice to the Prince: ". . . Princes who have set little store by their word, but have known how to overreach men by their cunning, have accomplished great things, and in the end got the better of those who trusted to honest dealing." He continues, "There are two ways of contending, one in accordance with the laws, the other by force; the first of which is proper to men, the second to beasts. But since the first method is often ineffectual, it becomes necessary to resort to the second. A Prince should, therefore, understand how to use well both the man and the beast" (1532, p. 127). Said further: ". . . [A] prudent Prince neither can nor ought to keep his word when to keep it is hurtful to him and the causes which led him to pledge it are removed. If all men were good, this would not be good advice, but since they are dishonest and do not keep faith with you, you, in return, need not keep faith with them; and no prince was ever at a loss for plausible reasons to cloak a breach of faith" (1532, p. 128).

Aristotle also notes that people may deliberate well about how to achieve evil things (*Nicomachean Ethics,* 1142b20–25). Therefore, practical knowledge must be about which ends are good to pursue. Aristotle famously claims in the beginning of the *Nicomachean Ethics* that all practices (praxis) "*seem (dokeo)* to aim at some good" (1094a1). The third norm of practical knowledge, then, would have the sense of what is traditionally called the natural law: *pursue good and avoid evil.* As Aquinas notes, "the natural law stands in relation to practical matters, as the first principles to matters of demonstration." He argues that ". . . good is the first thing that falls under the apprehension of the practical reason, which is directed to action: since every agent acts for an end under the aspect of good. Consequently the first principle in the practical reason is one founded on the notion of, viz., that *good is that which all things seek after*" (1265–1274, *Summa Theologica,* Vol. I, Part I–II, Q. 94. Art 2).

In order for practical reasoning to be morally conducive, to come close to what Wallace calls practical knowledge and what Aristotle calls *phronesis,* the three norms have to be weaved together in a certain order. This overarching norm can be expressed in the following way: *what ought to be done is what is right to do that is also likely to attain what is good to pursue.* The norm parallels what was previously articulated for the norms of good practices. Since practical reasoning is the principal reasoning of practices, then this alignment is necessary in order to have good practices.

However, this overarching norm stands as an empty formalism since it does not specify what *is* good and right. Aristotle's account of it is no better in this respect: "[G]ood deliberation [about means] is rightness of such deliberation which brings about a good" (*Nicomachean Ethics,* 1142b21). The ends that *phronesis* seeks "is what should or should not be done" (*Nicomachean Ethics,* 1143a9); "virtue makes the end in view right, *phronesis* makes the means towards it right" (*Nicomachean Ethics,* 1144a7). Saying that people should seek good ends in the right way doesn't say anything about what people actually ought to do.

Problems as Moral Guidance

The whole purpose of ethics has been to provide guidance for moral decision making. But the overarching norm of practical knowledge hardly does so. What does provide guidance are the practices of the communities to which people belong, each of which fills in the content of this overarching norm, relative to the specific ends which the practice pursues. Practices pick out ends and prescribe the means to attain them. But even if they provide guidance, this does not mean that, in their current forms and varieties in different cultures and communities, they are settled as the right thing to do.

There is a way, however, that practices can be considered sufficient guidance and to help with figuring out whether the ways and means and ends are going the right way. If Wallace is right, practices originate as solutions to certain problems, and they persist or change depending on how well they continue to address those problems. *Problems can serve as a proxy for the good.* As Dewey says, "when things are going completely smoothly, desires do not arise, and there is no occasion to project ends-in-view, for 'going smoothly' signifies that there is no need for effort and struggle. . . . There is no occasion to investigate what it would be better to have happen in the future, and hence no projection of an end-object." On the other hand, if things are not going smoothly, there is something the matter, "there is something lacking, wanting, in the existing situation as it stands, an absence which produces conflict in the elements that do exist" (1939, *LW* 13, p. 220).

Almost any practice is proposed as a solution to a problem, in the sense of how to attain certain ends or goals and what ends to attain. Agricultural practices propose the best way to grow food; medical practices the best way to remedy illness; political practices the best way to govern; educational practices the best way to teach and learn—and so on. The ends of nourishment, health, educating the young, and the governance of societies are found, among others, in every society. As already noted, a problem is typically defined as an impediment or obstacle to a goal. A practice, if working, has found a way to overcome that obstacle or impediment; and, if it is not working, it has failed to do so. "Just what response does this social arrangement, political or economic, evoke," Dewey says about practices, "and what effect does it have upon the disposition of those who engage in it? Does it release capacity? If so, how widely? . . . in an extensive and equitable way? Is the capacity . . . also directed in some coherent way?" (1920, *MW* 12, p. 197). As Hook emphasizes, "Dewey maintained that once men set out to put knowledge and intelligence to use, the relevant test of all social institutions becomes their impact upon the quality of human life and experience" (1959, p. 1016).

Problems can be thought of in a positive or negative sense. In its positive sense, so long as practices are working, that is, if there is an absence of significant problems, then the ends and means of those practices can be counted provisionally as good ends and righteous means—at least until if or when they do cause problems. This is consonant with Peirce's convergence theory of truth (Liszka, 2021, pp. 114–118). It is also consistent with Peirce's notion of fallibilism, the claim that there is no absolutely true belief, but that there is no reason to doubt any belief until there is a reason to doubt it (c. 1905, *CP* 1.148).

Recall that Peirce expresses convergence in three different but equivalent ways. For Peirce, one indication of true claims is that they approximate to the truth, in the sense that further inquiry by inductive tests do not refute it, and it continues to be supported by future inquiries (1878, *CP* 2.748). Similarly, it might be said that one indication of a good practice is that it cannot be improved upon, that significant changes to it makes it worse and, as such, it has approximated to the limit of its improvability. Another sense of convergence to the truth in Peirce is the idea that any inquirer with good methods should reach the same conclusion, if the claim is true (1878, *CP* 5.407). In this regard, one indication that a practice is working would be if different communities, unknown to each other, have adopted and retain similar practices. The third sense of convergence claims that a growing consensus among *inquirers* is an indication of the truth of the claim (1877, *CP* 5.407). Similarly, an indication of a good practice would be that more and more people adopt it as a standard or best practice over time. More specifically, one indication of this would be that people prefer a change in practice to the old ways. This is not too far off the mark from what Philip Kitcher argues. He makes the claim that "ethical truths are those acquired in progressive transitions and retained through an indefinite sequence of progressive transitions" (2011, p. 7).

This is clearly exemplified in the case of technology. Consider the development of the computer. Its core architecture of logic gates has not changed over time, based on George Boole's binary logic. However, the means to execute that architecture has changed rapidly over the last hundred years in light of solving certain problems with speed of calculations, size of computers, and energy use. As a result, the technology changed from the use of vacuum tubes as capacitors to regulate the gates, to transistors, to the integrated circuit—and the chip keeps increasing in capacity. The point is that no one building a computer uses vacuum tubes anymore. The tendency is to move toward technology that solves more problems more efficiently than its predecessors.

In a negative sense, just as fallibilism dictates that people should doubt beliefs when there is a reason to doubt them, so people should question the goodness and rightness of practices when they are not working and causing significant problems. As Dewey argues, when problems are understood as a lack or need, they can "serve as positive means for formation of an attainable end or outcome" and become ". . . the method by which warranted . . . desires and ends-in-views are formed" (1939, *LW* 13, p. 240). The ends that are good to pursue are solutions to the most pressing problems of the day. Problems tend to select ends to pursue, although negatively, as what is to be corrected. "The value of different ends that suggest themselves is estimated or measured by the capacity they exhibit to guide action in . . . *satisfying* . . . existing lacks" (1939, *LW* 13, p, 232). He argues, "Just as the problem which evokes inquiry is related to an empirical situation in which the problem presents itself, so desire and the projection of ends as consequences to be reached are relative to a concrete situation and to its need for transformation" (1939, *LW* 13, pp. 239–240). Given that desires and ends-in-view are "correlative," to the extent that desires are connected with what is valued, the valuation of an end ". . . takes place only when there is something the matter; when there is some trouble to be done away with, some need, lack, or privation to be made good, some conflict of tendencies to be resolved by means of changing existing conditions" (1939, *LW* 13, p. 221). "Considering the all but omnipresence of troubles and "evils" in human experience (evils in the sense of deficiencies, failures, and frustrations)," Dewey is puzzled that "theories of human activity have been strangely oblivious of the concrete function troubles are capable of exercising when they are taken as *problems* whose conditions and consequences are explored with a view to finding methods of solution" (1939, *LW* 13, p. 233).

Frederick Will agrees with Dewey that problems focus ends. "The faltering, failing, and confusion" brought on by the exercise of a practice "may provide not only motivation for revision of these procedures, but also indications of the general location where revision is called for and the general direction the revisions should take" (1997, p. 144). In this manner, problems serve as guides for selecting ends and correcting means. For example, Dewey points out that "when standards of health and of satisfaction of conditions of knowledge were conceived in terms of analytic observation of existing conditions, disclosing a trouble statable in a problem, criteria of judging were progressively self-corrective through the very process of use in observation to locate the source of the trouble and to indicate the effective means of dealing with it. These means form the content of the specific end-in-view, not some abstract standard or ideal" (1939, *LW* 13, p. 233). This indirectly creates the right ends to pursue, namely, solutions to those problems and, simultaneously, identifies what's wrong with the means.

Chapter 5

Normative Science

Practices at their morally best prescribe righteous ways to attain good ends. Aristotle acknowledges that there are "numerous practices" and the "ends are correspondingly numerous" (*Nicomachean Ethics,* 1094a3–4). His strategy is to suppose that there is higher end, a higher good, to which all such ends are subordinate. Will the knowledge of this supreme good, he says, ". . . not better enable us to attain what is fitting, like archers having a target to aim at?" (*Nicomachean Ethics,* 1094a20–25). The pragmatists consider the situation differently—the archers don't know where the targets are. They must first find the clues to its location. It has been argued here that the absence or presence of problems in these many practices provides the clues as to where the targets lay. The presence of problems indicates something not working with the practice, and their absence an indication of the right direction.

Still, there is the problem of how to know whether some practice is working or not and, if not, why it isn't working. That knowledge would be needed in order to fix problems. This knowledge, to quote Aristotle, "will better enable us to attain what is fitting." By all accounts, the best sort of knowledge-getting practice available to us is science, since science in Larry Laudan's words "delivers the epistemic goods." Is it *plausible* to consider ethics scientifically? The core of ethical reasoning as championed here is practical knowledge and, as Wallace argues, "practical reasoning, including reasoning involving moral considerations, is a form of problem solving" (2009, p. 18). The task, then, centers on the *plausibility* of treating practical knowledge scientifically. If, plausible, whether it could become a working science is another practical question.

Both Peirce and Dewey thought there could be something like a science of ethics. Dewey asks "whether scientific propositions about the direction of human conduct, about any situation in to which the idea of *should* enters, are possible; and, if so, of what sort they are and the grounds upon which they rest" (1939, *LW* 13, p. 192). Dewey argues that ethics "is ineradicably empirical, not theological nor metaphysical nor mathematical. Since it directly concerns human nature, everything that can be known of the human mind and body in physiology, medicine, anthropology, and psychology is pertinent to moral inquiry" (1922, *MW* 14, p. 204). As Phillip Kitcher describes Dewey's project in this regard, just as the development of the experimental method in the seventeenth century liberated the investigation of nature from the dogmatism of *a priori* reasoning and metaphysics, so the experimental method applied to ethical matters could achieve the same transformation in the human sphere (2012, p. 333).

Peirce also proposed a normative science (1903, *CP* 1.191; Liszka, 2021, pp. 58–63). Peirce was interested in it primarily because of his interest in logic. Logic is normative because it is a practice that prescribes how people *ought to* think, rather than how they actually do think (1902, *CP* 2.144). However, Peirce envisioned normative science as more of a formal science, whereas Dewey had more of an empirical one in mind. If ethics is to be scientific as Dewey suggests then, given that practical knowledge is the sort of practical reasoning that is morally conducive, it would have to be shown how practical knowledge can be *scientific* knowledge.

Aristotle says explicitly that it cannot (*Nicomachean Ethics*, 1142a24). His principal reason is that *phronesis* has to do with judgments about particulars, that is, particular situations that are changing and variable, while science (*episteme*) involves universals, regularities that are uniform and do not change (*Nicomachean Ethics*, 1140b, 1142a11ff). The laws of gravity are universal, but what justice demands can vary from situation to situation. A second obstacle to making it scientific, as Aristotle sees it, is that *phronesis* is more of a skill than knowledge. Like any skill, *phronesis* requires intuitive perception (*aesthesis*) (*Nicomachean Ethics*, 1142a15–20), experience (*Nicomachean Ethics*, 1142a15), correct deliberation (*bouleuesthai*) (*Nicomachean Ethics*, 1142b30), good judgment (*krinein*) (*Nicomachean Ethics*, 1143a15), cleverness (*deinoteta*) (*Nicomachean Ethics*, 1144a25), understanding (*synesis*) (*Nicomachean Ethics*, 1143a15–20), and these are not acquired by intelligence as one does in science. This is why, Aristotle says, young men can be good at mathematics but lack *phronesis* (*Nicomachean Ethics*, 1142a15). Additionally, the claim that practical knowledge or *phronesis* could become scientific raises the more contemporary problem of normative naturalism, understood in some sense as the reduction of the normative to the empirical. Practical knowledge is not concerned with just what will likely attain an end, but the right way to attain a good end, and these are normative claims that do not appear to be reducible to or dependent on empirical ones. These three issues must be addressed in order to argue for the plausibility of a normative science.

The General and the Particular in Practical Knowledge

The first problem for a normative science has to do with Aristotle's claim that *phronesis* is about judgment of particular situations and not the study of generals. For this reason, people knowledgeable about particular facts may do better in the matter of action than those who just know general principles (*Nicomachean Ethics,* 1141b20–25). Put more conveniently, *phronesis* is not about following moral rules mechanically, as prescribed by some practice, or the way in which one might follow an algorithm in mathematics for solving a problem, but in making good moral judgments, given the nuances and complexities of moral situations. Dewey strove to dispel this received view that ethical judgments had to do with individual cases and science with general rules that had nothing to do with particular situations (1916, *MW* 10, p. 8). Wallace follows Dewey on this, so it might be helpful to follow him.

Rather than arguing directly with Aristotle, Wallace chooses to contest Martha Nussbaum's position on this matter in *Love's Knowledge.* There she characterizes Aristotle's *phronesis* as a wisdom concerning how to negotiate the particulars of life-situations in order to achieve the right outcome. It involves a perception, a discernment of the particular situation that is "finely aware and richly responsible" of its nuances and complexities. As a result, Nussbaum argues for "the priority of the particular" over any general norms or precepts in *phronesis* (1990, p. 37).

Wallace does a close reading of Nussbaum's close reading of Maggie's deliberations in Henry James's *The Golden Bowl,* concerning her choice between remaining a companion to her beloved father or maintaining her marriage with her straying husband, whom she continues to love. In examining casuists, such as Albert Jonsen and Stephen Toulmin (1988), ethical particularists, such as Jonathan Dancy (2004), and thinkers such as Michael Walzer (1994), Wallace makes an important point. He argues that Nussbaum's claim of the *priority* of the particular over general norms is overstated. Rather, neither is prior to the other. Such a relation is better characterized as a dialogue between the particulars of the situation and general rules which might guide the situation (2009, p. 107). "It is the perceptions," he says, "together with practical knowledge consisting of general norms that together guide the decision and provide the basis for assessing the decision" in Maggie's case (2009, pp. 108–109). Granted there are many cases where problems are unique or nuanced, there are many that are not and fall into standard problems. Good plumbers do not come to the job with a blank slate and muck around with the particulars of the situation until they figure out the problem. General knowledge provides a guide as to how to identify the problem, and how to fix it. A seasoned plumber will gain general knowledge from many encounters with these problems, but that also helps the plumber to solve similar problems in the future. Wallace comes to the conclusion that,

> Practical knowledge of better and worse ways of doing things, arises from people's encounters with the world and their sharing with others, what they learn on these occasions. The encounters are particular events, but what is learned is general. What is learned is also normative. The knowledge provides guidance for action and standards for evaluation and criticism. The use of the practical knowledge so acquired is to enable people to cope with the next particular problem—and the next. (2009, p. 83)

Thus, practical knowledge is an interplay of general and particular (2009, p. 84). As Aristotle himself declares, *phronesis* is both about knowledge of general principles, and particular facts (N*icomachean. Ethics,* 1141b15). In his example, people must know both that light meats are wholesome *and* that chicken is a light meat. Both are forms of knowledge, one is a knowledge of facts, the other of general rules. But that's the same sort of division of labor in any science.

Wallace suggests that there are two aspects to this dialogue between general and particular: people acquire some general knowledge from engagement with the particular situations of a practice, but that also practices involve the application of general rules to particular and novel situations.

Diana Heney, who defends what she calls a pragmatist metaethics makes some telling points against particularists such as Jonathan Dancy. If the particularists are right and there are no invariant ethical rules that can be used to good effect in particular situations then, first there could be no moral learning that would carry from one situation to another (2016, p. 132). Each moral situation would have to be learned anew, and, of course, that is not what people observe in practical life. Second, if there cannot be something like general moral knowledge or rules, then collective practices would not be possible since they prescribe in general terms, righteous ways and means to good ends (2016, p. 133). Thus, particularlism would gainsay what is commonly observed in practical life. She cites with approval Brad Hooker's thought experiment that, in a community of particularists, no one would be sure of what anyone one would do in any situation. Practices have the function, whether they accomplish it or not, of converging people toward the better ways of doing good things (2008, p. 28; Heney, 2016, p. 133).

Wallace's colleague Frederick Will provides some insight into the sort of reasoning that goes on in the application of general rules to particular situations. He calls such reasoning *pragmatic rationality* (1997, p. 142). It is the sort of collective reasoning that results from practices-in-use, continuing application of practices as they are modified through solving problems in those practices. Will argues that such reasoning is not deductive, as the subsumption of a case under a general rule. As Will says, deduction alone would not be sufficient "to determine whether birth control or abortion (even in the cases of rape or incest) violates the Mosaic commandment 'Thou shalt not kill' " (1997, p. 145). The novelty in abortion, of course, is that it concerns a zygote, embryo, fetus growing inside a woman's body, as opposed to ordinary circumstances of full-grown adults who have their own bodies, physiologically independent of others. The same matter could be related to other situations, for example, killing the enemy in war, acts of self-defense, the withdrawal of life-preserving medical treatment from a dying patient, or the wanton killing of sentient animals. Each of these particular situations presents nuances that are not addressed by the general rule and require adjustment of that rule.

Because such reasoning involves a novel situation, some of Will's commentators have noted that it's more like Peirce's notion of abduction (Tiles, 1998, p. 277). Abduction may be a good candidate to explain how novelty, nuance and surprise can affect adjustments to general rules. In explaining how scientific reasoning works, Peirce thought that besides induction—the kind of reasoning that tests hypotheses—there was also a process of reasoning that was concerned with the formulation of hypotheses (1903, *CP* 5.189). These were not formulated in a vacuum but arose precisely out of the problems with existing hypotheses as they encountered anomalies while being field or laboratory tested by induction. Abduction was the process of reasoning by which one observed a surprising fact and modified an existing hypothesis or proposed an alternative hypothesis to explain it (1878, *CP* 2.624).

Detection is a good case study of abduction, as several Peirce scholars have pointed out, and it can serve as a good model of how one applies or refines existing rules or hypotheses to particular situations (Sebeok & Umiker-Sebeok, 1983; Harrowitz, 1983; Liszka & Babb, 2020). For example, in the classic detective story *Murder in the Rue Morgue*, Edgar Allen Poe's detective, Dupin, begins with the general commonsense rule of detection that murders are committed by human beings. In his interviews with various witnesses who did not see the perpetrator but heard him, they all report that it was someone with a foreign accent, although they all disagree on what foreign language was spoken. Further surprising clues show that the perpetrator was unusually strong given the brutality of the crime; that the perpetrator was particularly agile, given the difficult entrance to and egress from the apartment; and that there seemed to be no motive, given that valuables were left behind. A couple of other surprising clues lead Dupin to the abduction that the perpetrator was not human, but an animal, a primate of some sort. Through a careful search of the news, he's able to identify the culprit as an escaped orangutan, owned by a local sailor.

What's important to note here is that this does not refute the hypothesis that murders are committed by human beings. This would continue as a working hypothesis for any detective; but this particular incident, as rare as it would be, makes a modification in that working rule of detection. Detectives may have enough general knowledge to hypothesize that a series of gruesome murders were committed by a serial killer, but given some subtle differences with a timely, subsequent murder, they may believe it was committed by someone other than the serial killer.

Will sees the same sort of reasoning involved in the application of an existing rule to a novel situation in case law, where laws or legal principles are applied to novel situations. Will thinks *Brown v. Board of Education* (347 US 483 (1954) is illustrative since the Supreme Court had to interpret the Fourteenth Amendment in a novel situation of "separate but equal" delivery of goods such as education. In citing E. H. Levi on his views of legal reasoning, Will concludes, "A most important kind of legal interpretation is one in which the rule that is interpreted is forged and hence modified in the interpretation, in which the classification system employed in the rule undergoes change as the interpretation proceeds" (1997, p. 150).

Case law on the First Amendment's free-speech clause illustrates this nicely. The First Amendment states the rule generally:

> Congress shall make no law respecting an establishment of religion, or prohibiting the free exercise thereof; or abridging the freedom of speech, or of the press; or the right of the people peaceably to assemble, and to petition the Government for a redress of grievances. (1791, Amendment I)

As history has shown, when people put to practice their freedom of speech, certain anomalies and problems arise that the general rule does not clearly address. As Russell Weaver and Donald Lively put it simply: "The volume of litigation that it [the First Amendment] has generated indicates a high residual of indeterminacy with respect to the First Amendment's ultimate meaning" (2009, pp. 17–18). In a clever way, Weaver and Lively show how the First Amendment should now read, given the history of those judicial interpretations of novel situations:

> No branch of government, federal, state, or local, shall abridge freedom of speech or of the press except (1) when expression has slight, if any, social value; (2) presents a direct, imminent, and probable danger of inciting unlawful conduct; (3) defames a private person at least negligently and a public official or figure with actual malice; (4) invades privacy in an unacceptable way; (5) advertises a good or service that is illegal, or does so falsely or deceptively; (6) represents commercial speech that is outweighed by a substantial state interest and governed by regulation that is narrowly tailored to achieve its objective; and (7) is sexually explicit (albeit not obscene) and readily available to children. Freedom of speech and of the press does not prohibit government from managing speech in a content neutral way or regulating conduct or effects associated with speech. The level of speech protection may vary with the nature of the speech or the medium. The establishment clause generally guards against unacceptable levels of interaction between church and state. The free exercise clause prohibits government from

> abridging religion unless it can satisfy the demands of strict scrutiny. (2009, p. 17)

As they suggest, "The First Amendment, for practical purposes, is a work in progress" (2009, p. 7). But the core of its general principle has not been discarded because of these qualifications.

If it is plausible that abduction helps to explain the sort of reasoning that goes on in the application of the general to the particular, and abduction is part-and-parcel of scientific reasoning, then the claim that practical knowledge can be scientific in that respect should not be rejected. Abduction is a process of reasoning that leads to the modification (or rejection) of a hypothesis based on the observation of anomalies, surprises, or novelties that are the result of a particular situation. It requires, like practical knowledge, a keen observation of particulars, experience and cleverness in formulating modifications to the existing hypotheses that would account for the anomalies discerned in the laboratory or field.

Know-How and Know-That

The second problem with making practical knowledge scientific is that Aristotle considers *phronesis* more of a skill than knowledge. Skills do not seem to rely on knowledge, but science is about knowledge in the form of hypotheses or generalities. Gilbert Ryle's distinction between *knowing-that* and *knowing-how* may be helpful here (Ryle, 1945). As discussed, know-that is primarily propositional and can be articulated as a set of action statements that are believed (or not), or intentionally acted upon (or not). In that regard, they are general. Know-how, on the other hand, is the ability to do something, such as riding a bike, that is, adjustment of know-that to a particular situation. Not all bikes are alike, but there is still something alike in riding any bike. Ryle's position is that know-how cannot be reduced to knowing-that, and are distinct kinds of knowing (1945, pp. 4, 10), although knowing-how cannot be done without some know-that (1945, p. 47). This is the received view among many philosophers, psychologists, and AI researchers. Hubert Dreyfus represents this position:

> Phenomenology suggests that, although many forms of expertise pass through a stage in which one needs reasons to guide action, after much involved experience, the learner develops a way of

coping in which reasons play no role . . . In general, instead of relying on rules and standards to decide on or to justify her actions, the expert immediately responds to the current concrete situation. (2005)

Jason Stanley points out that this position is similar to claims made by moral particularists such as Jonathan Dancy. They

> . . . hold that moral agents do not employ general, exceptionless moral principles in guiding their behavior; indeed they hold that there are no such exceptionless moral principles. They argue that the variability and novelty of the situations that the moral agent encounters entails that there are no exceptionless moral principles that apply to all cases. The moral agent must navigate the particularities of each situation without them. This is analogous to the argument from skilled action to the conclusion that skilled action is not guided by principles. (2011, p. 181)

In regard to practices, knowing-that would be manifested in policies, procedures, rules, laws, advice, and so forth, and constitutes, in general form, the ends and purposes of the practices and prescriptions and proscriptions for the ways and means to attain them. It's the starting point for most practitioners of a practice, and it is the way in which practitioners learn *about* the practice. Student drivers are taught first the rules for the road. Artists are taught techniques in the arts. Engineers are taught the mathematics and physics of engineering. Student teachers are taught the elements of good pedagogy. Would-be lawyers first study the law.

Know-how, on the other hand, is related to the *performative competence* of the practitioners. It is realized when the person does the task successfully and consistently in a variety of circumstances and situations and, so, becomes expert in the practice. Know-how is not achieved solely by acquiring knowledge of rules, policies, and procedures, but in carrying through that know-that to particular situations that realizes the end or goal of the practice consistently over time. People may know that to join two boards together, a nail will do the trick, but be lousy at using a hammer. Certainly, in basketball, one can know all of the rules for shooting a basket from the foul line yet still not shoot baskets very well. Being able to shoot baskets consistently relies on all the elements of performative competence, including emotional intelligence, perception, memory, ability, capability, skill, practice, experience, judgment, intelligence, and talent. Wallace seems to make the same point:

> These bodies of practical knowledge that we practice as specialists are social artifacts, too. They are also complexes of norms. What a specialist knows and practices is how to proceed so that tasks are done well rather than badly. The norms themselves, of course reflect the experience of many individual practitioners: what they have learned about how to proceed in various circumstances so that the activity will actually serve the particular interest that is its reason for being. (2009, p. 122)

This distinction between knowing-that and knowing-how is given some credibility by empirical work in cognitive psychology (Devitt, 2011) which, in turn, originated in work on artificial intelligence (Stanley, 2011, p. 151). As discussed, in the field of cognitive psychology, knowing-how and knowing-that are translated into the distinction between *declarative knowledge* and *procedural knowledge*. Skill is primarily a form of procedural knowledge, although declarative knowledge can be involved in it (Anderson, 1980, p. 223; Devitt, 2011, p. 209).

Knowing-that is a product of explicit memory that allows one to explain to others any procedural rules or norms one has learned from experience and skill in performing the practice, while knowing-how in many cases relies mostly on implicit memory. Skills, such as learning how to use a stick shift, can start with an explicit set of rules: Take the foot off the accelerator; depress the clutch; shift into first gear; slowly raise the clutch while pressing slowly on the accelerator, and so forth. But, as anyone who's tried to learn this practice knows, it takes abilities such as body coordination, a sensitivity to when the clutch is moving proportionately to the accelerator, and a great deal of practice. Experience adds to the know-how in terms of special situations, for example, performing the practice on a hill, in reverse. Some people may have more of a talent for such a practice and can acquire the know-how without declaration of the procedural rules. A. S. Reber calls this "implicit learning," where know-how is acquired through observation and a little practice (Reber, 2003, p. 486; Devitt, 2011, p. 209). This seems to be confirmed by a study by Ron Sun and his colleagues (Sun et al., 2001, p. 207; Devitt, 2011, p. 210). As noted, the Dreyfus model for skill acquisition suggests that, if know-how begins explicitly, that is, on the basis of knowing the rules, the development from novice to mastery still requires an intuitive stage, a tacit form of knowledge. The expert does not rely rigidly on rules and can use that expertise in the context of novel situations or problems (Dreyfus & Dreyfus, 1980).

If practical knowledge is expertise in moral judgment and such expertise does not rely on general rules or norms, then this would appear to be a strong case against the plausibility of counting practical knowledge as scientific knowledge. There are two strategies to counter that claim. The strongest would be to follow Jason Stanley's argument that know-how is knowledge, but knowledge of facts:

> . . . knowing how to catch a fly ball must fit into a more general account of knowing when to catch a fly ball and knowing where to position one's glove in order to catch a fly ball. More generally, we need an account of what one might call *knowledge-wh*: knowledge where, knowledge when, knowledge how, knowledge why, etc. . . . knowledge of facts is necessary and sufficient for knowledge-wh. (2011, p. xviii)

But foregoing this very interesting argument, there is a more obvious point to make. The practice of science like any practice involves skill and expertise. Skillful work in the lab and in the field is a hallmark of good science. The fact that practical knowledge requires skill does not disqualify it from becoming scientific to the extent that science also requires skill.

Although knowing-how plays a critical role in successful practices, so does knowing-that. For practices to function well, not only must their practitioners perform well, but the practice must be well-designed. Certainly, the functioning of a practice may suffer if the agents involved do not have know-how, but it may also suffer because the practice is flawed in terms of the design or organization thought best to achieve those outcomes. In the first case, the problem is with the performative competence of the practitioners—their know-how; in the second case, the problem is with the practice itself—the know-that. The two work hand-in-hand. No matter how a well-articulated practice is likely to achieve its intended outcomes, if the practitioners are incompetent, those outcomes are unlikely. Conversely, no matter how competent the practitioners, if what is performed by the practitioners is so designed that it is unlikely to achieve the outcomes, then the result is the same.

Practical Hypotheses

Much of what makes up practical knowledge are practical hypotheses. Following Ryle, know-that and know-how can be understood as practical hypotheses in its simplest form. When actions of a certain sort are taken in certain situations, results of a certain sort tend to occur (1945, p. 10). As Wallace emphasizes, "many practical choices, including ethical ones, culminate in a course of action to be *tried*. Only the result of the actual trial can conclusively establish that the reasoning was successful" (2009, p. 109). Wallace cites approvingly, Dewey's recommendation that "we think of precepts [of the practice] as hypotheses—generalizations that have proved useful but remain open to modification in light of further experience" (2009, p. 99). The proposed solutions to problems, understood as plans, measures, and policies, are for Dewey "but hypotheses" and demonstrate an "alignment of philosophy with the attitude and spirit of the inquiries which have won the victories of scientific inquiry in other fields (1946, *LW* 15, p. 166).

If practical hypotheses are hypotheses, they should be capable of being tested and verified in principle like any scientific hypothesis would be.

Peirce's thesis in the pragmatic maxim of the transposition of theory to practice would support this claim. It supposes that theoretical reasoning can be transposed into practical reasoning. If a theoretical hypothesis predicts that a certain intervention in the world will likely produce certain effects then, if that is true, attaining those outcomes can be achieved by means of that intervention. For example, if it can be shown, through clinical trials, that a certain medical intervention cures the disease in a statistically significant number of cases, then practical reasoning would dictate use of the medicine if the goal is to cure the disease. In this way, the test of a practical hypothesis is the truth of the theoretical hypothesis from which it is transposed. *Practical knowledge, in this respect, rests on scientific reasoning.*

As noted, Peirce thought that scientific practice involved a triad of reasoning processes that worked with each other to formulate, test, and correct hypotheses, with the result, over time, of hypotheses that were less prone to error and more reliable for that reason. In other words, what made science better than other forms of inquiry was its ability to self-correct. Abduction was the reasoning by which new hypotheses were developed on the basis of anomalies with existing ones; deduction, in this context, was determining the testable consequences of hypotheses so formulated; and induction was the means by which hypotheses were tested for problems and anomalies. Peirce summarizes this nicely:

That which is to be done with the hypothesis is to trace out its consequences by deduction, to compare them with results of experiment by induction, and to discard the hypothesis, and try another, as soon as the first has been refuted; as it presumably will be. How long it will be before we light upon the hypothesis which shall resist all tests we cannot tell; but we hope we shall do so, at last. (1901, *CP* 7.220)

Similarly, practices can be considered to go through such processes. Originally, they may be established in order to solve a certain problem encountered in practical life. Over time, they get refined as they encounter novel situations or new problems and are thrown into the mix of other practices striving to attain similar goals. In some cases, they become so problematic that they are discarded in favor of a more viable alternative that results in fewer problems and more reliable outcomes.

Consider as an example the case of Head Start. It is an educational practice that has the following end with a generalized means: "to promote the school readiness of low-income children by enhancing their cognitive, social, and emotional development" (Sec. 645[42U.S.C. 9801](a)(1)). The abduction is that making their early learning environment as close as possible to privileged kids will help them succeed as much as privileged kids do. The practical hypothesis is to get these kids at an early age into educational programs and social contexts that will improve their math and literacy scores while helping their parents acquire educationally supportive skills, and that will make a positive difference in their educational success. How to know whether it works?

A look at the successive studies of the program by Deming (2009), Puma, et al. (2010), Heid and Peck (2012) and Phillips, Gormley, and Anderson (2016) shows mixed results, with the identification in the last study of places that exhibit best results and best practices. The studies employ standard clinical trial methodologies, including random selection of subjects to test, control groups, double-blind arrangements, and standard statistical analysis of the results. In other words, the intervention is tested like any medical intervention would be, although, given that it's a field study, the effort is much more complicated.

Consider another example. Among political practices in America, many feel that polarization is a problem. One hypothesis is that such polarization is due to the election of extreme ideological candidates on the Right and the Left. Consequently, one solution proposed is to change political practices, particularly in the practice of primaries, to promote more moderate candidates. One proposed solution was to open primaries to both independent voters and voters from the opposite party. The idea was that a wider representation of voters would more likely ensure that more moderate candidates would win primary elections. Several states have adopted such a strategy. A recent study by Eric McGhee and his colleagues shows that the change in practice had little effect on electing more moderate candidates in the primaries (2011). The failure of an intervention, of course, can also be determined empirically.

The lesson here is that there is no reason not to treat a practical hypothesis as anything different than an empirical hypothesis.

Normative Naturalism

Although it can be argued that some aspects of practical knowledge can be treated empirically and, so, scientifically, the normative bits cannot. These would include questions about righteous means and good ends, the heart of practical knowledge. This is the last obstacle to the claim that a normative science is plausible.

Most arguments against normative naturalism are versions of G. E. Moore's "open question argument" (1903, sect. 10). Moore claimed that all naturalist properties are descriptive, and descriptive claims, such as the utilitarian claim that the good is pleasure, are subject to the open question of whether pleasure is good. David Hume presented a second argument that normative claims cannot be derived from empirical ones, an "ought" cannot be derived from an "is" (1739, p. 335). A similar argument was leveled by Morton White against Dewey's effort to naturalize ethics. Normative claims are prescriptive, White argues, asserting what people *ought* to do. But empirical claims are descriptive and assert what *is* or is not the case. For that reason, the findings of what is would appear not to bear on the findings of what ought to be. No conclusion about what should be can follow from matter-of-fact propositions. If there's no "ought" in the premises, then there can be no "ought" in the conclusion. White complains about Dewey's scientific ethics that "here we have generated a normative or *de jure* proposition by performing a suitable operation on merely *de facto* propositions" (1949, p. 214).

More recently, Derek Parfit also advocates for the irreducibility of the normative to the empirical. "There is a deep distinction . . . between all natural facts and . . . normative facts" (2011, vol. 2, p. 310). The natural and the normative are simply "in two quite different, non-overlapping categories" (2011, vol. 2, p. 324). Parfit argues that normative claims are based on reasons for actions, and acting on reasons can't be understood in naturalistic terms. Parfit's strongest argument against naturalism is a somewhat modified version of the open question argument. He argues that no natural fact can provide a normative reason for action. The fact, for example, that jumping from a burning building will best fulfill the desire not to die in a fire is still not necessarily a reason why one *ought* to jump (2011, vol. 2, pp. 326–327). Presumably, there is a bottomless set of normative claims behind the empirical one, namely, that one ought to save your life and, ultimately, the prudential norm, namely, that people ought to do what is likely to achieve what they desire. Thus, even though practical reasoning will lay out what is likely to achieve what is desired, that alone doesn't imply that the action ought to be done. Normative naturalism would have to find a way around these significant problems.

Normative naturalists are of two sorts. Analytic naturalists, such as Frank Jackson (1998) and Michael Smith (2000), hold that the identity claims between normative and natural concepts are analytical truths. Jackson argues that if something is right, then it has a certain pattern or organization of natural properties. It is analogous to the way in which density is conceptualized as a ratio of mass and volume (2012, p. 78). Because moral properties are analytically identical to natural ones, the open question argument has no sway here. Just as insight into the concept of density is obtained by showing that it is nothing more than the ratio of mass and volume, then showing that the good is maximizing utility, for example, is just as insightful and not circular, as the open question holds. Jackson has a functional account of the good that is similar to James and argues that "what is a priori according to moral functionalism is not that rightness is such and such a descriptive property, but that A is right if and only if it has whatever property it is that plays the rightness role in mature folk morality, and it is an a posteriori matter what that property is" (1998, p. 151).

Nonanalytic naturalists, on the other hand, argue somewhat differently. David Copp, for example, holds that the relation between normative and natural properties is empirical (2012). If a property is natural, then evidence for any beliefs about it is established "by means of empirical observation and standard modes of inductive inference" (2004, p. 13). As such, they can be the subject of, and explained by the natural sciences. This was also the conclusion (and worry) of the non-naturalists. G. E. Moore said plainly that if ethics is considered naturalistically as ". . . an empirical or positive science: its conclusions could all be established by means of empirical observation and induction" (1903, sects. 25, 91). Parfit claims it as well (2011, vol. 2, p. 305). So, too, with Russ Shafer-Landau" (2003, p. 59; Copp, 2012, p. 27). Gilbert Harman defined it similarly as the position that "the place of value and obligations [is] in the world of facts as revealed by science" (2000, p. 79).

David Copp argues that normative facts are simply those facts that will solve normative problems. One important normative problem is the problem of sociality. It is the problem of how to minimize conflict so as to maximize cooperation, reminiscent of what James proposes in "the Moral Philosopher and the Moral Life." There are some moral codes that will solve this problem better than others, and the determination of which is better is an empirical question (2012, p. 38).

Another sort of normative naturalism, espoused by Larry Laudan, sidesteps the ontological issue of whether normative properties are of a natural kind. Instead, he argues that normative claims share the same epistemology as empirical ones, so they get their warrant and justification from empirical ones (1987, p. 24). He argues that neither a normative nor a descriptive claim is ". . . eliminable or reducible to its counterpart; yet both behave epistemically in a very similar way, so that we do not require disjoint epistemologies to account for [normative] rules and [empirical] theories" (1990, p. 56). Whatever subjective beliefs people have for attaining particular ends are trumped by evidence that certain actions do, in fact, lead to certain ends more likely than alternatives. As Peirce puts it, ". . . truth is neither more nor less than that character of a proposition which consists in this, that belief in the proposition would, with sufficient experience and reflection, lead us to such conduct as would tend to satisfy the desires we should then have" (1877, *CP* 5.375n2).

This is the position that will be taken here. *The normative force or warrant for a normative claim is an empirical one.* This is echoed by Dewey, according to Jennifer Welchman: "Since inference has the same form or structure in moral and scientific judgments, Dewey concludes there is no reason to suppose that moral inquiries and judgments cannot be made 'scientific'" (1995, p. 43). Dewey says that normative claims are better evaluated if they "rest upon scientifically warranted empirical propositions and are themselves capable of being tested by observation of the results actually attained as compared with those intended" (1939, *LW* 13, p. 212). Ralph Wedgewood argues somewhat similarly in saying that although normative facts are not natural ones, they "are realized in natural ones" (2007, p. 6).

Because normative claims are not reducible to empirical ones, this avoids the naturalistic fallacy. Practical knowledge, the reasoning of problem solving, has both a normative and an empirical dimension. But *the norms of practical reasoning get their normative force, their warrant in corresponding empirical claims*. This, of course, has to be explained.

The Empirical Warrant for Prudential Norms

Recall that practical knowledge involves three interwoven norms: a prudential norm that people ought to do what is most likely to attain their ends; a norm of good ends and a third of righteous means.

Following Laudan's logic, the prudential norm is warranted only if the action recommended does in fact likely attain the end specified in particular practical reasoning. This follows from Peirce's theory-to-practice thesis, namely, that practical hypotheses are transposed from theoretical ones, and the truth of the practical hypothesis rests on the truth of the empirical one. If a college education is the best means to a rewarding, good-paying career, then that rests on the truth of the empirical hypothesis that college graduates tend to have rewarding, good-paying careers, compared with those who don't have a college degree. Presumably, that can be inductively tested and statistically verified. For this reason, the test of the truth of a practical hypotheses would seem to be subject to the same methodologies as any scientific hypothesis. If a practical hypothesis proposes certain means to attain an end, for example, that needle exchanges will reduce the incident of HIV among drug users, then, in principle, that can be tested like any hypothesis on the basis of those predictions.

To make this clearer, the prudential norm can be incorporated into the practical reasoning of some practice in the following way. Keep in mind that practical reasoning in this context is not made by individuals but is carried by practices. As such the ends and the means proposed are not subjective:

If people desire some end, E; and

If a practice claims an action, A, is the means most likely to attain E;

Since people ought to do that which will likely attain that end;

Then People ought to do A.

The salient reason for doing the action is the empirical claim that it will likely attain the desired end. It is not the prudential norm. The prudential norm, that people ought to do that which will likely attain that end, is not the reason to act *unless* the practical hypothesis in the second premise is true. The warrant for following the norm is the truth of the empirical claim. What warrants the claim that people ought to get vaccinated against COVID-19, is the empirical claim that the vaccinations (of various sorts) reduce the chance of getting the disease to a very low probability. Suppose it is false that the action prescribed will attain the end desired. Clearly, advising someone to do what is unlikely to attain what they want makes no sense, rationally speaking. Although one can certainly advise them not to what they desire, that relies on norms related to ends, rather than means.

Using an earlier example, one might give prudential advice to hikers in bear country to stand their ground, make themselves known to the bear, and not run away—which kicks in the bear's chase instinct. All of these claims about what to do are based on the best available studies on bear behavior. Jake, who encounters a bear while hiking believes instead that climbing a tree would help him safely escape the bear. As a matter of fact, black bears can climb trees quite easily, so Jake would have been ill-advised to climb the tree if the bear was a black bear. What Jake *ought* to have done is stand his ground, since the bear is more likely to walk away from such a circumstance and more likely to attack if the person flees—since that triggers the pursuit-instinct in the bear. This allows people to make a normative claim based on an empirical one. It also makes possible an objective claim as to why people ought or ought to not do something. It can be objectively said that Jake ought to not do something because the means by which he wants to accomplish his end is empirically false. As Larry Laudan argues about such prudential "ought" claims, "it is clear that such rules, even if they do not yet appear to be truth-value bearing statements themselves, nonetheless depend for their warrant on the truth of such statements" (1987, p. 24).

The Empirical Warrant for Good Ends and Righteous Means

Prudential norms only address one aspect of the normative character of practical knowledge. It's about attaining an end, but it doesn't seem to address the matter of which ends are good to pursue. Walter Lippmann says, "it is not easy to explain why a thing we desire is so righteous" (1927, p. 23).

Nor does the prudential norm say what constraints should be placed on the way in which they are attained. A concept of the good typically plays the role of identifying proper ends. But, among the pragmatists, James and Dewey in particular dismiss the idea of the possibility of an overarching good or ideal as a target for ethical archers to hit, as Aristotle suggests. Instead, the argument here has been that the presence or absence of problems can serve as a proxy for the good.

There are two interconnected arguments to be made in this case for showing how problems figure in the empirical warrant for ends. The first concerns identifying something as a problem, which seems to be an evaluative, normative claim. Counting something as a problem seems to be counting something as bad, morally speaking, which implicitly calls up some sense of the good. There also appears to be another implicit norm related to problems as ends, namely, that people ought to solve problems.

The first argument, that there is an empirical warrant for counting something as a problem, relies on the thesis of ethical supevenience—that normative properties supervene on natural ones. The thesis was first articulated by R. M. Hare (1952) and has many current supporters (McPherson, 2012; Rosen, 2020)—although some have doubts (Roberts, 2018). Something that is counted as good or bad supervenes on natural properties if the two co-vary, such that a change in the natural properties results in a change in their evaluation, normatively speaking. This shows a necessary relation between the evaluation and the natural properties associated with that evaluation: if two possible entities are alike in all base respects, they are alike in all ethical respects (McLaughlin, 1995, p. 24).

The supervenience thesis is certainly intuitive. If two problems were exactly the same in regard to all their physical properties, yet one was counted as bad and the other good, people would say this would entail a patent inconsistency on the part of the evaluator. If the problem of famine is bad, it is because it has certain natural properties and empirical markers, such as death or ill health as a result of starvation. If famine led to good health, and had no other ill effects, it would certainly not be counted as bad. Thus, the warrant for claiming something bad is that it has certain natural properties and, since problems are counted as bad things, it would also hold for identifying something as a problem.

Just as people can be wrong about what they ought to do based on the empirical claim of what will likely attain their ends, people can also be wrong about what is problematic, based on empirical facts. For example, New York State, like other states, is considering bail reform (Merkl, 2019).

Many residents are against it because they think the current bail system works. It keeps people accused of crimes, who they believe are likely to have committed those crimes, off of the street. But one reason for the reform is that the current system favors the wealthy. Poor people who cannot meet bail must languish in jail until their trial is set—which can take months, if not longer. Some, of course, are convicted of a crime, but others are not. Many people are not aware of the empirical fact about the difference between the wealthy (among those who are granted bail) and the poor. That empirical fact can then be the basis for a re-evaluation of the practice as problematic or not. Similarly, over time, empirical facts about homosexuality have emerged that have been crucial in re-evaluating it as a problem or not for the general population. For example, the claim that homosexuality is a choice has been reasonably disproven, or that it is the result of parental molestation; that gay men molest children disproportionately to heterosexual men, as well, and so forth.

As a bonus, empirical markers can also serve to rank problems and provide further direction for priority in solving problems. This becomes important later when the matter of moral progress is discussed. Some of the more important variables, as T. M. Jones has argued, would be the number of people affected by the problem; its magnitude in terms of the scale and kind of consequences; how likely it will happen; how imminent; which people or groups might be affected (1991). All of these variables can be empirically determined. Although one variable might trump another in certain situations, if a problem has all these markers, then its intensity and urgency would be quite clear to people.

If the empirical markers of a situation are what warrants counting it as a problem, there is still the question of what warrants the norm that people ought to seek solutions to problems. Why should they make things better? Peirce's notion of evolutionary love and Dewey's meliorism assume that people ought to act to make things better, but should they? Why not leave the problems of climate change for future generations to deal with? To the extent that something is identified as a problem, it is also identified as bad, and the norm of good ends says people ought to avoid what is bad. But what warrants that norm?

An argument can be made that also shows that the warrant for melioristic norm is also empirical. To the extent that something is counted as bad, it can be assumed that people count that as an undesirable state of affairs. Consequently, to the extent that something is considered, objectively, to be a likely solution to that problem, then that is identified as a desirable state of affairs. Since, by the norm of prudential reasoning, people ought to do what is likely to attain what they desire, then people ought to do what is likely to solve their problems. But since the warrant for any prudential norm is an empirical one, then the normative force for pursuing the solution to a particular problem is also empirical, to the extent that the proposed solution is likely to solve the problem.

There is, finally, the norm of righteous means to consider. What warrants that norm? Given Wallace's claim that practices are inherently normative since they prescribe and proscribe right ways to attain the ends of the practice, it would follow that, assuming the ends good, the ways prescribed are not right if they tend make the practice problematic. Since problems are identified by the supervenience thesis by their empirical markers, and the warrant for counting something as a righteous means would be based on the problems they cause, then the warrant for claiming means to be righteous or not rests on those empirical markers.

Since problems have empirical markers associated with the intensity or seriousness of the problems, then this could also be a measure of the seriousness of the problems. For example, consider the case of fraud as a means to whatever end is envisaged. *Forbes* magazine reports that losses due to credit card fraud alone are around $190 billion annually. Banks lose about $11 billion and bank customers around $5 billion to fraud. As Haydn Shaughnessy intuitively notes, "those losses are scary, and present a deep systemic problem . . ." (Shaughnessy, 2011). Every year the Association of Certified Fraud Examiners releases a report on their study of occupational fraud and abuse (Dorris, 2018). In their 2018 report, they studied a sample of nearly 2700 cases of fraud around the globe. The empirical findings included a loss of $7 billion dollars from that sample, with a median loss of $130,000. Nearly 22% of the cases caused losses of $1 million. This is a problem.

But the report also makes empirical claims that could be helpful in preventing fraud in practices. Corruption among officials was the most common type of fraud. They also showed that even though owners or executives accounted for a small percentage of fraud cases, the median loss in those cases was $850,000, higher than the total median loss of all cases. Nearly half of the fraud cases were due to weaknesses in internal control. Most tips about fraud come from organizations that have hotlines. Fraudsters who had been with their company longer stole twice as much. Only 4% of perpetrators had a prior fraud conviction. Men were much more likely than women to commit fraud.

The fewer the problems, and the less intense the problems that are generated by a certain means, the more likely the means are righteous *and* effective. Since the prudential norm claims that people ought to do what is likely to attain what they desire, and it is desirable to have relatively problem-free practices, then people ought to retain those practices that work and fix those that cause problems. But, again, the warrant for that prudential norm is an empirical one—that as an empirical truth, the corrective means will likely fix the problem.

In Dewey's view, the advance in ethics is dependent on the proper partnership with science: "The consequent divorce of moral ends from scientific study of natural events renders the former impotent wishes . . ." (1922, *MW* 14, p. 162). As a concluding remark in favor of the case of a normative science, Dewey writes:

> In doing away once for all with the traditional distinction between moral goods, like the virtues, and natural goods like health, economic security . . . and the like . . . experimental logic when carried into morals makes every quality that is judged to be good according as it contributes to the amelioration of existing ills. And in so doing, it enforces the moral meaning of natural science. When all is said and done in criticism of present social deficiencies, one may well wonder whether the root difficulty does not lie in the separation of natural and moral science. When physics, chemistry, biology, medicine, contribute to the detection of concrete human woes and to the development of plans for remedying them and relieving the human estate, they become moral; they become part of the apparatus of moral inquiry or science. The latter then loses its peculiar flavor of the didactic and pedantic; its ultra-moralistic and hortatory tone. It loses its thinness and shrillness as well as its vagueness. It gains agencies that are efficacious. But the gain is not confined to the side of moral science. Natural science loses its divorce from humanity; it becomes itself humanistic in quality. It is something to be pursued not in a technical and specialized way for what is called truth for its own sake, but with the sense of its social bearing, its intellectual indispensableness. (1920, *MW* 12, pp. 178–179)

Consider one last example that incorporates the various points here. In a well-known article, "Famine, Affluence and Morality," Peter Singer argues:

"I begin with the assumption that suffering and death from lack of food, shelter, and medical care are bad" (2001, pp. 106–107). Second, "if it is in our power to prevent something bad from happening, without thereby sacrificing anything of comparable moral importance, we ought, morally, to do it" (2001, p. 107). Third, giving to charitable organizations that address famine meets the second premise; therefore, not doing that is morally wrong.

In this first premise of his argument, Singer is identifying something as "bad," that is, a problem. Why is it bad? Empirically, starvation causes ill health that has life-long effects, if it does not kill in the meantime. If it were the means to good health, people would be hard-pressed to label it bad.

Singer's next premise is a matter of righteous means: Coming to the aid of another is right if the cost to the helper is relatively insignificant. Not only ought one come to the aid of another if it costs the helper little, but it is more likely that people will come to the aid of others if there is little cost. The third claim is a prudential one; namely, a means by which one can likely prevent people from starving to death is to donate to effective charities with that purpose. In other places, Singer calls this "effective altruism" (2009). In this way, Singer identifies a problem as an end and proposes a righteous way that is likely to resolve it. This argument, many would say, has much more normative force than simply declaring that people ought to come to the aid of those in dire need.

Chapter 6

Communities of Inquiry

Practices are the results of experiments of living over time, established to solve a problem by providing the better means to an end. They are collective efforts. It is through the very acts of pursuing the ends, acting on the means, and abiding by the norms prescribed by practices, that people come to weigh in on those practices. Based on the problems that such practices create or solve, and by the means afforded them, they aim to correct, change or continue the practices that constitute their lives. It is in this way, as James argues, that all people ". . . contribute to the [human] race's moral life" (1891, p. 595).

If practices evolve to solve problems, there has to be a way to determine whether the solutions they propose truly solve, or at least ameliorate the problems they are designed to solve. This is a matter of their governance. The better governance processes are those capable of evaluating the practice's effectiveness in solving problems, have the capacity and means to improve it where needed, retain what works, or forego the practice altogether. The core of the governance process, then, is self-correction. Without this capability to correct itself, problems will grow and solutions will be lost.

To evaluate solutions to problems and propose alternative practical hypotheses where these solutions fail, practices and their practitioners must engage in inquiries. But inquiry itself is a practice with ends, means and norms concerning those means. The insight of the pragmatists, both the classical thinkers and those contemporary philosophers sympathetic to the tradition, is that inquiry itself engenders a certain sort of community. It is one that prescribes ends and means to those ends most conducive to self-correction and, thereby, improvement in its condition. As such, it can serve as a model for an effective problem-solving community.

The Ends and Means of Inquiry

What is the end of inquiry? Inquiries make claims about the subject of the inquiry as a result of the inquiry. The end, however, is not just to make claims but to assert the claims are true. Of course, how to determine whether a claim is true is a difficult question, but that does not detract from its aim. It would be strange to say that the goal of inquiry is to produce false claims, unless the inquiry is a pretense. The aim of truth is implicit in the practice of inquiry. Cheryl Misak says this plainly: "Truth . . . is internally related to inquiry . . ." (2000, p. 73).

Thinkers such as Karl-Otto Apel (1980), Jürgen Habermas (1990), Robert Brandom (1994), and Cheryl Misak (2000), all point to the implicit end of truth in inquiry by means of analyzing what inquirers do, namely, make assertions, truth claims. They argue from somewhat different theoretical frameworks but circle around the same conclusion. They are also inspired by Peirce's notion of community of inquiry and his fledgling speech act theory (except for Brandom who points to Dewey as a source) (1994, pp. 289ff.). Peirce argued that making an assertion commits the speaker to provide evidence for the assertion to the listener, much like making an affidavit before a notary, that what is asserted is true under some penalty (c. 1895, *CP* 2.335; 1905, *CP* 8.313; Boyd, 2016).

If inquiries end in claims, then it can be presumed that inquirers are asserting those claims. Assertions, if genuine, imply that assertors believe in some way, for some reason, on some basis, that the assertion is true. This is certainly the position of Robert Brandom. "The attitude of taking-true is just that of *acknowledging* an assertional commitment." He argues that it is an "attitude that grounds consequential undertakings of such commitments" (1994, p. 202). "What is it that we are *doing* when we assert, claim or declare something?" he asks. "The general answer is that we are undertaking a certain kind of *commitment*" (1994, p. 167). He writes that ". . . the characteristic authority on which the role of assertions in communication depends is intelligibly only against the background of a correlative *responsibility* to vindicate one's entitlement to the commitments such speech acts express" (1994, p. xii).

Misak concurs. She writes, "First, when I assert or believe that p, I commit myself to certain consequences—to have expectations about the consequences of p's being true." What follows is:

> These will be specified in terms of actions and observations: "if p, then if I do A, B will be the result." And, as Peirce stressed, some of these consequences will be consequences for belief. When I assert or believe that p, I find myself bound up in a web of inferential connections. If, for instance, I believe that p, and p entails q, then I am committed also to q. (2000, pp. 73–74)

Misak seems to agree with Habermas that, in asserting a claim, people are also committed to the claim that anyone should believe the assertion as they do (Misak, 2000, p. 74; Habermas, 1990, p. 65). This is the justification for Misak's own assertion that the illocutionary force of speech acts of belief and assertion not only commit people to inquiry, but it also commits people to *communities* of inquiry (2000, p. 95). Making an assertion to others enjoins them to make their own inquiries about what is asserted, resulting in their own assertions or counterassertions. For Habermas, an assertion is a call by the assertor for all to believe as the assertor does. It is an address to some community of inquirers. As Peirce argues, "no sensible man will be void of doubt as long as persons as competent to judge as himself differ from him. Hence to resolve his own doubts is to ascertain to what position sufficient research would carry all men" (1869–1870, *W* 2, p. 355). Misak no doubt agrees with Peirce:

> Belief involves being prepared to try to justify one's views to others and being prepared to test one's belief against the experience of others. Thus, the differences of inquirers—their different perspectives, sensibilities and experiences—must be taken seriously. If they are not, reaching the best or the true belief is not on the cards. (2000, p. 94)

Robert Talisse provides a good summary of Misak's position. First, to believe some claim is to believe that the claim is true. Second, to hold the claim true, is to claim that it would meet all challenges to its truth. But to hold that claim is to engage in a project of inquiry. But, last, inquiries are ongoing collective efforts that require squaring one's beliefs and assertions with others (2005, p. 103).

Inquiry is a collective, intergenerational effort over time. Peirce stresses that "probability and reasoning rests on the assumption" that inquiry will happen over time. He emphasizes that such inquiries "must embrace the whole community," communities to come, and communities anywhere. For that reason, "logic is rooted in the social principle," and inquirers must see their interests identified with those of an "unlimited community" (1878, *CP* 2.654; Liszka, 2021, pp. 137–138).

If truth is the end of inquiry, then what about the means? Following the overarching norm of practical knowledge—what ought to be done is what is right to do that is also likely to attain what is good to pursue--there are two questions in regard to the means of inquiry. What means to the end of truth are most *effective*, that is, most likely to attain the end of sorting out false from true claims? Secondly, what are the *righteous* means to the pursuit of truth? That is, what are the norms for sorting out false from true claims? As it pertains to the matter of practices, these two questions are more specific. What are the most effective means for determining which practical hypotheses will solve or ameliorate the problems related to a practice? What are the righteous ways to conduct such inquiries?

Compared to alternatives, it is widely recognized that the most effective means of inquiry, the method that delivers the epistemic goods, is the scientific method, broadly understood. However, students of science are loathe to identify any *specific* set of features of the method, since methods can vary from discipline to discipline (Gauch, 2003, pp. 4-5). Nonetheless, there are some general features that have gained widespread acceptance among scientific practitioners, as indicated by how it is represented in science education (Carey, 2012), by professional scientific organizations, such as the American Academy for the Advancement of Science (Gauch, 2003, pp. 5-6), and in the format of professional, peer-reviewed scientific journals (Jirge, 2017; American Association for the Advancement of Science, 2021; International Committee of Medical Journal Editors, 2021). These include the formulation of a hypothesis to explain an observed anomaly or problem. The framing of the hypothesis in testable form, usually in the form of predictions that can be observed in some experimental setting. The careful testing and statistical analysis of the results of those experiments as to determine whether what is predicted has or has not occurred to a statistically significant degree. A careful consideration, based on that analysis, as to whether the hypothesis should be rejected or not, that is, good methods in detecting erroneous hypotheses. Most importantly, continued testing of the hypothesis over time to the point where the hypothesis is considered to be established by the most relevant scientific practitioners.

Not only is the scientific method, so-called, thought to be the most effective means of inquiry, it is also thought by many students of science to be essentially a method of problem solving, therefore, ideally suited to the matter of problem-solutions (Laudan, 1977, pp. 4-5; Darden, 1991; Bechtel & Richardson, 1993). The prudential norm argues that people ought to do what is likely to attain their ends. If so, then the effectiveness of science in sorting out true from false hypotheses in problem solving, would argue that scientific methods ought to be adopted as far as possible in addressing the problems of practices.

But what about *righteous* means of such inquiries? True to Wallace's claim, the practice of science, like any practice, is normative and so promotes certain ethical norms for its practice. Good science is ethical science. It's hard to imagine good science done by dishonest scientists. How is it possible that truth could emerge from the deliberate adoption of false data, or the manipulation of data to fit a hypothesis? Peirce emphasizes that inquirers must have the right sort of epistemological virtues for inquiry to be successful (1903, *CP* 1.49; Liszka, 2021, pp. 158–159).

Robert Talisse claims that among the most important of these virtues of inquiry are honesty, modesty, charity, and integrity (2005, pp. 112–113). Honesty is "the disposition to follow evidence and weigh various factors relevant to a problem, and a willingness to base decisions upon such considerations. . . . The . . . honest deliberator follows reasons and arguments, not bare interests or preference" (2005, p. 112). The humble inquirer understands proposals "not as ultimate resolutions, but as hypotheses to be tried and evaluated in terms of their effects." Charitable interlocutors "accept as a default position that their opponents are not simply stupid or misguided or corrupt, but possibly correct" (2005, pp. 112–113).

As Peirce sees it, inquirers who lack integrity corrupt inquiries (1898, *CP* 1.619). There are sham inquiries, for example, an inquiry into a corrupt politician by equally corrupt or politically motivated investigators that intends to exonerate that politician or scientists who are paid by corporations to find scientific support for a vested interest. People often feign belief in order to manipulate or achieve some particular end. Inquirers who have more of an interest in proving their point than the truth about their claim may engage in what is often called confirmation bias, cherry-picking evidence that supports the claim and ignoring evidence that does not. But all of these are a failure in achieving the end of inquiry as much as if one were to fail for methodological reasons. Misak adds another virtue, which might be associated with the virtue of humility: inquirers are expected to forego their belief in the face of overwhelming evidence against it (2000, p. 74).

The commitment to these virtues of honesty, humility, and integrity are warranted because as a matter of empirical fact, inquiries that aim at truth are more likely to attain truth if inquirers have these virtues. Consequently, if, by the prudential norm, people aim at truth, then they should employ the scientific methodologies (as far as possible) honestly and with integrity. Accountants could not have accurate books if they are dishonest, doctors could not cure diseases if they prescribed worthless drugs because of kickbacks. Scientists, as in the past, would not find the truth about the link between cancer and smoking if their research was paid for by cigarette companies.

If these are some of the virtues of inquirers, what are the norms of communities and practices of inquiry? Recall the earlier discussion of Peirce's account, in "The Fixation of Belief," of the norms of differing communities of inquiry, those based on authority and dogmatism, and those based on science. Presumably, communities want to have their citizens believe that the means and ends of the various practices that constitute the community are good, righteous, and efficient, even if they have their problems. Since, as Peirce argues, beliefs engender action, then doubts foster inaction, dilute solidarity, and weaken cooperation. If everyone or nearly everyone is on board about the means and ends of practices, then that is the basis of solidarity, and the ends of the practice are more likely to be accomplished (Liszka, 2018).

Fixing beliefs on the basis of authority engenders an *ethos* that favors strong hierarchies, emphasizes the virtues of obedience and loyalty, discourages curiosity, cultivates a blind trust of authority, and stresses top-down, asymmetrical communicative practices (1877, *CP* 5.381–382). Obviously, such communities do not foster the virtues needed for good inquiries. Indeed, inquiry in such communities does not really seek truth but seeks to legitimate the beliefs that the authorities want its members to believe. This could result in general stability and a certain solidarity in the short run, but false beliefs, particularly if they make predictions that are false, or misguide believers, tend not to work out in the long run (1877, *CP* 1.60).

People could also choose to hold on to their beliefs by ignoring or censoring all contrary beliefs and finding ways to rationalize away or dismiss any evidence contrary to those beliefs. If people chose to live with other like-minded people only and insulate themselves from other-minded people, this might stabilize their beliefs in the short-run, but not in the long run. Like authoritative communities, such communities must be highly censorious and manipulative in order to maintain solidarity and belief stability (1877, *CP* 5.378). If people are swayed by public opinion, such opinion is fickle, changes with the times, and is based on what other people think or say, so long as there is enough of them (1872, *W* 3, p. 15).

Communities of inquiry, modeled on scientific communities, engender an ethos contrary to these other methods of fixing belief. Science requires a community that is open to inquiry (c. 1899, *CP* 1.135) and relies on reasoning rather than authority. Scientific inquiry requires an opportunity to criticize and evaluate beliefs, and commits those who assert beliefs to publicly accessible demonstration of those beliefs (1877, *CP* 5.384).

This is not to say that science as it is practiced does not become authoritarian at times, that scientists never practice the method of tenacity, or that they are never dishonest or fraudulent or capable of being bought. There is something about the general methodology of science that, because it engages in public demonstrations that can be replicated and observed, allows these errant actions to be corrected, so that false hypotheses and claims eventually go by the wayside.

Recall in an earlier discussion that John Dewey argues for an alliance between scientific and democratic method (1939, *LW* 13, p. 135). Misak seems to agree. She claims that the norms of communities of inquiries constitute a kind of "epistemological democracy" (2000, p. 96). "The requirements of genuine belief show that we must, broadly speaking, be democratic inquirers" (2000, p. 106). "The pragmatist thus supports a kind of radical democracy in inquiry" (2000, p. 94), mainly because without the norms that require the justification of one's beliefs, and recognition of others to challenge those beliefs, true beliefs will not emerge in the process (2000, p. 94). She quotes Hilary Putnam approvingly: "[D]emocracy is a requirement for experimental inquiry in any area. To reject democracy is to reject the idea of being experimental" (Borradori, 1994, p. 64; Misak, 2000, p. 94).

Surely, however, neither Putnam nor Misak can mean that inquiry is democratic in the sense that people vote on what is true, or that majority rules. Although Peirce talks about consensus of beliefs as an indication of truth, this is certainly not meant in the constructivist sense. Truth is not born out of agreement; rather, agreement is an indication of truth because inquirers doing inquiries well done tend to come to the same conclusion about the subject of their inquiries in the long run.

Misak and Putnam may have in mind something similar to the distinction that Dewey makes between democracy as a political entity and as a social idea. For Dewey, the fundamental norm of social democracy is governance by the governed. People have a responsible share in forming and directing the practices in which they participate, relative to their capacity to do so (1927, *LW* 2, p. 325). Rights of free speech and equality particularly aid in that realization.

However, there are some conflicts between the norms of democracy and the norms of inquiry in this respect. The First Amendment guarantees freedom of speech with, of course, a number of qualifications that have evolved over time through case law. There is also an equal right to free speech in the sense that it applies to every citizen. But it does not qualify free speech in terms of true beliefs, only that people have a right to assert whatever they wish, regardless of whether it is true or even regardless of whether they believe it is true. They can distort the truth, spread misinformation, slander public officials, and a number of other speech practices not conducive to truth-making, and would not do in practices of inquiry.

Democratic norms of free speech and equality as applied to inquirers would have to be qualified. Discourse ethics as developed by Apel and Habermas makes some of these qualifications clear. Discourse ethics also captures the fundamental norm of democracy as a social idea since what is morally true and right comes out of agreement from participation in a discourse about those matters, a discourse structured by giving reasons and justifications for what is believed to be right and good. Habermas makes an important distinction between strategic communication and communication that aims at securing agreement (1990, p. 44). Strategic communication uses claims, whether true or false, not to come to a genuine agreement with others, but to get others to believe something that is in the interest of the strategist. Propaganda, of course, is the exemplar of strategic communication, and it is hardly conducive to truth-getting inquiries. One of the greatest propagandists in the United States, Edward Bernays, understood implicitly that democracies, with their emphasis on public opinion, were highly vulnerable to forms of strategic communication such as propaganda. Manipulation of the opinions of the masses is the "unseen mechanism" of society, and constitutes "an invisible government," led by a few who are "the true ruling power" of the country. "This is a logical result of the way in which our democratic society is organized" (1928, p. 37).

Securing agreement on the other hand requires that the communication partners can, of their own accord, understand the reasons for believing a claim to be true or false, and each has an interest in getting others to an agreement about their respective beliefs on that basis. An inquirer *wants* others to believe as that inquirer believes. Inquiry practices are more like practices that secure agreement than strategic ones.

The norms of discourse ethics are translated in a more practical way by Robert Alexy, and in a manner that shows some of the differences between democratic notions of free speech and equality, and those notions as they are considered in discourses that secure agreement (1990). The free speech of inquirers would be constrained by the inferential commitments of their assertions, including general rules of logic, such as noncontradiction (1990, p. 163), something as noted by Brandom and Misak. Free speech would also be qualified by sincerity commitments (1990, pp. 163–164). People are free to make their claims or assertions, so long as they sincerely believe them. This would prevent forms of strategic communication, claims that are not sincerely held to be true, but used to manipulate people towards certain other beliefs or actions. This is especially relevant in the age of the internet where fabrication and misleading information is rampant. Inquiries, on the other hand, are often cases where people may inquire not because they sincerely believe that a hypothesis is correct, but because they think it plausible. Inquirers should hold judgment on a hypothesis until the evidence weighs in. Scientists who sincerely believe their hypotheses true before an inquiry to justify them often lead to confirmation bias. Peirce was particularly concerned about this and developed techniques of predesignation in statistical analysis to avoid this, something that presaged similar developments in the methods of frequency theory in statistics (1902, *CP* 2.775).

The democratic norm of equality would be translated into discursive practices that aim at securing agreement in something like the following sense. All inquirers should have the same opportunity to make claims, raise issues, criticize the claims of others, defend their claims, ask questions, and so forth (1990, pp. 166–167). If this norm was not heeded, then people with important criticisms or great insights might be excluded from the inquiry, hampering the goal of reaching a true claim.

However, this raises the issue of differentials in knowledge or expertise in such inquiries (1990, p. 180). If there is a dispute about whether immunizations cause autism, it would seem that people would want those that have the most expertise in that area to have more opportunities and play a larger, leading role in investigations. It would seem intuitive that if there is a health problem with cancer, that people would want those trained in the relevant medical research to be principals in the inquiry and lead it. So wouldn't this also be true in regard to any problem? The principal democratic norm is citizen participation in the government's governance of its citizens. The norms of a community of inquiry would seem to imply something different, that the governance of practices of inquiry should favor or privilege expertise. This creates a conflict between expertise and democratic norms.

Another important norm of discursive practices aimed at securing agreement is nonexclusion. This also expresses the fundamental norm of the social idea of democracy, that people have a right to participate in decisions about the rules and policies that will govern them. For this reason, people cannot be excluded from discourses about these matters because of what they claim or, certainly, who they are (1990, p. 167). To allow such exclusions could easily lead to cherry-picking inquirers who happen to agree with the prevailing beliefs of those engaged in the discourse.

But when it comes to inquiries, should certain beliefs be seriously entertained and everyone included in inquiries? If, for example, there are inquiries about how to prevent something like the Holocaust from happening again, should Holocaust deniers be seriously considered or even excluded from the inquiry? If the inquiry is how to mitigate climate change, should climate-change deniers be part of the inquiry? If there is an inquiry into the mitigation of COVID-19, wouldn't it be prudent to have only the experts involved and discount any popular view not held to be plausible by the experts? Should people believe the scientists about the lack of causal connection between immunizations and autism, or some Hollywood actors? The economy of research would suggest that, given that time is short and problems must be addressed, then implausible claims should be excluded from inquiries (1990, p. 180). This was certainly part of the role of abduction in Peirce's notion of the economy of research, namely, to sort out the plausible from the implausible hypotheses *before* research began (c. 1901, *CP* 7.220). Not everybody's wild-eyed conspiratorial hypothesis can be considered, but that would appear to violate the fundamental norm of the social idea of democracy.

A third important norm is noncoercion. Coercion is the hallmark, as Peirce argues, of authoritative communities, not scientific ones. Attempts to intimidate a minority by a majority of believers could lead to false results. History shows that sometimes it is the belief that is contrary to the prevailing opinion that wins the day. Threats and sanctions against those who hold certain contrary beliefs could also derail the search for truth. Think of the plight of Galileo and the history of evolutionary theory, which is still controversial in many quarters today.

Apel and Habermas claim that the norms of discourse ethics fall out of the very nature of securing agreement. Apel thinks these norms are transcendental in the sense of necessary presuppositions of participants in such discourses. To deny these presuppositions results in a performative contradiction analogous to the performative contradiction in asserting that one does not exist (1990, p. 43). Habermas is skeptical about Apel's claim and proposes a quasi-empirical foundation to these principles, modeled after theories such as Kohlberg's and Chomsky's that aim to show a universal basis to moral judgment, on the one hand, and linguistic competence on the other (1990, p. 15). But those theories are still empirical theories about claims of a universal human capacity.

Misak is skeptical about both Apel's and Habermas's justifications. Her alternative is not much better. Instead, she offers prudential advice to people:

> . . . [O]ne of my arguments for that method [the democratic method]—that adopting a method which ignores the experience of others is a bad means for getting belief which best accounts for all experience and argument—has no transcendental ring at all to it. It does not suggest that the possibility of language or communication depends on a certain conception of how to live (i.e. freely and equally). Rather, it is a hypothetical imperative of the sort: if you want beliefs which will withstand the force of experience, then do such-and-such. The additional empirical or sociological claims is then added—virtually everybody claims to be after such beliefs." (2000, p. 107)

Misak is relying on the prudential norm that people ought to do what will most likely attain their ends, and if participating in discourses with democratic norms is likely to result in true beliefs, then, if people desire true beliefs, then they should participate in these kinds of discourses. Prudential norms alone, as discussed, do not have the normative force that other sorts of norms do. People can take the advice or not. It's also doubtful that everyone is chomping at the bit to acquire true beliefs. They are often more interested in defending their beliefs, true or not. Leon Festinger showed that, when people encounter cognitive dissonance, where evidence may contradict one's belief, people have a tendency to favor their existing beliefs in proportion to their personal investment in those beliefs. In those cases, people tend to ignore contrary evidence, or find ways to rationalize it away (1962).

If the justifications of Apel and Habermas are to be rejected, a better alternative may be Brandom's account. Brandom argues that making assertions or claims commits people to the implicit norms of certain discursive practices. This has more normative force, since people can be chastised or sanctioned on the basis of those norms by other interlocutors. Refusals to justify beliefs, ignoring evidence, or making contradictory claims, allows other interlocutors to call those people on the carpet. With prudential advice, people can take it or leave it. Imagine the difference between prudential and practical norms in the courtroom. If all involved, judge, jury, prosecutor, defendant, and witnesses were tasked to determine whether the defendant is guilty or innocent on the basis of prudential advice, who knows what would result, depending on who elected the advice and who did not. To have jurors take an oath to be impartial is a commitment to the practice by the jurors and, should they fail in the commitment, they can be sanctioned accordingly. The warrant for the commitment is the empirical warrant of the norms of impartiality, weighing evidence, and the like. They are more likely than alternatives to determine whether or not the defendant is truly guilty or innocent of the crime.

The Problem of Epistemarchy

One important matter that came to light in the previous analysis centered on the norm of nonexclusion. In effect, it expresses the fundamental norm of the social idea of democracy, namely, that the governed should have the right to participate in matters pertaining to the rules and policies that govern them. As Joshua Cohen expresses this ideal, ". . . [O]utcomes are democratically legitimate if an only if they could be the object of a free and reasoning agreement among equals" (1996, p. 73). This more or less expresses the Rawlsian position that what is right is the outcome of a fair, deliberative process, one not tainted by interests (1971). But inquiries that aim at truth and knowledge, particularly science-based inquiries, are conducted by experts, so that participation in such inquiries to be successful should privilege those with the relevant knowledge and expertise. This condition for successful inquiries seems to conflict with the norms of democratic practice. Philip Kitcher raises this very important issue in the context of scientific inquiry itself, whether science experts should exclusively direct the ends and means of scientific research, or should those affected by such research also have a role in those considerations (2001; 2012). If this question were extended to the political realm, then the issue becomes whether experts in the political practices that pertain to legislation and policies, transportation, energy, education, security, international affairs, and all such matters, everything that affects people in their practical lives, should have a larger role in such matters.

Robert Talisse calls this the *epistemarchy principle*. "If political wisdom is knowledge of some object, then it is unclear why one should need public discussion to discover it rather than, for example, the research of a few well-trained (political) scientists" (2005, p. 101). He formalizes it in the following way:

> **Epistemarchy Principle.** Political wisdom entitles the politically wise person to a share of political power directly proportionate to his wisdom. Conversely, those lacking political wisdom should lack political power. (2005, p. 99)

Political power here should be understood as the ability to participate in decisions about the rules and policies that will govern people in a community. The same could be said about Wallace's notion of practical knowledge. Does Misak's idea of "epistemological democracy" also lead to epistemarchy?

Talisse attributes this position to Plato: ". . . [A]s the *Republic* shows, a politics expressly aimed at truth and wisdom will be hostile to democracy" (2005, p. 100). Dewey makes the same point. The problem of modern democracies is the threat of an "intellectual aristocracy" (1927, *LW* 2, p. 362):

> The essential fallacy of the democratic creed, it is urged, is the notion that a historic movement which effected an important and desirable release from restrictions is either a source or a proof of capacity in those thus emancipated to rule, when in fact there is no factor common in the two things. The obvious alternative is rule by those intellectually qualified, by expert intellectuals. This revival of the Platonic notion that philosophers should be kings is the more taking because the idea of experts is substituted for that of philosophers, since philosophy has become something of a joke, while the image of the specialist, the expert in operation, is rendered familiar and congenial by the rise of the physical sciences and by the conduct of industry. (1927, *LW* 2, p. 363)

Kitcher attributes this view to Plato as well: "Plato offers a portrait of an allegedly ideal city, a *kallipolis,* in which the lives of all go well because wise and good experts understand what is best for each type of person and design institutions and laws that promote the best for everybody (2012, p. 366). Certainly, that is a better proposal than having the ignorant and evil make such determinations, but it cuts out the possibility of a better alternative that some pragmatists like James, Dewey, and Kitcher want to promote. This harks back, ironically, to the opening of this book, in which the pragmatists took aim at Plato's notion of imposing an ideal good on an imperfect community. Yet, a certain strain of pragmatism, based on Peirce's notion of the community of inquiry, appears to lead to the very claims that pragmatism had hoped to cast aside. As David Estlund frames the issue, how is it possible to "let truth be the guide without illegitimately privileging the opinions of any putative experts" in the various practices that constitute a democratic community? (1997, p. 183).

Dewey's struggle with epistemarchy's claim of rule by expert takes shape in his debate with one of its strongest advocates, Walter Lippmann. Dewey's *The Public and Its Problems* is a response to Lippmann's provocative book *The Phantom Public,* characterizing the state of democracy as it had come to be practiced by his time. Many would say that it rings true especially today. *The Phantom Public* was a best seller at the time but shocked many with its straight-talking, *realpolitik* account of American democracy.

Lippmann studied at Harvard and was influenced by William James. As a journalist, he won two Pulitzer Prizes for his work and helped to found *The New Republic,* for which he served as editor. He also held positions in government. Lippmann was especially concerned how propaganda was influencing public opinion, which motivated another well-received book, *Public Opinion.*

Lippmann argues that purveyors of democracy are under two illusions. The first is that the government expresses the will of the people and that there is such a thing as a public that supposedly has such a will. People generally don't know what's going on or where things are being carried by the government (1927 p. 3). Only a small proportion of eligible voters vote, and fewer still participate in the affairs of government (1927, p. 6). The citizen, he avers, is not to blame for how is it possible to have an opinion on all the problems of government, labor, transportation, banking, finance, rural, urban, educational, agricultural, international, educational, "while he is earning a living, rearing children and enjoying life?" (1927, pp. 13–14). The ideal of democracy rests on the possibility of an omnicompetent citizen, but that's impossible. No one comes close, not even the president of the United States can attain this ideal (1927, p. 11).

Voting, demonstrations, and voicing opinions are not governing; they are expressions that only reward or punish those who govern. The public does not devise laws and policies but is presented with alternatives or choices that they can say yes or no to. They rarely, if ever, create or administer what they have in mind (1927, pp. 41–42). It is always a matter of something that has been done or is planned to be done (1927, p. 45). The public does not select the candidate to be nominated, write the platform, or outline the policy. It takes what is presented and goes from there (1927, p. 47). The public does not originate these things; it aligns itself for or against them. The various publics, it is hoped, should "support the Ins when things are going well" and "support the Outs when they seem to be going badly" (1927, p. 116). "[The public] must choose between the Ins and Outs on the basis of a cumulative judgment as to whether problems are being solved or aggravated" (1927, p. 119). There is no ethical superiority to majority rule, but it is a mechanism for a civilized society to ameliorate the force which resides in "the weight of numbers" (1927, p. 48). It's a good substitute for fighting (1927, p. 49).

So what is the role of the public, such as it is? There is not *the* Public, but various publics that form when certain problems that interest them become manifest. "At certain junctures problems arise. It is only with the crises of some of these problems that public opinion is concerned. And its object in dealing with a crisis is to help allay that crisis" (1927, p. 56). Interestingly, Seyla Benhabib says something similar: "[T]he public sphere comes into existence whenever and where ever all affected by general social norms of action engage in a practical discourse, evaluating their validity" (1992, p. 105). The government consists of a body of officials, some elected, some appointed, who presumably have the practical knowledge to deal with the various and complex facets of governing. Where those who are supposed to manage these practices fail, the public intervenes. "When the officials fail, public opinion is brought to bear on the issue (1927, pp. 62–63). They are a bellwether for the workability of a rule, policy, or action. In some cases, the public may not even know there is a problem until someone objects. If things are going smoothly, and there are not objections, then there's no problem as far as the public is concerned (1927, p. 94). "It only deals with the failures" (1927, p. 97).

The role of public opinion is to discern by signs and other indications who, among those governing, can solve the problem and advocate a workable solution rather than those who are just pursuing their own self-interest. "Public opinion in its highest ideal will defend those who are prepared to act on their reason against the interrupting force of those who merely assert their will" (1927, p. 59). The purpose of public debate, for example of candidates for political office, is to expose those who are self-interested from those who have some genuine public good in mind (1927, p. 104).

How do the various publics deal with problems of interest to them? First, they identify the rule, policy, or action as defective, and characterize its defect, as how that problem affects them. Second, they petition in some way the agency that is most likely to mend it. "These are, I should maintain, the only two questions which the public needs to answer in order to exert the greatest influence it is capable of exerting toward the solution of public problems" (1927, p. 98). In light of this, those who govern must propose rules, policies, procedures, and actions that are clear and specify the way they can be amended without revolution (1927, p. 126).

The sort of epistemarchy that Lippmann envisions has obvious significant differences with the political mechanisms that Plato imagined in *The Republic* since it is tempered by the political mechanisms of democracy. For one thing, the "Ins" can be replaced if the public does not find their work satisfactory or to their liking. There are feedback mechanisms by which various publics can register problems and affect the course of action of the experts. Expertise is not centered in a single philosopher-king, but among many experts in many areas among many different governmental practices. In that way, expertise in one area can be working well, but in another area problematic. The laws, policies, actions and procedures do not come down from a philosopher-king on high without public input or consideration, but have mechanisms for public input and amendment as its application requires.

Dewey was greatly affected by Lippmann's book and sought to give a defense of a more participatory sense of democracy. About a year later, he gave a series of lectures on the matter at Kenyon College in Ohio. It was published as *The Public and Its Problems* in the following year. Lippmann's reaction to the book was dismissive, and, indeed, the book was written in Dewey's typical verbose style that did not have the punch or succinctness that Lippmann's journalistic, to-the-point, laconic writing mastered.

Dewey conceded Lippmann's points about the public, but he insisted that it was in "eclipse" rather than nonexistent. Dewey attributed the eclipse to several factors. One was an inherent contradiction in the principles of democracy, which favored a form of individual rights that diminished the sense of community needed to foster a public (1927, *LW* 2, p. 307). Capitalism, particularly its Adam Smith-inspired, invisible hand ideology, reinforced this individualism by claiming that the pursuit of individual interests will result in public good (1927, *LW* 2, p. 312). The industrial age is another cause of the eclipse of the public since it has been the cause of the loss of small communities (1927, *LW* 2, p. 314). Another factor was the increase in the number, variety and cheapness of types of amusement and entertainment that serve as a distraction from public affairs by the masses (1927, *LW* 2, p. 321). Finally, another factor was the way in which science was used in current society, instrumentally for "the interests of its consequences for a possessing and acquisitive class" (1927, *LW* 2, p. 344).

How is the public to come to light again? Dewey insists that there has to be a return to the core ideas of a democracy; the Great Society must be transformed into the "Great Community" (1927, *LW* 2, p. 327). There is a difference between democracy in the political sense with all its governance mechanisms, such as separation of powers, voting, majority rule, and the like, and the social concept of democracy. The social idea of democracy entails a certain set of relations among individuals, between individuals and the groups to which they belong and, second, a certain kind of relation among the various groups. The relation among individuals is its face-to-face communication in small communities, characteristic of neighborhoods and local communities (1927, *LW* 2, p. 368). The relation of individual to group "consists in having a responsible share according to capacity in forming and directing the activities of the groups to which one belongs and participating according to need in the values which the groups sustain" (1927, *LW* 2, pp. 327–328). From the standpoint of the group, the role is to promote the growth of individuals within that group, relative to their goods and interests (1927, *LW* 2, p. 328). Furthermore, the role of all groups is to ensure a flow among the groups with which they interact (1927, *LW* 2, p. 328). If "practices" are substituted for "groups," then Dewey is more or less characterizing democracy as a social idea in terms of the governance of its practices. These features more or less define the very idea of a community. Dewey concludes that "regarded as an idea, democracy is not an alternative to other principles of associated life. It is the idea of community life itself" (1927, *LW* 2, p. 328).

This sense of democracy is contrasted with the sort of epistemarchy—rule by experts—that Lippmann envisions. There are several problems with such a governance model for democracy. Among the most important is that "a class of experts is inevitably so removed from common interests as to become a class with private interests and private knowledge, which in social matters is not knowledge at all" (1927, *LW* 2, p. 364). As a result, an epistemarchy would tend to further separate the public from participation in its own governance, the fundamental norm of democracy.

However, Dewey concedes that the political mechanisms of democracy currently in place, and which Lippmann notes, would temper the more negative aspects of an epistemarchy. Political mechanisms such as voting, majority rule, "to some extent. . . . involve a consultation and discussion which uncover social needs and troubles" (1927, *LW* 2, p. 364). Citing De Tocqueville, such mechanisms "force a recognition that there are common interests, even though the recognition of *what* they are is confused; and the need it enforces of discussion and publicity bring about some clarification of what they are. The man who wears the shoe knows best that it pinches and where it pinches, even if the expert shoemaker is the best judge of how the trouble is to be remedied" (1927, *LW* 2, p. 364). "But what is more significant" about voting, Dewey says, is that counting of heads compels prior recourse to methods of discussion, consultation and persuasion . . ." (1927, *LW* 2, p. 365). What would improve this role of the public is enhancing what leads up to the vote. "The essential need, in other words is the improvement of methods and conditions of debate, discussion and persuasion. That is *the* problem of the public" (1927, *LW* 2, p. 365). If this could be corrected, then the basis of Lippmann's complaint about the public, and the call for a democratized epistemarchy would have less weight.

So how is that to be enhanced? Dewey argues that "this improvement depends essentially upon freeing and perfecting the processes of inquiry and of dissemination of . . . [the experts'] conclusions." Dewey admits that the work of the inquiry "devolves upon experts," but the expertise does not extend to "framing and executing policies, but in discovering and making known the facts upon which the former depend." Experts are only technical experts, not experts in judging "the bearing of the knowledge supplied" (1927, *LW* 2, p. 365). However,

> . . . one great trouble at present is that the data for good judgment are lacking; and no innate faculty of mind can make up for the absence of facts. Until secrecy, prejudice, bias, misrepresentation, and propaganda as well as sheer ignorance are replaced by inquiry and publicity, we have no way of telling how apt for judgment of social policies the existing intelligence of the masses may be." (1927, *LW* 2, p. 366)

The results of inquiries are "but tools after all," and their actuality is accomplished in face-to-face relationships. "Logic in its fulfillment recurs to the primitive sense of the word: dialogue" (1927, *LW* 2, p. 371). The findings in the inquiries of experts can only be fulfilled in "the relations of personal intercourse in the local community" (1927, *LW* 2, pp. 371–372). The problem with scientific and social inquiry is that it is applied to society by interests rather than incorporated in society for the purposes of its deliberation (1927, *LW* 2, p. 344). What is needed in order to foster democratic community is what is characteristic of democracies, as found in small communities—face-to-face interactions. The solution to the problem of the public is the reconstruction of face-to-face communities (1927, *LW* 2, p. 368).

This is actually not too far from the conclusion that Philip Kitcher makes in regard to ethical discussion: "We should seek a notion of mutual engagement as well suited to the renewed ethical project as the original version of mutual engagement—the deliberations among band members—was to the original venture" (2011, p. 340). In Kitcher's anthropological reconstruction of the ethical project, he argued that small human bands—hunter-gather types—developed egalitarian models for the deliberation of the rules that were to govern their lives, which involved a high degree of participation and mutual engagement of the sort that is conducive to solving problems among the group.

Given that Dewey was born and raised in Vermont, he may have had the model of the town hall meeting in mind as the hallmark of democracy and something exemplified in Jefferson's sense of democracy (1939, *LW* 13, pp. 175–176). Since Dewey invokes De Tocqueville, it's interesting to note his observations about New England folk:

> The New Englander is attached to his township, not only because he was born in it, but because it constitutes a social body of which he is a member, and whose government claims and deserves the exercise of his sagacity. . . . Another important fact is that the township of New England is so constituted as to excite the warmest of human affections, without arousing the ambitious passions of the heart of man. . . . the township serves as a centre for the desire of public esteem, the want of exciting interests, and the taste for authority and popularity, in the midst of the ordinary relations of life; and the passions which commonly embroil society change their character when

they find a vent so near the domestic hearth and the family circle. (1835, pp. 84–85)

Problems and the Governance of Practices

So what comes out of the Lippmann-Dewey debate that is relevant to problem-based ethics? Perhaps De Tocqueville can be invoked again: "The great privilege of the Americans does not simply consist in their being more enlightened than other nations, but in their being able to repair the faults they may commit" (1835, p. 257). One matter that is important to the goodness of practices is how they self-correct, that is, how they solve their problems. What is critical for the governance of any practice, large or small, whether its domain is the wider public or a narrower constituency, is whether it has established reliable mechanisms for doing four commonsense things in this respect:

(1) Devising ways and means to identify its problems and having those who suffer or endure the problems to voice their concerns;

(2) Developing the expertise to propose and devise feasible solutions to those problems;

(3) Employing reliable methodological means to assess and test the results of those solutions;

(4) Establishing ways and means to amend or discard proposed solutions as required, based on the results in (3) and, if discarded, procedures for moving on to the next proposal.

This is not too far afield from Peirce's characterization of the scientific method as the interworking of abduction, deduction, and induction. Abduction concerned with identifying the problems and conflicts in a practice, and formulating plausible solutions. Deduction concerned with figuring out ways in which the better practical hypotheses can be implemented. Induction concerned with figuring out the best ways to assess the interventions to see if they are working.

Each of these aspects of governance may involve different types of discourses and practices. Identifying problems and the concerns of those who suffer the problems involve conversations as well as inquiries, the former giving voice to those who are troubled by the practice's ways and means and as a way to create sympathy and understanding among the participants. But it has to be accompanied by effective inquiries into the causes and nature of those problems, if the plausible solutions are to be discovered—and that often requires expertise. There is no reason why those who wear the shoes, as Dewey says, cannot say where they pinch and suggest a fix, but the shoemaker has to make it so and likely knows better than the wearer how to fix them. Similarly for the other stages of good governance.

Practices can organize themselves as practices of inquiry into the best ways and means of attaining its ends and managing the various conflicts that occur both internally to the practice and, externally, with other practices. If done right, this governance process can create a proper relation of governance between expertise and the practice's public

Consider as a model the educational practice as institutionalized in colleges and universities. It may not be the best, but it is certainly not the worst model. This practice has practitioners, those who execute the practice, and beneficiaries, those who receive the goods of the practice. For the sake of illustration, suppose the focus is on one of its principal goods, education, and set aside research and other ends it claims to achieve. Teachers are thought to be practitioners of educational practices, and students are thought to be the direct beneficiaries. There are indirect beneficiaries, of course, parents above all, who are relieved that their children will be employable, knowledgeable, and better people as a result. Most other practices are indirect beneficiaries of education since educated people have the skills, training, and knowledge needed to carry out these practices. Thus, the community as a whole is thought to benefit from educated people, and this is why people pay for it through their taxes. Parents, employers, and people generally speaking want students to be educated because of the observable outcomes of education. The direct and indirect beneficiaries of a practice may be counted as the practice's public.

As practitioners, teachers are presumed to have a level of practical knowledge, both know-that and know-how, in educational practices. For that reason, they are typically counted as having the expertise to educate students. They are presumed to be experts in the subject matter they teach and good at teaching it. Their know-that, in turn, may be based on the inquiries of others experts in the field, psychologists, sociologists, education professors, who do theoretical work and experiments on the subject of education. This informs the practice of teachers, and if teachers are good teachers, they are motivated to improve their practice from these sources of knowledge and their own experience in the classroom.

These practices are housed within institutions that have a certain governance structure. This typically includes administrators and regents or trustees, as well as the college's faculty and, to some degree, its staff. The hallmark of most American public universities is what is called shared governance between faculty and administrators. Sometimes a division of governance roles between faculty and administrators is made in the institutions, and sometimes there's quite a bit of overlap, so that faculty have significant input into most aspects of the institution's governance. The regents provide public oversight since they are drawn mostly from the public.

There can be a number of problem areas within the university. Internally, there can be performance problems with faculty. There can be problems between faculty and students, faculty and administrators, administrators and regents, regents and faculty, and so forth. There can be external problems between universities and state funders and legislators, between parents and faculty and administrators, complaints from employers and agencies, and so forth.

If colleges are well governed, they work to minimize these problems, and they do so through mechanisms for interaction between the practice and its publics. But depending on the problem, its solution is handled by the appropriate expertise. If the problem is with the performative competence of faculty, then faculty have organized processes by which performance is evaluated and corrected where possible and, in some cases, recommending termination. Students have opportunities for input into teaching performance. Faculty may work with hospitals, schools, businesses, agencies, and others to meet their needs through curricular changes, and those same publics have opportunities to register complaints or inadequacies in the education of the students they get as employees. Administrators may confront faculty with changes that are needed to maintain enrollments and meet student demand. Through their own governance process, faculty may confront administrators on policy or procedural problems and, if unionized, on labor issues. Students typically have their own governance organization and publish a student newspaper to voice concerns, register complaints, and keep an eye on administrative doings. The public's regents have, in many cases, high authority to approve policies, curriculum, and direction of the college. On top of this, regional accreditors, professional accrediting organizations, insist on periodic evaluation of the institutional effectiveness of the college. Academic programs are regularly reviewed by academics external to the institution. Both state and federal governments impose a number of rules, regulations, and reporting requirements on the institution. This may be enough to get the picture. Good governance of practices has a way of incorporating the issues and complaints of its publics into the governance process in an effective way that allows it to identify problems and uses the expertise of its practitioners to solve those problems, measures the effectiveness of those solutions, and acts to correct the corrections, if needed.

Chapter 7

Change for the Better

One central theme of pragmatist ethics is that moral progress is not measured by a fixed end, an ideal conception of the good but, as Philip Kitcher claims, "progress *from*" a problematic state to one less so (2011, p. 288). As Colin Koopman argues, the focus should be on moral melioration, rather absolute moral rightness (2015, pp. 11–12). If that is so, how is progress to be measured? If the governance of practices demands self-correction, are the changes that practices make progressive and moving in the right direction or regressive and heading in the wrong one? How do people know that change is for the better? What makes a change an improvement? The claim here is that progress is to be measured in problems solved and the problem-solving effectiveness of the practices that solve those problems. Intuitively, solving problems makes things better, and practices and communities that can solve their problems are better for it.

Progress as Preference for Ways of Life

Phillip Kitcher raises an interesting question: Are changes to human practices and institutions "mere change," one thing after another, or is there a way to count certain changes as progressive and others as regressive? (2011, p. 138). It would seem intuitive to count the abolition of slavery or the suffrage of women as progressive changes in the United States, but, at the time, there was enough controversy about the first to cause a bloody civil war and a protracted campaign by most men to prevent the second from happening for some 130 years. So it wasn't intuitive back then.

Kitcher discusses one criterion that is often used to measure progress. To say that the abolition of slavery or the establishment of equal rights for women in America is a progressive step is based on people's preferences for such changes. Despite the great and difficult resistance to these changes, once the changes settled in, it seems that people in America—or at least nearly everyone—do not want to return to the practice of slavery. Of course, there are outliers on every issue. For example, a January 2016 *Economist* poll found that nearly 20% of Trump supporters did not approve of the abolition of slavery (White, 2016). It seems unimaginable today to disenfranchise women voters or to take away certain gains in equal rights for women in civic life and the workplace. The new ways caused a painful disruption of the old ways, but it's a welcome disruption because most, if not all, prefer the new way to the old.

As Kitcher expresses this criterion: a change is progressive "just in case those who live after the change prefer life in the later world to life in the earlier one" (2011, p. 175). In other words, progress is measured by how people vote with their feet. But he also points out, directly, the problems with this criterion as stated. First, transitions created by the change may be very rocky, so there needs to be a reasonable period for assessing the change. The abolition of slavery solved the slavery problem, but the attempt to integrate former slaves into white-dominant society generated problems of racial conflicts and tensions, discrimination, pervasive segregation, Jim Crow laws, lynching, race riots, much of which lasted for at least a century, until the formal passage of civil rights legislation. Of course, legislation did not eliminate racial conflicts, racism, tensions, discrimination, and more subtle forms of segregation that are still very much present. At the same time, without the abolition of slavery, there could not have been the scaffolding to civil rights reform for African Americans. Despite 150 years of such problems, it's doubtful that African Americans would want to return to slavery for the obvious reasons that all the problems experienced over the years were even more intensely present in the institution of slavery.

Jared Diamond called the change from hunting and gathering to agriculture about 13,000 years ago "the worst mistake in the history of the human race" (1987, p. 64). According to Mark Cohen (2002), the hunter-gatherers' way of life was on a whole better in regard to nutrition, prevention of disease, and ease of labor, compared with its early agricultural counterparts. Hunter-gatherers had better nutritional intake of vitamins, minerals, and protein. The mobility of small populations reduced parasitic diseases. The more sedentary and larger populated agrarian societies exhibited more infectious and parasitic diseases, anemia, and mineral deficiencies. Also, the labor-to-leisure ratios were lower for hunter-gatherers as opposed to early agrarians. They also tended to be more egalitarian in their group organization. Cohen asks: "[I]f agriculture provides neither better diet, nor greater dietary reliability, nor greater ease, but conversely appears to provide a poorer diet, less reliably, with greater labor costs, why does anyone become a farmer?" (1977, p. 141). Good question.

Jared Diamond has an explanation: although there were a few hunter-gatherer groups that adopted farming, most were simply displaced by farmers, primarily to the advances in technology and war-making (1999, p. 112). The history of the conquest of North American indigenous peoples shows that although Native Americans adopted some of the invader's technology of war, they did not abandon their ways of life and fall in with European ways. Force rather than preference seemed to be the primary reason for the eventual decline of the hunter-gatherer way of life in the Americas. Many of the Athabascan, Inupiat, and Yupik peoples in Alaska today, for example, still seem to prefer their quasi-subsistence lifestyle to the ways of the city. After all, the defeat in the Civil War forced slave owners to give up the practice of slavery. They did not prefer to do so. So it was mere change after all.

If preference is measured at the point of change, many changes are so controversial that those changes would never be counted as progressive. It would seem more reasonable to wait until the dust has settled. This entails a period of time in which the practical consequences of the changes have taken root sufficient to see whether the new or old way is to be preferred. But when does the dust settle? And is this a case of just getting used to something? Kitcher supposes that advocates of this criterion for progress would have to argue that the preference must also endure "in the limit." However, he shows a number of problems with that criterion (2011, p. 176). For example, Diamond estimates that the hunting way of life dominated human culture for somewhere between 46,000 and 70,000 years before agriculture first took root (1999, p. 104). Agriculture is a mere 13,000 years old at most. It seems that hunting-gathering endured longer than agriculture. Slavery endured for at least three thousand years of recorded history, and it is only recently in the last 150 years that it has been legally abolished in all countries, although proxies of it exist in different forms.

Of course, what has to be looked at is the preference relative to alternatives. Agriculture did not develop during this early period in human history, so there was no way for hunter-gatherers to compare. Hunting-gathering and agriculture lived side by side for a relatively short period of time before agriculture came to dominate. But, if Diamond is right, this was the result of violent change, where agricultural societies could put together larger armies and develop technology at a greater rate than the hunter-gatherers. The North was slavery free for several decades before the Civil War and co-existed with the slave-owning South, but that did not change the preferences of the South. Again, the change was not by preference, but by force.

But if, after the dust has settled and people have a chance to live in the new ways for a period of time, if the change was forced, and there are opportunities to change back, then the evidence of preference would be whether there are few regressions to the older way of life over time. There doesn't seem to be a movement on the part of most people to return to hunter-gatherer practices. When the Eighteenth Amendment passed, many Americans celebrated this as making things better. However, when the consequences of the prohibition became manifest, the amendment was repealed just a few years later.

But if it takes some time to experiment with the change and live in the consequences, then it can't be just the preference, but *why* people prefer the new to the old ways. It must have something to do with the palpable, practical consequences of the change. If mere preference were the criterion, then the 20% of Trump supporters who want to return to slavery would be just as justified as the 80% who don't.

The Cumulative Theory of Progress

One proposal for what counts as progress is related to the sorts of problems existing practices cause and what sorts of solutions changes to the practice involve. R. G. Collingwood says the character of a historical period can be evaluated by how it solves its particular problems (1956, p. 87). Collingwood developed a *cumulative theory of progress* to sort this out.

Although Collingwood did not think that there was progress in art and morality, he did seem to think so for science. His criterion for scientific progress was clear: A theory not only had to solve all or most of the problems of that which it replaced, but also it solved even more problems than what it replaced. Collingwood expresses this in the following way:

> If thought in its first phase, after solving the initial problems of that phase, is then through solving these, brought up against

others which defeat it; and if the second solves these further problems *without losing its hold on the solution of the first,* so that *there is gain without any corresponding loss,* then there is progress. (1956, p. 329)

Collingwood seemed to think that philosophy could be counted as progressive in the same way: ". . . . Philosophy progresses in so far as one stage of its development solves the problems which defeated it in the last, without losing its hold on the solutions already achieved" (1956, p. 332).

Applying this criterion to practices, it could be said that, if any change in a practice involves solutions to a group of problems that it could not solve prior to the change and still retains the working solutions to past problems, then the change is progressive (1956, p. 333).

As Larry Laudan notes, this is the simplest and clearest account of progress since it does not require counting or weighting solutions to problems. If all the solutions to previous problems are retained in the change, plus solutions to problems not solved in the *status quo*, then that is obviously progressive just on the face of that fact (1977, p. 148). Cohen complains that the change to agriculture was regressive because it did not solve the problems of proper nutrition, disease control, and labor-to-resource ratios as well as hunting and gathering did, even if it did solve the problem of sustaining larger populations and defense, among others. One assumes that if early agriculture had solved these problems as well as or better than hunting and gathering and, additionally, had solved other problems that hunting and gathering could not—such as feeding larger populations—then he would have to count the development of agriculture as progressive.

However, Laudan thinks that scientific progress in Collingwood's sense is rare. It simply does not reflect the historical record. It is unusual for a scientific theory to solve all of the problems of its predecessors, so that even if there are problem gains, there are also corresponding problem losses (1977, p. 148). If this criterion held, hardly anything would count as progressive, yet science seems to progress nonetheless. There are many examples. Newton's optics failed to solve the problem of refraction in Iceland spar crystals, which had been explained by Huyghen's theory. There was the failure of nineteenth-century caloric theories of heat to account for heat convection and generation, which was solved previously by Rumford in the eighteenth century. Many of the problems in chemistry that had been solved by the theories of elective affinity were not solved by Dalton's atomic theory, and so on (1977, pp. 148–149). Speaking more generally, democracy couldn't be counted as a progressive political development, compared to monarchy, since it did not solve all the problems monarchies did, such as the efficiency of decision making. Moreover, it created all sorts of new problems not native to monarchies. These include problems of an uninformed or uneducated voting public, inertia due to political party conflict, gerrymandering, balance of powers, tyranny of the majority, and the several problems that Lippman discusses.

If hunting-gathering solved some problems, it was unable to solve the emerging problem of sustaining larger populations, which the agrarian communities were able to do better over time. There was a necessity in the sense that the problem had to be solved, or the hunter-gatherers would indeed outgrow their resources, and their nutritional advantages would soon disappear. Agrarian societies were able to solve that problem adequately but at the cost of not solving the nutritional and health problems as well as smaller bands of hunter-gatherers had been able to do. People had to work harder at getting fewer nutritional and health benefits from the work, but the agrarian societies solved a number of other problems that the foragers could not.

Thus, as Laudan argues, there is often both problem-solution gain and loss in such changes, but the *saliency* of which problems are solved also matters in the calculation. Agrarian societies were able to solve the very serious problem of growing populations and scarcer food sources much better than hunters-gatherers were able to do. At the same time, larger populations brought certain advantages to a community that smaller ones could not provide. But the agrarian societies lost the more egalitarian forms of governance and more leisurely life style. This led to more communicable diseases. Jared Diamond recognizes that the practices of agriculture ". . . bestowed on farmers enormous demographic, technological, political and military advantages over neighbouring hunter-gathers. The history of the past 13,000 years consists of tales of hunter-gatherer societies becoming driven out, infected, conquered or exterminated by farming societies in every area of the world suitable for farming" (2002, p. 702).

For this reason, the emergence of agrarian societies created another problem for hunter-gatherers they could not solve—the problem of defense of their way of life. Call this sort a problem an existential crisis, that is, a problem which, if not resolved, would result in the end or replacement of the practice, institution, or community. Certainly, bands of hunter-gatherers warred among each other—but they were more or less on equal par in terms of weapons and population. However, agrarian societies could produce surpluses of food that could support more people, that permitted labor stratification so that people could focus on developing technical skills that led to advancements that could produce more food, better weapons, standing armies, and other means for the necessities of life—and support more people. In other words, as noted, such societies were able to grow autocatalytically (2002, p. 701). More complex organizations could develop large-scale coordination of efforts, adding to the advantages. Forager bands remained relatively stable in size, but so did their technology and social organization.

Progress as a Function of Problem-Solving Effectiveness

The regime change to agriculture does not satisfy the cumulative problem criterion since it did not solve well all of the problems that foraging societies did. There is another way of looking at problems involved in such transitions. Even if agrarian societies could not solve all the problems that foraging ones did, they were able to solve certain critical emerging ones that foraging societies could not. Even if they generated new problems, they were also capable of solving many of these problems fairly well. As a result, agrarian societies came to dominate the human landscape because they were more effective at solving problems over a wider range of domains. Suppose, as Collingwood says, the character of a historical period can be measured by how it solves its particular problems (1956, p. 87). This implies that, even if a new regime generates new problems, so long as it is able to solve those new problems consistently at a sufficient rate and in a manner that builds on the earlier ones, that could also be an indication of progress. Larry Laudan suggests that progress results from enhancing what he calls *problem-solving effectiveness* (1977, p. 5).

Since science is a practice that is ostensibly progressive and, as he says, "delivers the epistemic goods," Laudan thinks that studying how science makes progress might not only be interesting in itself, but might be instructive in explaining progress among other practices and practical life as a whole (1977, p. 7). Assuming it's possible to generalize his findings over domains, this could be applied not only to a scientific practice but to other practices and communities as a whole.

From Laudan's point of view, science *is* essentially problem solving, so how well a scientific theory does solve problems is a measure of progress (1977, pp. 4–5). More specifically, since any theory is embedded in an existing network of theories, ontological assumptions, and methodological procedures, it's more accurate to speak of progress relative to a *research tradition*—a concept somewhat cognate with Thomas Kuhn's classic notion of *disciplinary matrix* (1977, p. 78).

If the key to progress is problem-solving effectiveness, then how is a research tradition—or any practice—considered more effective at solving problems than its predecessors or contemporaries? Laudan advocates for a noncumulative theory of progress based, first, on how problems and their solutions are *weighted* in terms of their importance and, second, what might be called the general *efficacy* by which a theory or research tradition solves important problems. Certainly, a change in a practice or regime would not be considered progressive if it solved a bunch of trivial problems and left the more important ones unresolved. Second, a change in a practice or regime might initially solve an important problem, but not many others, while generating many more problems than it could resolve, and earlier solutions are left orphaned—in the sense that they do not serve as scaffolds to solutions for later problems.

In regard to the first criterion, Laudan notes that science is generally concerned with both empirical and conceptual problems. Following Peirce's notion of abduction, Laudan defines an empirical problem as one that poses a puzzle, a surprise, an anomaly of some sort. Offspring bear resemblance to their parents; alcohol left standing in a glass soon disappears, the planets are spherical in shape, heavy objects fall to the ground with a certain regularity—"more generally, anything about the natural world which strikes us as odd, or otherwise in need of explanation, constitutes an empirical problem" (1977, p. 15). Empirical problems are divided into three types: solved, unsolved, and anomalous. The latter are "problems which a particular theory has not solved, but which one or more of its competitors have." Unsolved problems are those that no theory has yet solved (1977, p. 17). These may include long-standing problems, basic or "archetypal" problems, problems that are common or generalized across domains (1977, pp. 32–36).

Additionally, there are two types of conceptual problems: internal, due to inconsistency or contradiction within a theory, and, external, due to a conflict among theories about similar concepts. As an example of the latter, Ptolemy's concept of orbit was at odds with the older concept in Aristotle and Eudoxus (1977, p. 51). As an example of the former, Faraday's theory of electrical interaction had hoped to explain away the problem of action-at-a distance but, in fact, still employed it in his explanation (1977, pp. 49–50). In general, a research tradition makes progress if it solves a maximum of these sorts of empirical problems and minimizes significant conceptual problems, relative to alternatives (1977, p. 119).

The second condition—the *efficacy* of a research tradition—is determined by at least four important factors: (1) problem-solving ability persists over time, so that a comparison between the latest solutions and the earliest ones show comparable successes; (2) the rate at which salient problems are solved is at least constant, if it does not increase over time; (3) the numbers of problems, anomalies, and inconsistencies that solutions generate over time is not disproportionate to the number of solutions; (4) scaffolding, so that later solutions tend to be built on earlier ones (1977, pp. 107, 119).

The problem-solving effectiveness of a practice involves not just the ways and means of attaining its ends, but also what sorts of problems it creates or solves as those means and ends affect other practices and people. As Collingwood emphasized, there's an important difference between improvement and progress. An improvement may ameliorate one problem but create others in the same practice. Nuclear plants generate cheap energy but create problems of storage of nuclear waste and increase the danger of nuclear accidents. An improvement may ameliorate a problem but leave more serious ones unresolved. Homeless shelters may help in the short-term in getting people off the streets, but do not address the root problem of homelessness. A change may improve one practice but worsen another with which it is networked. Big box stores reduced costs of consumer goods but ruined locally owned stores and decimated small downtown centers. The amelioration of a problem may affect an entire way of life. The development of the internet solved the problem of rapid communication but increased the dangers of the widespread dissemination of false or misleading information.

Moral Progress

If the problem-solving effectiveness of practices is to be the measure of progress, it has to be effective at solving all the different kinds of problems associated with a practice. To be effective, it has to be effective not only at solving problems of means, but problems with the norms of its ways and means and the ends at which it aims. Agrarian societies solved many problems but also adopted authoritarian and hierarchical governance practices and exercised expanse by force and cruelty in many cases, decimating the ways of life of other peoples.

Such matters create what Philip Kitcher calls altruism problems—how the arrangements of practices, their means and ends, create conflicts among people in the pursuit of those ends. Kitcher sees "altruism failures" as the principal problem that ethical norms and rules address (2011, p. 6). Altruism can be of different sorts. Behavioral altruism is reciprocity based on self-interest, so that people adjust their behavior toward others because they hope it will serve their own interests (2011, p. 19). The sort of altruism that is more conducive to ethical behavior is the case where people are motivated to act on what they perceive as the wants and desires of others, with no expectation that it would promote their own particular wants and desires (2011, p. 22). To see injustice done to others but not to oneself, yet acting to correct that injustice, is the hallmark of ethical altruism. It is also the glue that creates social stability (2011, p. 222).

"The original function of ethics," Kitcher argues, "is to remedy *those altruism failures provoking social conflict . . .*"; to allow a "smoother, more peaceful, and more cooperative social life, through remedying altruism failures and, more specifically, through clearing up those altruism failures involving the most urgent endorsable desires on the part of the potential beneficiaries" (2011, p. 223). David Copp calls this the problem of sociality, how to discover the norms that maximize cooperation in people's pursuit of ends while minimizing the conflicts in the pursuit of those ends (2012, p. 38). When altruism fails, some people's ends are frustrated, and conflicts can arise. When altruism problems are resolved, Kitcher argues that "group members satisfy more of their desires and protest less" since there tends to be more cooperation, coordination, and stability in goal pursuit (2011, p. 222). In other words, moral progress hinges on the solutions of the problems of sociality. It harks back to James's problem of fighting against the tragic sense of life, finding that optimum that maximizes people's goods with a minimum of conflict. A change is progressive "just in proportion to its success in solving this 'problem of maxima and minima'" (James, 1907, p. 61).

Since Kitcher agrees with Dewey that "the notion of progress is understood in terms of problem-solving" (2012, p. 336), it seems he would agree with Laudan that the mark of progress is the problem-solving effectiveness of communities, especially their effectiveness in solving altruism problems. According to Kitcher, Dewey sees problem solving as "moral experiments [that] consist in changing the social world. . . . [and] We judge the outcome of these changes by trying to live with them, checking whether their consequences fit with our other habits and impulses, leaving us in a situation that is less problematic for us than that in which we began" (2012, pp.

336–337). Based on Dewey's insights, Kitcher argues for an *originary* versus a *teleological* view of progress, where the former is directed by improvement and progress from the current states of affairs, rather than movement towards some ideal, as in the latter (2015, p. 478). Kitcher argues, in particular, for what he calls *pragmatic progress,* which "consists in overcoming problems in the current state" (2015, p. 478).

The first step in solving altruism problems is to determine which desires for ends are *endorsable*. These are ones that can or should be pursued with a minimum of disagreement. Desires for certain ends can be endorsed by a group because, in principle, each member of the group can recognize these as desirable for itself (2011, pp. 122, 223). These would certainly include what John Rawls calls *primary goods*. These are goods that people can agree are desirable for anyone no matter what else is desired, such as food security, wealth, companionship, liberty, freedom from fear, among others (Kitcher, 2011, pp. 223 n. 14, 105 n. 1; Rawls, 1971, p. 396).

Altruism problems occur when people are prevented or constrained by the arrangement of practices to pursue these endorsable desires in a way that guarantees reasonable success. The wide permission to pursue endorsable desires tends to create cooperation. For example, if people are pursuing the same endorsable ends, such as food security, and the one recognizes what is desired as just as legitimate for the other, and all involved can agree on the best means for attaining that end, this creates a solidarity, making their cooperation more likely, and more likely to achieve what is desired by both than working alone. If the desired ends of people are different but do not conflict, and one recognizes the other as a means to that end, then mutual cooperation in achieving each of the ends is more likely and will work out better than refusing to cooperate. Alternatively, if the desired ends do not conflict, then allowing others to pursue those goals without interference would, one supposes, also be endorsable. Where desired ends do conflict, then consensus about how those conflicts can be adjudicated and which desires should be constrained or interferes with the goals of others should also be endorsable. When an arrangement of practices and institutions is more inclusive of endorsable ends but minimizes conflict compared to alternatives, then that arrangement is progressive (2011, pp. 221–222). Kitcher calls this effort *expanding the circle* (2011, pp. 216–217).

Correspondingly, altruism failures occur, and arrangements of practices and institutions are regressive, when they are designed so that some people with the same endorsable ends as others are excluded or constrained from achieving those endorsable ends. The abolition of slavery was progressive since it changed practices so that formerly enslaved peoples could share in the same common, endorsable ends—liberty—goods that others already had (2011, pp. 153ff.). For the same reason, women's suffrage and equal rights in the home and the workplace was progressive since they expanded the circle of those who have these same basic citizenship rights (2011, p. 135ff.). On the other hand, the Jim Crow laws were regressive, because they constrained endorsable ends such as voting, employment and educational opportunities for African-Americans, but not for white peoples. Recall William James's thought on this matter, worth repeating, that "the course of history is nothing but the story of men's struggles from generation to generation to find the more and more inclusive order" (1891, p. 610). What ameliorates the tragic sense of life is discovering arrangements of practices and institutions that "expand the circle" for "endorsable" ends.

Like Laudan's notion of efficacy, the mechanisms by which altruism problems are solved must be effective. "Ethical progress consists *in functional refinement*, first aimed at solving the original problems more thoroughly, more reliably, and with less costly effort . . ." (2011, p. 221; 2012, p. 316). "We make progress by solving problems, by introducing or refining devices that fulfill the pertinent functions" (2012, p. 316). Indeed, he likens solving altruism problems like a "social technology," and like any technology, progress "is readily understood as functional refinement. We start with a function to be fulfilled and an initial device that does the job. From first success descends a sequence of improvements, things performing the task more reliably, more quickly, more cheaply, and with less demands on the user," and "in ways that generate fewer problems for potential users" (2011, pp. 218–219, 212, 315).

Like Laudan's notion of saliency, functional refinement also needs to be directed toward the more significant and urgent problems of the day and addressing the difficulties involved in weighing the relative importance of problems (2015, p. 479). What counts as significant is itself problematic (2015, p. 485). Kitcher argues that the notion of what counts as significance evolves:

> The criteria of significance . . . evolve with the changing conditions of human life. To make a judgment about the significance of a problem is to adopt a stance about what matters to a group of people, living at some particular place and time." (2015, p. 488)

Kitcher emphasizes that each change in practical arrangements creates conflicts in that enhancements to some practices are at the cost of others. Kitcher argues that in these cases, extremes should be avoided. Progress cannot be made if there is no cost to some practice, nor would there be progress if the enhancement of a few practices is achieved no matter what the cost to others (2012, p. 317). The assessment of the advantages of different sets of losses and gains requires a collective deliberation of the community so affected. "The ethical project," as he says "is something *people work out together*" (2012, p. 323). Sometimes he refers to this as a *Deweyan conversation*, best described as collective deliberation that also works to disclose biases, interests, and the emotional investment of the participants in the matter of hand, with the aim to take on the view of impartial spectator, as far as possible, in resolving problems (2012, pp. 339–340). Such conversations build empathy and sympathy in understanding how people are affected by the problems with the current organization of practices and institutions. As he says elsewhere in the context of which scientific problems to address: it is an ". . . *informed* discussion among *representatives of all available perspectives* aiming to reach an evaluation of scientific questions *with which all parties can live*" (2015, p. 489).

If communities are to form these practices of inquiry, and engage in experiments of living, what will warrant keeping the experiment going or abandoning it? How will they know that the norms they're proposing are true in some sense of moral truth? Kitcher argues that the truth of ethical norms is measured by the progress they entail (2011, p. 7). Kitcher argues that "truth is what you get by making progressive steps (truth is attained in the limit of progressive transitions) . . ." (2011, p. 210). Ethical truths are "the descriptive counterparts of prescriptions that would be stable under progressive conditions (2012, p. 318). "Reliability in the production of ethical truth gives way to reliability in the genesis of progressive transitions" (2011, p. 213). Or, as he says elsewhere, "ethical truths are the stable elements in progressive practices, as people deliberate together to solve the problem of living" (2014, p. 101).

Kitcher's account of moral truth has a family resemblance with Peirce's convergence theory of truth (2011, p. 176 n. 4; Liszka, 2021, pp. 130–133). Just as Peirce thought truth was the end result of inquiry over time, Kitcher thinks that moral truth is what remains stable in progressive normative changes over time through experiments of living.

Recall that Peirce had three senses of convergence in terms of approximation (1901, *CP* 7.216), the consensus of inquirers (1893, *CP* 6.610), and independent discovery (1871, *CP* 8.12). Each of these different senses of convergence might serve as an indicator of moral truth of the norm in question (Liszka, 2021, pp. 114–119). Peirce's first sense of convergence as approximation might be thought of as scaffolding in this context. For example, in the history of the United States, basic political rights applied only to white men. This served as a scaffold upon which to extend these to men of color, and eventually to women. Historically, it would be reasonable to see this as progressive in the sense of approximations to a more inclusive circle of people counted as bearer of rights. As Kitcher characterizes it, "progressive transitions occur exactly when the modified code contains precepts enjoining altruism of wider scope or greater range than the code it replaces" (2011, p. 215). Of course, these transitions were not simply a matter of a historical unfolding, but they were brought about through enormous hardship and struggle. Nonetheless, the scaffolding was there to make such progress possible.

The second sense of convergence in this context would be a practical consensus, in the sense that the norms persist in successive transitions, so that more and more people over time come to the same conclusion that the norms are worth retaining. As he argues, ". . . ethical rules count as true just in case those rules would be adopted in ethical codes as the result of progressive transitions and would be retained through an indefinite sequence of further progressive transitions" (2011, p. 246). This might be the place where preference plays something of a role. It would be indicated by deliberate adoption by subsequent generations or, at least, their willing conformity of behavior to the code. This could serve as a reasonable indicator of moral truth in the context of other indicators.

Peirce's third sense of convergence would suggest that communities, independently of one another, would have their progressive transitions converge to similar norms in the long run. Although there are certainly cases where similar practices evolve in disparate communities, Kitcher thinks that ethical pluralism is a real possibility. Two different ethical traditions could make progressive transitions with little commonality in their moral codes in the long run (2011, p. 248). As he writes, "rival traditions offer different elaborations of the ethical project, alternative cultural lineages, and societies. We can imagine two different ethical traditions proceeding indefinitely, making a series of progressive transitions, without its ever being possible to integrate their differing accomplishments." In other words, there can be *weak* versus *strong convergence*. Strong convergences are practically identical; weak convergences are those that settle on a finite set of alternatives among a number of possibilities. Polygyny, monogamy, and polyandry constitute a finite set of solutions to the problem of parental investment but differ in terms of the ways and means and the norms associated with that end.

But if there is divergence as Kitcher suggests, then their respective ethical codes would be incommensurable and, if incommensurable, there would appear to be no basis to judge one against the other. But such debates are critical to progress. If there was no basis for abolitionists to criticize slaveholders then, indeed, violent overthrow is the only alternative—may the force be with you. In some cases, this might be the only resolution.

Alaine Locke addresses this issue of pluralism and the possibility of "ideological peace." Locke studied at Harvard at the turn of the twentieth century and took a particular interest in William James. In "Values and Imperatives" (1923) and "Cultural Relativism and Ideological Peace" (1944), he developed a pluralistic ethic, based on some of James's ideas that could serve to solve the problems Kitcher discusses. The gist of Locke's argument is that, under the right sort of governance structure, dialogue and conversations between different value and norm-holders can walk through different phases that lead to the betterment of each of the conflicting groups.

For Locke, ". . . the gravest problem of contemporary philosophy is how to ground some normative principle . . . of objective validity for values without resort to dogmatism and absolutism on the intellectual plane, and without falling into their corollaries on the plane of social behavior and action, of intolerance and mass coercion" (1923, p. 678). A pluralistic attitude may have more success than an absolutist one at arriving at some "ideological peace" among conflicting norms and practices, since it adopts a fallibilistic attitude towards its own values and, therefore, is open to correction (1944, p. 70).

Locke's argument is that such dialogues should have the following guidelines (1944, p. 73). First, look to the common norms and ends. It's unlikely that two traditions have nothing in common. Michael Walzer talks about the notion of minimal morality: "[I]t consists in principles and rules that are reiterated in different times and places, and that are seen to be similar even though they are expressed in different idioms and reflect different histories and different versions of the worlds" (1994, pp. 16–17). In citing Walzer, Wallace argues that human beings are alike in that they live in communities, use language, and cooperate with one another. Community, language, and cooperative activity are features of every culture, and certain norms are absolutely necessary for such cultural artifacts" (2009, p. 74).

Short of explicit commonality, conflicting communities should seek to identify values and norms that are functionally equivalent. For example, whether marriage is heterosexual or same-sex, its functional constancy is the same, in the sense that it promotes certain norms of commitment and other sorts of family values. Moreover, the same object may be valued in different ways, and different objects can be valued in the same way. Marriage may be valued morally, religiously, or aesthetically.

Cultural reciprocity is the second guideline, in the sense that dialogue should promote the exchange of ideas and practices, so that the better ones may be recognized. The last guideline is a limit to cultural convertibility, the right of each of the differing communities to retain their identity, to inhibit assimilation of one by the other, and to avoid judgments of superiority (1944, p. 73).

To employ this process effectively, conflicting communities or practices with ostensibly incommensurable norms must go through a developmental process. The first prerequisite is to adopt an attitude of peaceful coexistence, a mere tolerance of differences without mutual respect. If all goes right, this should evolve into a growing respect for those differences. At this stage, there can be the possibility of reciprocal exchange, interaction and mutual respect. From this attitude it is possible to discover commonality of purpose, while still holding to differences (1923, pp. 684–685).

Has There Been Progress?

Steven Pinker thinks that what counts as progress is "one of the easier questions to answer" (2018, p. 51). In his book, *Enlightenment Now: The Case for Reason, Science, Humanism and Progress*, he lists a number of goods that people intuitively prefer to their opposite: life is better than death, health better than hunger, abundance better than poverty, peace better than war, safety better than danger, freedom better than tyranny, and so on. Most people would say intuitively that these are endorsable goods in Kitcher's sense of the term. "All these things can be measured," Pinker notes, and "if they have increased over time, that is progress" (2018, p. 51). If the "circle" of these endorsable goods is "expanded," then this would count as progressive in Kitcher's sense. If more people are happy than before, if more people are healthier than before, there's more abundance and greater wealth than poverty, fewer wars, less violence in communities, and less oppression, then cumulatively that amounts to progress. If this can be shown empirically, then that provides the warrant for continuing whatever ways and means are in place and abiding by the norms that guide them.

Pinker claims that such progress can be empirically verified. Through statistical evidence, historical research, and otherwise, he argues that indeed, for the most part, over the last two centuries people have experienced a relatively steady increase in these endorsable goods worldwide. More recent generations, statistically speaking, are happier, wealthier, healthier, more secure, and less oppressed than previous ones. Consequently, by the criterion Pinker establishes, the case for progress has been made.

This progress, Pinker claims, has been steady since the Enlightenment in the eighteenth century. He thinks a good starting guess as to the principal causes of such progress is something about the Enlightenment. Pinker claims that the ideals of the Enlightenment account for such progress. Above all, it is the use of reason as opposed to dogmatism, understood primarily as holding beliefs accountable to objective standards (2018, p. 8). The second is the use of science (2018, p. 9), particularly its characteristic "fallibilism, open debate, and empirical testing" as a model of "how to achieve reliable knowledge" (2018, p. 10). The third is the norms embedded in secular ethics, based in humanism, with a focus on transforming the practices and institutions of practical life, especially toward democratic practices (2018, p. 10). The fourth factor is the adoption of meliorism, the belief in progress, that things can be made in such a way as to make them better (2018, p. 11).

If this is all true, it's good news for pragmatists. The pragmatists argue that inquiry, as modeled by the empirical methodologies of science, and that communities of inquiry, with their openness, norms of debate and criticism, fallibilistic attitudes, guided by certain democratic-like norms, are the most promising ways to fix problems and make lives go better. In fact, Dewey seems to agree with Pinker's understanding of the Enlightenment ideals, "the faith that human science and freedom would advance hand in hand to usher in an era of indefinite human perfectibility" (1939, *LW* 13, p. 160.) If Pinker is right about the indicators of progress and the norms that guide it, then the pragmatists are right that people should use reason, science, and democratic norms as the ways and means to continue practical life in the progressive direction it's going.

Pinker makes a good case. Not many people would prefer to return to times when the prospect of living a long healthy life was less likely, and that it was more likely that they would see at least one or more of their children die in infancy. It is the same for the other indicators of well-being he discusses at length.

However, Pinker has been criticized on a number of fronts, both in terms of the statistical analyses supporting his claims, and the more historical and philosophical explanation of the role of Enlightenment ideals in that progress. Pinker may have a point that some intellectuals and politicos have a vested interested in disclaiming progress and emphasizing what is bad rather than good since they make a living off of predictions of doom and gloom, and their theories for change (2018, pp. 39ff.). But several reputable scholars, economists, and social scientists do make credible criticisms of his position.

Pinker presents strong evidence of overall increases in those goods that most people count as constitutive of well-being. It's hard to deny, on the evidence, for example, that life expectancy, access to health services, and a number of other indicators have been on the rise. The problem with Pinker's statistics is that they fail in many cases when disaggregated. For example, he tends to minimize the impacts of gross inequalities in income distribution, even if wealth has generally increased overall in the United States. Yes, wealth has increased, but the disproportionate concentration of wealth in the few is a problem. The data also does not reflect recent economic declines in certain regions of the country, nor in terms of racial divides (Goldin 2018). The measure of how much inclusiveness in the benefits of these goods is questionable.

Another problem with Pinker's statistical evidence is that it fails to elaborate on the complex systems that result from the interactions among each of the variables that count as well-being. The analysis fails to heed Collingwood's warning that not all improvements lead to progress. Economic growth that is at the source of increases in wealth and declines in poverty come at the expense of healthy ecosystems. Globalization creates more risks such as cascading financial crises and crippling cyberattacks, with the ability of small groups to do great damage and exacerbate political polarizations (Mariathasan, 2015; Goldin, 2018). Not everything is as rosy as Pinker thinks.

There are also problems with his historical and philosophical analysis of the underlying Enlightenment ideology he claims has led to such progress. All good statistical analysis knows that just because one thing precedes another, what precedes is not necessarily the cause of what follows. In reviewing Pinker's book, some reputable Enlightenment scholars have pointed out that Enlightenment figures were not always consistent with so-called Enlightenment ideals, and many things now counted as immoral, such as racism, colonialism, imperialism, slavery, and the like were justified or rationalized by Enlightenment thinkers. The French Revolution of 1792–1799, supposedly inspired by Enlightenment ideals, ended in authoritarianism and barbarity (Hanlon, 2018). In some cases, figures not associated with the Enlightenment were more optimistic about progress than many of the core Enlightenment figures. Those who advanced science the most, such as Newton, were not particularly enlightened in the Enlightenment sense (Bell, 2018).

Dewey wrote *Freedom and Culture* in 1939, at the intersection of three worrisome political movements and regimes—fascism, Nazism, and

Stalinism. He cautioned that "it is no longer possible to hold the simple faith of the Enlightenment that assured advance of science will produce free institutions. . . ." He thought its technological application in mass production of goods "has created a vast and intricate set of new problems. It has put at the disposal of dictators means controlling opinion and sentiment of a potency which reduces to a mere shadow all previous agencies at the command of despotic rulers" (1939, *LW* 13, p. 156).

Pinker also seems to slight the struggle of peoples in the march toward progress. Much of what has been achieved has come not through some smooth path of following Enlightenment ideals, like following a map to a destination. Rather, the norms that have proven themselves—many of which are what some Enlightenment figures presaged—are those that have been wrought through the struggles, blood, sweat, and tears of people to make changes to better their lives. Although certainly some were inspired by the Enlightenment, many ordinary folk were not necessarily conversant with Enlightenment ideals but knew the problems they faced and understood what would fix them. Change had to be cut through the thickets of problems and troubles, rather than travel on the paved road to progress, as exemplified by the struggle for women to have the simple basic right to vote and the struggle of African Americans for ordinary civil rights (Bell, 2018).

The point of many pragmatists—both in the past and currently—is that it is not the ideals of the Enlightenment that are the *causal* factors in progress. Rather, in the context of experiments of living, some of these ideals were proposed and contextualized as practical hypotheses, that would solve certain problems and better the human condition. But they had to be worked out in the experiments of life to demonstrate their worth. It is how the practices of science and the practices of democracies corrected themselves and proved themselves over time in solving problems that warms many people to them, not the rhetoric of lofty ideals. It is their problem-solving effectiveness that matters. They must continue to prove themselves by being able to solve and continue to solve their more salient problems more effectively and continue to do so by expanding the circle of those who benefit from such solutions.

Generalizing Problem-Solving Effectiveness

Progress is made through the ability of practices to self-correct. Self-correction entails problem-solving effectiveness. It is the ability to detect erroneous practical hypotheses and develop ones that are more likely to achieve their ends than those previously adopted. It is adept at correcting failing norms by which such means are carried out, and to change direction or refine ends as warranted.

If problem-solving effectiveness is the key to progress, what are its general features? With some extrapolation, the work of Laudan and Kitcher can be used to develop a hybrid model of problem-solving effectiveness, which would appear to have two important features: *saliency* and *efficacy*:

1. *Saliency.* The ability to identify and resolve those problems that have the greatest impact on a community;
2. *Problem-solving efficacy*:
   a. *Scaffolding.* Later solutions are better than earlier ones but are built on earlier ones in a recognizable chain that makes the later solutions more likely;
   b. *Solution rate.* Solutions to problems persist or increase over time, so that new problems are solved in a timely fashion;
   c. *Proportion.* Solutions tend not to generate more problems than they solve.

To be counted as progressive, changes in the means, ends, or norms of practices should be capable of solving their most salient problems in a manner that builds on previous solutions, but with greater efficacy, such that it does not generate more salient problems than it solves.

Consider the first feature, *salience*. It is clear that if the more significant problems of a community are not addressed, then this will lead to more problems of greater import rather than less. Since it is people who are affected by problems, then people—through whatever deliberative, demonstrative or governance practices they have at hand must select problems for resolution and make changes accordingly. Not only are there problems about which problems to select and how to prioritize them, but there may be problems with the governance practices by which such decisions are made.

Although communities must identify their salient problems as Kitcher argues, it is possible to provide some guidance for the selection of problems. T. M. Jones's notion of moral intensity, discussed earlier, might serve as a good start. After all, the more morally intense the problem, the more salient, and the more salient, the more motivated people are to resolve it (1991). Jones argues that the factors that figure in moral intensity include the magnitude of the consequences, how likely and how far into the future those consequences will occur, whether they are concentrated in a few or in many, and the proximity of the problem to people's lives or community. Based on this criterion, and some of the types of problems identified by Laudan and Kitcher, consider the following list:

1. *Existential problems:* These are problems that threaten people's lives or an entire people's way of life. Their solution often involves dynamic change to many practices. Each generation seems to face an existential crisis, world war in the 1940s, nuclear holocaust in the 1960s and 1970s, and now climate change and the COVID-19 pandemic, currently. Examples are wars, famines, pestilence, fatal communicable diseases, pandemics, sweeping natural disasters, and genocide.

2. *Problems of sociality*: These are problems concerning cooperation and solidarity in a community; how to avoid or minimize conflict and polarization, how to achieve consensus, agreement or compromise on means and ends. These are fundamental problems that must be resolved if a community is to solve any of its problems.

3. *Common problems:* These are problems that are shared by different groups across the community or among communities. Examples are food security and access to health care. If a problem affects just one part of a community, even if it is serious, it would not be considered common.

4. *Base problems*: These are problems in a practice upon which many other practices are dependent. Examples are unemployment, inflation, and market crashes since the well-being of many other economic practices can be affected by these problems. Constitutional crises would be a base problem for democratic governments.

5. *Problems of scale:* This is the number of people affected by the problem. According to the World Health Organization, a quarter of the world's population is affected by mental health problems. Half of the world's population lives on

less than $2.50 a day. About 3.7 billion people in the world have either poor access to clean water or lack the means of basic sanitation. A scaled problem may not necessarily be common. Everyone in a sizable community might be affected by a problem—Syria's civil war is an example.

6. *Imminent problems*: These are problems that are happening now or clearly about to happen.

7. *Difficult problems:* These include relatively long-standing *unsolved problems*, such as cancer. They also include *intractable problems*, problems that are structurally inherent in a practice or network of practices, such as cycles of recession in a capitalist economy or the continuing presence of war. Although they may not be solvable, they may be managed. *Anomalous problems* are another subtype. These are problems that are the result of either internal consistencies in the operation of the practice or inconsistency between the practice and other practices, such as the conflict between the constitutional right to liberty and the practice of slavery in antebellum America, or between liberty and security.

The more of these characteristics a problem has, the more salient the problem, and the more weighted its call for a solution might be considered. If unemployment affects large numbers of people across nearly every community in a society now, then it hits nearly all the buttons for a salient problem.

As an example of the reasonableness of this list, consider how the medical community determines the saliency of diseases and causes of death. The World Health Organization, for example, ranks ischemic heart disease at the top of the list, with nearly 9.4 million deaths worldwide, and a death rate of 1,655 per 100,000. Stroke is second with 5.8 million deaths and a death rate of 77. Pulmonary disease is third with 3.0 million deaths and a death rate of 41, followed by lower respiratory infections, Alzheimer's and dementia, lung cancers, diabetes mellitus, road injury, and diarrheal diseases. Tuberculosis is last with 1.3 million deaths worldwide and a death rate of 17 per 100,000 (World Health Organization, 2016). Clearly, the scale of the disease is a factor in the ranking, but also the fact that these can be fatal. These are also common diseases, in the sense that they affect every human community. They are happening now, and people are dying as a result. Also, it is well known that some of these diseases are difficult to treat. In contrast, although eczema is a common disease and significantly widespread (with as much as 18.1% of the population affected in America alone), as well as difficult to treat, it is still considered less salient because it is not fatal (National Eczema Association, 2015).

Efficacy is the second feature of problem-solving effectiveness. Efficacy is indicated by the scaffolding of solutions, the rate of solutions, and the proportion of solutions to new problems. Technological improvements are good illustrations of these criteria. Kitcher often points to improvement in technology as a model for explaining certain aspects of ethical progress (2011, p. 7). Peirce for one notes that improvement in invention is similar to the process by which science advances (1902, *CP* 2.86). There's little doubt about the progress in computer technology, so consider the history of its improvements, as outlined by Paul Ceruzzi (2003), as a good illustration of the various aspects of efficacy.

Consider the case of scaffolding. The core architecture of computers involves logic gates, based on George Boole's 1854 algebra—an advance on Leibniz's binary logic. Logic gates are efficacious since they involve seven basic processes, which, when compounded, can express almost any complex computing operation. The problem was how to realize logic gates mechanically. Charles Peirce is thought to be the first to describe how these logical operations could be carried out by electrical switching circuits, so that opening or closing the circuit would express Boole's binary logic (1886, *W* 5, pp. 421–22).

The earliest computer, the Z1, developed by Konrad Zuse in 1936, used mechanical operations to do so, but this proved very unreliable. His Z3, along with the Atanasoff-Berry machine developed some years later, used vacuum tubes as capacitors to solve the logic gate problem. The vacuum tubes could control the voltage levels sufficiently in the circuits to open or close the gates. As more and more vacuum tubes were needed in order to increase the speed of calculations, by the time the ENIAC computer was developed some years later, it had something like 17,000 vacuum tubes which, along with the thousands of switches, wiring, soldering and other materials, weighed 30 tons and occupied 1800 square feet of space.

Even with the improvements made to the vacuum tube, it was still the size of a light bulb and frequently burned out. The development of the transistor in 1947 by John Bardeen, William Shockley, and Walter Brattain at Bell Labs solved this problem. The transistor used semi-conductor material to perform the same function as the vacuum tube, but was more capable of controlling electronic current to perform the logic gate functions, with much more efficiency of space, reliability, and less use of energy.

With the demand for more speed in calculation, large numbers of transistors linked in complex circuits had to be used, which created massive wiring problems. The invention of the integrated circuit in 1958 by Jack Kilby solved this problem by integrating all of these various components onto a silicon chip, which when modified could serve as a directed semi-conductor. In 1969, a team of scientists working for Intel developed a way to integrate not only the components of computers into one chip but to integrate the various functions of the computer for keyboard scanning, display control, printer control, and so forth, onto one such chip. Although the chip was only $1/8^{th}$ inch by $1/6^{th}$ inch, it had all the power of the original ENIAC.

Scaffolding typically has a catalytic effect on improvements, so that the rate of problem-solving generally goes up over time, often exponentially. An early solution delimits the problem, so that is easier to find better solutions to the problem. The time between development of computing technology, say from the abacus to Leibniz to Boole to Babbage, drawn out over centuries, versus the time between the development of vacuum tubes, transistors, and integrated circuits, accomplished over decades, is a remarkable difference in the rate of solutions. Certainly, Moore's law illustrates this best. He predicted in 1965 that the number of transistors that could fit on an integrated circuit would double each year. He thought the rate would drop off in 10 years, and after 1980, there would be a doubling every two rather than one year. But only now does it appear to be leveling off, with the hope that parallel computers or quantum computers might be the next best solution to increasing such capacity (Moore, 1998; Dubash, 2005; Cardinal, 2015).

The history of computer technology nicely illustrates the idea of problem-solving efficacy. As computing technology advanced, it created problems of size, efficiency, and cost. Starting with the Z1 and culminating in the massive, energy-sucking ENIAC computer, the problem of size was paramount. Additionally, other problems emerged, such as speed of calculations, programmability, memory storage, and the like. Eventually, in short order, most of these problems were solved sufficiently, so that even as new problems were generated, they were relatively quickly resolved. Thus, the proportion of solutions to new problems were favorable, so that the technology was not overwhelmed by the problems it generated.

Changes to practices are progressive if they can generate solutions that outpace their problems. Problems can be internal to the practices themselves.

Practices may no longer function as well as they did. Problems can result more systemically and arise from how practices work together with other practices. Problems can also emerge from changes to the larger environment in which they operate. The key to outpacing these problems is the problem-solving effectiveness of the practices that constitute the life of a community. To be effective, practices must have a governance structure that is adept at self-correction, one that gives them the ability to correct their most salient problems of means, ends and norms efficaciously.

Conclusion

The effort here has been to make a case for a pragmatism-inspired, problem-based ethics—to demonstrate its logic and normative force. The claim of such an ethic is simple: solve problems and good follows. Problems abound just about anywhere in any community. Some are small, some large, some aplenty, some fewer, and the fewer the better. Sometimes there are practices that help solve these problems, and sometimes they are the problem. Practices come about to solve problems and not to create them, but they don't always work. The goal is plain then: keep those practices that work until they don't work; and change those that don't work until they do. And if that doesn't work, then build a new one that does. History has shown that sometimes an entire system of practices has to go if the human condition is to get any better. Problems are the stones in the river that help the weary traveler ford the river. They give direction and genuine solutions to transform lives for the better.

Solutions to problems can serve as a proxy for the good. Problems can play a normative role like any concept of the good in identifying what is wrong in the world, with solutions telling us what is right. Problems have clarity, specificity, and serious ones have urgency. Concepts of the good are vague, general, and uncertain as to whether they are right. People respond more to problems than ideals. There is little hesitation in finding a solution to an urgent problem, but people are less certain about which ethical principle to follow.

Problems have a way of troubling people even if they are not themselves suffering the problem. Problems not solved are like a malaise that seeps into the community, changing its ethos until a tipping point is reached. They color the community, wipe away the veneer, expose the flaws. The moral character of people and the ethos of their communities are manifested in how they address their problems. Solving the problems of others is the beginning of a moral stance, the possibility of altruism. Justice is not realized until those not affected by a problem act to solve it for those who are.

Problem-based ethics engenders meliorism. It is not a naive optimism that thinks progress is inevitable, that the next generation will be better than the previous, marching toward some utopian ideal. It is certainly not the laziness of a cynical pessimism, where people find comfort in thinking that nothing changes for the better—so why try? Meliorism recognizes that changes for the better are not everything at once up the stepladder of progress. Progress is more analogous to an equalizer, adjusting the frequencies and figuring out what needs boosting and what needs cutting to achieve a better moral sonority. Rather than moving toward some ideal, focus on making the current situation better.

People tend to reason practically. They are goal-directed beings: here are the things desired, and here's the way to get them. The way to get them is always constrained by the ways and means of the configuration of practices relevant to that end. Practices are collectively formed and evolve over time. They are meant to be problem solvers, solving the problem of how to get what is collectively endorsable. Practices provide a visualization of the end, and they lay out the means to attain it. What people desire is rarely novel, and the culture's practices provide a set of ends that are thought worth pursuing. In fact, if it were not for the culture, people would not desire certain ends. Practices not only lay out how to attain an end, but they implicitly or explicitly make normative claims that these are the best and righteous ways to attain those ends, and these are the ends that are worthy of pursuit—and that is why the practice is what it is. Practices are inherently normative in that they prescribe or proscribe what are claimed to be effective and righteous ways to attain good ends. Practices fill in the content of the overarching norm of practical reasoning: what ought to be done is what is good to do that is likely to attain what is good to want.

But, of course, not all practices fulfill their purpose. If a practice is problematic, it is often found in one or more aspects of its practical reasoning. It may be the case that the ways and means prescribed no longer work to get the end-in-view. The end may no longer be what people want or should want. The normative constraints on the ways to the end may be the source of trouble.

Solving problems is ultimately an empirical matter, based in lived experience, the experiments of living. To fix a problem, to improve a practice is an intervention, and the test of the intervention is whether it can be shown that it made a change in the practice or system of practices sufficient to ameliorate its problems. If solving problems is an intervention, science can help since it is the best method known for solving problems. However, the use of science should not devolve into social engineering. Expertise has a vital role, but inquiries into what fixes a problem must include those affected by the problems, and they should not be simply the passive subjects of an experiment. John Dewey's faith is perhaps best expressed by Eddie Glaude: the work of pragmatism is "to express a profound faith in the capacity of everyday ordinary people to transform their world" (2007, p. 7).

On the other hand, the ignorance of those who do not abide the norms of logic and evidence, who subscribe to outlandish conspiracy theories, should not prevail in a situation where serious problems need to be solved, lives are at stake, and the quality of lives is on the line. There's a difference between freedom of speech and speech that leads to truth. The former is a prerequisite for the latter, but the howl of opinions rarely leads to truth. The debate between John Dewey and Walter Lippmann is still relevant today for this reason. Democracy needs to refine its practices in order to get better at figuring out the play between expertise and the role of the public in solving its problems. The norms and methodologies of a community of inquiry can model what should be the norms of communities and practices generally, if they are to be effective in their problem solving. Both science at its best and democracy at its core share similar norms, but, as Dewey noted, there are many aspects of democracy that lend themselves to what most people think is right as opposed to what is right.

What is needed in a community is problem-solving effectiveness, the capacity for self-correction. That is what makes progress more likely. Problem-solving effectiveness is identifying the more salient problems in a community and solving them efficaciously. This includes the problem of sociality, how to create sufficient solidarity to work together in solving problems, how to minimize conflicts, avoid polarization, and get to consensus, agreement and compromise. The most efficacious method for solving problems is the scientific method, generally understood. If the pragmatists are right, scientific inquiry also models the norms and virtues that will most likely find the better solutions to problems. Consequently, prudence would argue that science and empirical methods should be used as far as possible to remedy problems and test solutions. Effective problem solving builds on the better solutions that have come before, lets go of failed ones, and is able to solve problems at a rate greater than the problems solutions may engender. It has the capacity to adapt to novel problems.

Still, people have to live with the realization that life is tragic. Not all that people hold desirable and good can work together in the same order of things. For every change, for every new order of things, someone's good is diminished or ruined, even if others gain. The goal is to manage this human condition by finding arrangements of practices and institutions that can maximize goods and expand the circle of those enjoying the goods that others do, while minimizing problems. Life is tragic also in the sense that the order of things is oppressive, that there are things that happen beyond human control, and things happen that could not be anticipated. Progress is not inevitable. Regress is just as possible. History does not unfold like the inexorable path of Hegel's *Geist*.

Colin Koopman seems right in saying that "ethics for James and Dewey . . . is not so much about determining what is right or wrong in advance of action . . . as it is about the effort to live better lives where there are no rules guiding us in advance" (2015, p. 149). This is true to a point. There is guidance in the form of the practices that constitute communities that have filled in these rules to guide lives. But these are also the source of problems and troubles. "The point of pragmatist moral theory," he continues, "is not develop rules of morality that must be followed in practice but rather to develop tools for inquiry that we can employ within experience in order to improve it" (2015, p. 149).

If solutions to problems are the way to progress, what is needed are good studies of problems and problem solving. Pragmatist ethics of the sort championed here needs to address this matter of problem solving. Certainly, there is some theory to this, but it encourages thinkers to get their hands dirty in the problems of life. All theoretical ethicists should be engaged in a real-life problem, so as to guide their theory making. In making Richard Rorty's point, Colin Koopman writes that philosophers ". . . should no longer think of their activities in their remote academic corners as the intellectual and moral center of the universe. Philosophy has its own history and its own set of problems, but we have no better reason for thinking that solving these problems will save humanity than we do for thinking that writing a really good poem or making a really good film will do the trick" (2015, p. 30). The model for the ethicist in the pragmatist mold is more Jane Addams, who worked to solve the problems of immigrants, John Dewey, who created an experimental school to transform education, or Alain Locke, who imagined and realized the Harlem Renaissance. It is an approach better than those who engage in a sort of cultural criticism that admires the problem, but let others do the hard work of finding the solution. The world needs critical thinking, but it needs problem-solving skills more.

Problem solving also has to be recognized as an inherently interdisciplinary effort. Serious problems are almost always complex problems that require social, political, scientific, and psychological address. This sort of work requires cross-disciplinary communication and the ability to translate theoretical vocabulary and concepts into common frameworks. It requires teamwork rather than the solitary hero-thinker.

"Humans are problem solvers," Maria Kronfeldner stresses, "they often change their ideas, behaviors and material artifacts according to certain goals that define the problems they want to solve. . . . Through social transmission, it becomes possible that others can in turn improve on these solutions. If this happens, cumulative cultural evolution takes place (Kronfeldner, 2007, p. 508). The best that can be hoped for is that those who come before us have given us a scaffold upon which to reach a bit higher in ameliorating the works and troubles of the human condition.

References

Notes on References

References are in APA Style, with the following exceptions. References are dated with the original publication or composition of the author, where appropriate, and indicated in parenthesis (date). The edition or translation of the work from which the material is cited, if different, is indicated by brackets [date]. The original dates of the publication of Plato and Aristotle are not listed because of their uncertainty. The dates of the translations of these works are listed in brackets.

Agre, Gene (1982). The concept of problem. *Educational* Studies, 13(2), 121–142.
Alexy, Robert (1990). A theory of practical discourse. In Seyla Benhabib & Fred Dallmayr (Eds.), *The communicative ethics controversy* (pp. 151–192). MIT Press.
American Association for the Advancement of Science (AAAS) (2021). Instructions for preparing an initial manuscript. https://www.sciencemag.org/authors/instructions-preparing-initial-manuscript.
Anderson, John (1980). *Cognitive psychology and its implications.* W. H. Greeman.
Andrade, Jackie, May, Jon, van Dillen, Lotte, & Kavanagh, David (2015). Elaboration intrusion theory. Explaining the cognitive and motivational basis of desire. In Wilhelm Hofmann & Loran Nordgren (Eds.), *The psychology of desire* (pp. 17–35). Guilford Press.
Annas, Julia (2006). Virtue ethics. In David Copp (Ed.), *The Oxford handbook of ethical theory* (pp. 515–536). Oxford University Press.
Anscombe, G. E. M. (1963). *Intention.* Cornell University Press.
Apel, Karl-Otto (1980). *Towards a transformation of philosophy* (Glyn Adey & David Frisby, Trans.). Routledge and Kegan Paul.
Aquinas, Thomas (1265–1274) [1947]. *Summa theologica.* Fathers of the English Dominican Province, Trans.) (3 Vols.). Benziger Brothers.
Aristotle. *Nicomachean Ethics* (Hippocrates Apostle, Trans.). D. Reidel [1984].
Aristotle. *Rhetoric* (W. Rhys Roberts, Trans.). The Franklin Press [1981].

Atkinson, J. W. (1957). Motivational determinants of risk taking behavior. *Psychological Review*, 64(6), 359–372.
Audi, Robert (2006). *Practical reasoning and ethical decision.* Routledge.
Aydin, Ciano (2009). On the significance of ideals: Charles S. Peirce and the good life. *Transactions of the Charles S. Peirce Society*, 45(3), 422–443.
Bain, Alexander (1865). *The Emotions and the will* (2nd edition). Longmans, Green.
Bain, Alexander (1889). *Logic: Deductive and inductive.* D. Appleton and Co.
Bandura, Albert (1977). *Social learning theory.* Prentice Hall.
Bechtel, William & Richardson, Robert (1993). *Discovering complexity.* Princeton University Press.
Bell, David (2018, April 2). The powerpoint philosophe: Waiting for Steven Pinker's enlightenment. *The Nation.* https://www.thenation.com/article/waiting-for-steven-pinkers-enlightenment/.
Benhabib, Seyla (1992). Models of public space. In Craig Calhoun (Ed.), *Habermas and the public sphere* (pp. 73–98). MIT Press.
Bergman, Mats (2012). Improving our habits: Peirce and meliorism. In Cornelis de Waal & Krzysztof Skowronski (Eds.), *The normative thought of Charles S. Peirce* (pp. 125–148). Fordham University Press.
Bernays, Edward (1928). *Propaganda.* Ig Publishing.
Bernstein, Richard (1971). *Praxis and action.* University of Pennsylvania Press.
Boisvert, Raymond (1999). The nemesis of necessity: Tragedy's challenge to Deweyan pragmatism. In Casey Haskins & David Seiple (Eds.), *Dewey reconfigured: Essays on Deweyan pragmatism* (pp. 151–168). State University of New York Press.
Borradori, G. (1994). *The American philosopher: Conversations with Quine, Davidson, Putnam, Nozick, Danto, Rorty, Cavell, MacIntyre, and Kuhn* (R. Crocitto, Trans.). University of Chicago Press.
Bourdieu, Pierre (1990). *The logic of practice.* Stanford University Press.
Boyd, Kenneth (2016). Peirce on assertion, speech acts, and taking responsibility. *Transactions of the Charles S. Peirce Society*, 52(1), 21–46.
Boyer, Eric (2010). John Dewey and growth as "end-in-itself." *Soundings: An Interdisciplinary Journal*, 93(1/2), 21–47.
Brandom, Robert (1994). *Making it explicit: Reasoning, representing, and discursive commitment.* Harvard University Press.
Brandom, Robert (2000). *Articulating reasons: An introduction to inferentialism.* Harvard University Press.
Bratman, Michael (1999). *Intention, plans, and practical reason.* CSLI Publications.
Brent, Joseph (1998). *Charles Sanders Peirce: A life.* Indiana University Press.
Burnet, John (1914). *Greek philosophy.* Macmillan.
Cardinal, David (2015, April 14). Moore's law at 50: Its past and its future. *Extreme Tech.* https://www.extremetech.com/extreme/203031-moores-law-at-50-its-past-and-its-future.
Carey, Stephen (2012). *A beginner's guide to scientific method.* Wadsworth.

Ceruzzi, Paul (2003). *History of modern computing.* (2nd ed.). MIT Press.
Chadwick, G. A. (1971). *Systems view of planning.* Pergamon Press.
Cohen, Joshua (1996). Deliberation and democratic legitimacy. In James Bohman & William Rehg (Eds.), *Deliberative democracy. Essays on reason and politics* (pp. 67–92). MIT Press.
Cohen, Mark (1977). Population pressure and the origins of agriculture: An archaeological example from the coast of Peru. In C. A. Reed (Ed.), *The origins of agriculture* (pp. 135–178). Mouton.
Cohen, Mark (2002). Were early agriculturalists less healthy than food collectors? In Carol Ember, Melvin Ember, & Peter Peregrine (Eds.), *Research frontiers in anthropology. Archaeology* (pp. 3–16). Prentice Hall.
Colapietro, Vincent (1998). American evasions of Foucault. *The Southern Journal of Philosophy,* 36(3), 329–351.
Collingwood, R. G. (1946). *The idea of history* (Jan Van Der Dussen, Ed.). Oxford University Press.
Collingwood, R. G (1956). *Essays in the philosophy of history* (W. Debbins, Ed.). University of Texas Press.
Copp, David (2004). Moral naturalism and three grades of normativity. In Peter Schaber (Ed.), *Normativity and naturalism* (pp. 7–45). Ontos Verlag.
Copp, David (2009). Toward a pluralist and teleological theory of normativity. *Philosophical Issues,* 19(1), 21–34.
Copp, David (2012). Normativity and reasons: Five arguments from Parfit against normative naturalism. In Susana Nuccetelli & Gary Seay (Eds.), *Ethical naturalism: Current debates* (pp. 24–57). Cambridge University Press.
Cornford, F. M. (1932). *Before and after Socrates.* Cambridge University Press.
Crocker, David (1997). *The ethics of consumption.* Rowman and Littlefield.
Dancy, Jonathan (2004). *Ethics without principles.* Oxford University Press.
Darden, Lindley (1991). *Theory change in science: Strategies from Mendelian genetics.* Oxford University Press.
Davidson, Donald (2006). *The essential Davidson.* Oxford University Press.
Davis, G. A. (1973). *Psychology of problem solving: Theory and practice.* Basic.
Deming, David (2009). Early childhood intervention and life-cycle skill development: Evidence from Head Start. *American Economic Journal: Applied Economics,* 1(3), 111–134.
De Tocqueville, Alexis (1835). *Democracy in America* (Henry Reeve, Trans.). Pennsylvania State University.
Devitt, Michael (2011). Methodology and the nature of knowing how. *The Journal of Philosophy,* 108(4), 205–218.
Dewey, John (1915). The logic of judgments of practice. *The Journal of Philosophy, Psychology and Scientific Methods,* 12(19), 505–525.
Dewey, John (1917). The need for a recovery of philosophy. In John Dewey, et al. (Eds.), *Creative intelligence: Essays in the pragmatic attitude* (pp. 3–69). Holt.

Dewey, John (2008a). *John Dewey: The middle works, 1899–1924* (Jo Ann Boydson, Ed.). (15 Vols). Southern Illinois University Press.

Dewey, John (2008b). *John Dewey: The later works, 1925–1953* (Jo Ann Boydson, Ed.). (17 Vols.). Southern Illinois University Press.

Diamond, Jared. (1987, May). The worst mistake in the history of the human race. *Discover Magazine*, 64–66.

Diamond, Jared (1999). *Guns, Germs and Steel.* W. W. Norton.

Diamond, Jared (2002). Evolution, consequences and future of plant and animal domestication. *Nature*, 418, 700–707.

Dorris, Bruce (2018). *Report to the nations. 2019 global study on occupational fraud and abuse.* Association of Certified Fraud Examiners.

Dreyfus, Hubert (2005). Overcoming the myth of the mental: How philosophers can profit from the phenomenology of everyday expertise. *Proceedings and Addresses of the American Philosophical Association*, 79(2), 47–65.

Dreyfus, Stuart, and Dreyfus, Hubert (1980). A five stage model of the mental activities involved in directed skill acquisition. University of California, Berkeley, Operations Research Center.

Dubash, Manek (2005, April 13). Moore's law is dead, says Gordon Moore. *Techworld*, 12 (32). http://www.techworld.com/news/operating-systems/moores-law-is-dead-says-gordon-moore-3576581/.

DuPuis, E. Malanie (2015). *Dangerous digestion: The politics of American dietary advice.* University of California Press.

Dykhuizen, George (1961). John Dewey at Johns Hopkins (1882–1884). *Journal of the History of Ideas*, 22(1), 103–116.

D'Zurilla, Thomas, Nezu, Arthur, & Maydeu-Olivares, Albert (2004). Social problem solving: Theory and assessment. In Edward Chang, Thomas D'Zurilla & Lawrence Sanna (Eds.), *Social problem solving* (pp. 11–27). American Psychological Association.

Eccles, J. S., Adler, T. F., Futterman, R., Goff, S. B., Kaczala, C. M., Meece, J. L., & Midgley, C. (1983). Expectancies, values, and academic behaviors. In J. T. Spence (Ed.), *Achievement and achievement motivation* (pp. 75–146). San Francisco, CA: W. H. Freeman.

Edel, Abraham & Flower, Elizabeth (1985) [2008]. Introduction. In JoAnn Boydston (Ed.), *John Dewey: The later works* (Vol. 7) (pp. vii–xxxv). Southern Illinois University Press.

Estlund, David (1993). Making truth safe for democracy. In David Copp, Jean Hampton & John Roemer (Eds.), *The idea of democracy* (pp. 71–100). Cambridge University Press.

Estlund, David (1997). Beyond fairness and deliberation. In James Bohman & William Rehg (Eds.), *Deliberative democracy* (pp. 173–204). MIT Press.

Feibleman, James (1969). *An introduction to the philosophy of Charles S. Peirce.* MIT Press.

Festinger, Leon (1962). Cognitive dissonance. *Scientific American,* 207(4), 93–106.
Frega, Roberto (2012). The practice-based approach to normativity of Frederick L. Will. *Transactions of the Charles S. Peirce Society,* 48(4), 483–511.
Frensch, Peter & Funke, Joachim (1995). *Complex problem solving: The European perspective.* Lawrence Erlbaum.
Gauch, Hugh (2003). *Scientific method in practice.* Cambridge University Press.
Gauthier, David (1986). *Morals by agreement.* Oxford University Press.
Gibney, Elizabeth (2020, April 27). Whose coronavirus strategy worked best? Scientists hunt most effective policies. *Nature.* https://www.nature.com/articles/d41586-020-01248-1.
Glaude, Eddie (2007). *In a shade of blue: Pragmatism and the politics of Black America.* University of Chicago Press.
Goldin, Ian (2018, Feb. 16). The limitations of Steven Pinker's optimism. *Nature.* https://www.nature.com/articles/d41586-018-02148-1.
Goldman, Alvin (1970). *A theory of human action.* Prentice-Hall.
Goldman, Alvin (1983). Epistemology and problem solving. *Synthese,* 55(1), 21–48.
Gould, John (1955). *The development of Plato's ethics.* Cambridge University Press.
Gutmann, Amy, and Thompson, Dennis (1996). *Democracy and deliberation.* Belnap Press.
Habermas, Jürgen (1990). Discourse ethics: Notes on a program of philosophical justification. In *Moral consciousness and communicative action* (pp. 43–115) (Christian Lenhardt & Shierry Nicholsen, Trans.). MIT Press.
Hanlon, Aaron (2018, May 17). Steven Pinker's new book on the Enlightenment is a huge hit. Too bad it gets the Enlightenment wrong. *Vox.* https://www.vox.com/the-big-idea/2018/5/17/17362548/pinker-enlightenment-now-two-cultures-rationality-war-debate.
Hare, R. M. (1952). *The language of morals.* Oxford University Press.
Harman, Gilbert (2012). Naturalism in moral philosophy. In Susana Nuccetelli & Gary Seay (Eds.), *Ethical naturalism: Current debates* (pp. 8–23). Cambridge University Press.
Harris Poll (2013, Dec. 16). American's belief in God, miracles and heaven declines. http://www.theharrispoll.com/health-and life/Americans_Belief_in_God_Miracles_and_Heaven_Declines.html.
Harrowitz, N. 1983.The body of the detective model: Charles S. Peirce and Edgar Allan Poe. In Umberto Eco & Thomas Sebeok (Eds.), *The sign of three* (pp. 179–197). Indiana University Press.
Harvard University (2015). John A. Paulson School of Engineering and Applied Sciences. Founding and early years. http://www.seas.harvard.edu/about-seas/history-seas/founding-early-years.
Hayes, John (1979). *The complete problem solver.* Franklin Institute.
Heid, Camilla & Peck, Laura (2014). *The role of program quality in determining Head Start's impact on child development,* Department of Health and

Human Services. http://www.acf.hhs.gov/sites/default/files/opre/hs_quality_report_4_28_14_final.pdf.
Heney, Diana (2016). *Toward a pragmatist metaethics*. Routledge.
Hofmann, Wilhelm & Nordgren, Loran (Eds.) (2015). *The psychology of desire*. The Guilford Press.
Holmes, John Haynes (1915). *Is death the end?* G. P. Putnam and Sons.
Hook, Sidney (1950). The desirable and emotive in Dewey's ethics. In Sidney Hook (Ed.), *John Dewey: Philosopher of science and freedom* (pp. 194–216). Dial Press.
Hook, Sidney (1959). Pragmatism and the tragic sense of life. *Proceedings and Addresses of the American Philosophical Association*, 33, 5–26.
Hook, Sidney (1959a). John Dewey—philosopher of growth. *The Journal of Philosophy*, 56 (26), 1010–1018.
Hooker, Brad (2008). Moral particularlism and the real world. In M. Lance, M. Potrc, & V. Strakovnik (Eds.), *Challenging moral particularism* (pp. 12–30). Routledge.
Hume, David (1739) [1978]. *Treatise of human* nature. L. A. Selby-Rigge & P. H. Nidditch (Eds.). Clarendon Press.
Hunt, Bruce (2010). *Pursuing power and light: Technology and physics from James Watt to Albert Einstein*. Johns Hopkins University Press.
International Committee of Medical Journal Editors (ICMJE) (2021). Preparing a manuscript for submission to a medical journal. http://www.icmje.org/recommendations/browse/manuscript-preparation/preparing-for-submission.html.
Jackson, Frank (1998). *From metaphysics to ethics*. Oxford University Press.
Jackson, Frank (2012). On ethical naturalism and the philosophy of language. In Susana Nuccetelli & Gary Seay (Eds.), *Ethical naturalism: Current debates* (pp. 70–88). Cambridge University Press.
James, William (1890) [1950]. *Principles of psychology* (2 Vols). Dover.
James, William (1891) [1992]. The moral philosopher and the moral life. In Gerald Myers (Ed.), *Writings 1878–1899* (pp. 595–617). Library of America.
James, William. (1892) [1992]. *Psychology: Briefer course*. In Gerald Meyers (Ed.), *Writings 1878–1899* (pp. 1–444). Library of America.
James, William (1898) [1992]. Philosophical conceptions and practical results. In Gerald Myers (Ed.), *Writings 1878–1899* (pp. 1077–1097). New York: Library of America.
James, William (1907). *Pragmatism*. Longmans, Green and Co.
Jirge, Padma (2017). Preparing and publishing a scientific manuscript. *Journal of Human Reproductive Sciences*, 10(1), 3–9.
Jones, T. M. (1991). Ethical decision making by individuals in organizations: An issue-contingent model. *The Academy of Management Review*, 16(2), 366–395.
Jonsen, Albert & Toulmin, Stephen (1988). *The abuse of casuistry: A history of moral reasoning*. University of California Press.

Kahneman, Daniel (2011). *Fast and slow thinking*. Farrar Straus and Giroux.
Kant, Immanuel (1785) [1959]. *Foundations of the metaphysics of morals* (Lewis White Beck, Trans.). Bobbs-Merrill Press.
Kant, Immanuel (1793) [1949] *Theory and practice concerning the common saying: This may be true in theory but does not apply to practice*. In Carl Friedrich (Ed.), *The philosophy of Kant*. Modern Library.
Kennedy, James & Eberhart, Russell (2001). *Swarm intelligence*. Morgan Kaufmann Publishers.
Kettner, Matthias (1998). Reasons in a world of practices: Reconstruction of Frederick L. Will's theory of normative governance. In Kenneth Westphal (Ed.), *Pragmatism, reason and norms* (pp. 293–340). Fordham University Press.
Kitcher, Philip (2001). *Science, truth, and democracy*. Oxford University Press.
Kitcher, Phillip (2011). *The ethical project*. Harvard University Press.
Kitcher, Phillip (2012). *Preludes to pragmatism: Toward a reconstruction of philosophy*. Oxford University Press.
Kitcher, Philip (2014). Extending the pragmatist tradition: Replies to commentators. *Transactions of the Charles S. Peirce Society*, 50(1), 97–114.
Kitcher, Phillip (2015). Pragmatism and progress. *Transactions of the Charles S. Peirce Society*, 51(4), 475–494.
Koopman, Colin (2015). *Pragmatism as transition*. Columbia University Press.
Korsgaard, Christine (1999). *Creating the kingdom of ends*. Cambridge University Press.
Kronfeldner, Maria (2007). Is cultural evolution Larmarckian? *Biology and Philosophy*, 22(4), 493–512.
Ladd-Franklin, Christine (1916). Charles S. Peirce at the Johns Hopkins. *Journal of Philosophy*, 13(26), 715–716.
Laudan, Larry (1977). *Progress and its problems: Toward a theory of scientific growth*. University of California Press.
Laudan, Larry (1987). Progress or rationality? The prospects for normative naturalism. *American Philosophical Quarterly*, 24(1), 19–31.
Laudan, Larry (1990). Normative naturalism. *Philosophy of Science*, 57(1), 44–59.
Lippmann, Walter (1927) [2011]. *The phantom public*. Transaction Publishers.
Liszka, James Jakób (1996). *A general introduction to the semeiotic of Charles S. Peirce*. Indiana University Press.
Liszka, James Jakób (2000). Peirce's new rhetoric. *Transactions of the Charles S. Peirce Society*, 36(4), 439–476.
Liszka, James Jakób (2014). Peirce's idea of ethics as a normative science. *Transactions of the Charles S. Peirce Society*, 50(4), 459–479.
Liszka, James Jakób (2018). The problematics of truth and solidarity in Peirce's rhetoric. *Semiotica*, 2018(220), 235–248.
Liszka, James Jakób (2019). Peirce's convergence theory of truth redux. *Cognitio*, 20(1), 91–112.

Liszka, James Jakób (2021). *Charles Peirce on ethics, esthetics and the normative sciences*. Routledge.

Liszka, James Jakób & Babb, Genie (2020). Abduction as an explanatory strategy in narrative. In Tony Jappy (Ed.), *The Bloomsbury companion to contemporary Peircean semiotics* (pp. 205–234). Bloomsbury.

Locke, Alaine (1923) [2000]. Values and imperatives. In John Stuhr (Ed.), *Pragmatism and classical American philosophy* (pp. 676–686). Oxford University Press.

Locke, Alaine (1944). Cultural relativism and ideological peace. In Lyman Bruyson, Louis Finfelstein, & R. M. MacIver (Eds.), *Approaches to world peace* (pp. 609–618). Harper.

Machiavelli, Niccolo (1532) [1955]. *The prince* (Hill Thompson, Trans.). The Heritage Press.

MacIntrye, Alasdair (1981). *After virtue*. Notre Dame University Press.

Mariathasan, Michael (2015). *The butterfly effect*. Princeton University Press.

Martin, Jay (2002). *The education of John Dewey: A biography*. Columbia University Press.

Mayer, Richard E. (1977). *Thinking and problem solving: An introduction to human cognition and learning*. Scott Foresman.

McGhee, Eric, Masket, Seth, Shor, Boris, Rogers, Steve & McCarty, Nolan (2011). A primary cause of partisanship? Nomination systems and legislator ideology. http://www.princeton.edu/~nmccarty/PrimarySystems.pdf.

McLaughlin, Brian (1995). Varieties of supervenience. In Elias Savellos & Umit Yalcin (Eds.), *Supervenience: New essays* (pp. 16–59). Cambridge University Press.

McPherson, Tristram (2012). Ethical non-naturalism and the metaphysics of supervenience. In Russ Shafer-Landau (Ed.), *Oxford studies in metaethics* (pp. 205–234) (Vol. 7). Oxford University Press.

Merkl, Taryn (2019). New York's upcoming bail reform changes explained. Brennan Center for Justice. https://www.brennancenter.org/our-work/analysis-opinion/new-yorks-upcoming-bail-reform-changes-explained.

Misak, Cheryl (2000). *Truth, politics, morality: Pragmatism and deliberation*. Routledge.

Moore, G. E. (1903). *Principia ethica*. Cambridge University Press.

Moore, G. E. (1903a) [1993]. Preface to the second edition. *Principia ethica* (T. Baldwin, Ed.). Cambridge University Press.

Moore, Gordon (1998). Cramming more components onto integrated circuits. *Proceedings of the IEEE*, 86(1), 82–84.

Morrow, Glenn (1954). The demiurge in politics: The *Timaeus* and the *Laws*, *Proceedings of the American Philosophical Association*, 27, 5–23.

Morse, Donald (2001). Pragmatism and the tragic sense of life. *Transactions of the Charles S. Peirce Society*, 37(4), 555–572.

Murphey, Murray (1961). *The development of Peirce's philosophy*. Harvard University Press.

Nagel, Thomas (1970). *The possibility of altruism*. Princeton University Press.

National Eczema Association (2015). Eczema facts. http://nationaleczema.org/research/eczema-prevalence/.

Nickles, Thomas (1981). What is a problem that we may solve it? *Synthese,* 47(1), 85–118.

Nussbaum, Martha (1990). *Love's knowledge.* Oxford University Press.

Papies, Esther & Barsalou, Lawrence (2015). Grounding desire and motivated behavior. A theoretical framework and review of empirical evidence. In Wilhelm Hofmann & Loran Nordgren (Eds.), *The psychology of desire* (pp. 36–60). Guilford Press.

Pappas, Gregory (2008). *John Dewey's ethics.* Indiana University Press.

Parfit, Derek (2011). *On what matters* (3 Vols.). Oxford University Press.

Peirce, Charles (1976). *The new elements of mathematics* (Carolyn Eisele, Ed.). (4 Vols.). Mouton.

Peirce, Charles (1978). *The collected papers of Charles Sanders Peirce.* In Charles Hartshorne, Paul Weiss & Arthur Burks (Eds.). (8 Vols.). Harvard University Press.

Peirce, Charles (1982-). *Writings of Charles S. Peirce* (Max Fisch, et al., Eds.). (7 vols.). Indiana University Press.

Peirce, Charles & Jastrow, Joseph (1885). On small differences in sensation. *Memoirs of the National Academy of Sciences,* 3, 73–83.

Phillips, Deborah, Gormley, William & Anderson, Sara (2016). The effects of Tulsa's CAP Head Start program on middle-school academic outcomes and progress. *Developmental Psychology,* 52(8), 1247–1261.

Pinker, Steven (2008, Jan. 13). The moral instinct. *New York Times Sunday Magazine.* http://www.nytimes.com/2008/01/13/magazine/13Psychology-t.html?_r=0.

Pinker, Steven (2018). *Enlightenment now: The case for reason, science, humanism and progress.* Viking Press.

Plato. *The Laws* (A. E. Taylor, Trans.). In Edith Hamilton & Huntington Cairns (Eds.), *Plato: The collected dialogues.* Princeton University Press. [1973]

Plato. *The Meno* (W. K. C. Guthrie Trans.). In Edith Hamilton & Huntington Cairns (Eds.), *Plato: The collected dialogues.* Princeton University Press. [1973]

Plato. *The Protagoras* (W. K. C. Guthrie Trans.). In Edith Hamilton & Huntington Cairns (Eds.), *Plato: The collected dialogues.* Princeton University Press. [1973]

Plato. *The Seventh Letter* (L. A. Post, Trans.). In Edith Hamilton & Huntington Cairns (Eds.), *Plato: The collected dialogues.* Princeton University Press. [1973]

Puma, Michael, Bell, Stephen, Cook, Ronna & Heid, Camilla (2010). *Head Start impact study: Final report.* Department of Health and Human Services. https://www.acf.hhs.gov/sites/default/files/opre/hs_impact_study_final.pdf.

Putnam, Hilary (1992). *Renewing philosophy.* Harvard University Press.

Putnam, Hilary (1995). Pragmatism and moral objectivity. In M. Nussbaum & J. Glover (Eds.), *Women, culture and development: A study of human capabilities* (pp. 199–224). Oxford University Press.

Putnam, Hilary (2004). *Ethics without* ontology. Harvard University Press.

Rawls, John (1971). *A theory of justice*. Harvard University Press.
Reber, A. S. (2003). Implicit learning. In Lynn Nadel (Ed.), *Encyclopedia of Cognitive Science* (pp. 486–491). (Vol. 2). Nature Publishing Group.
Richardson, Henry (1997). *Practical reasoning about final ends*. Cambridge University Press.
Roberts, Debbie (2018). Why believe in normative supervenience? In Russ Shafer-Landau (Ed.), *Oxford studies in metaethics* (pp. 1–24) (Vol. 13). Oxford University Press.
Robin, Richard (1967). *Annotated catalogue of the papers of Charles S. Peirce*. University of Massachusetts Press.
Rorty, Richard (1989). *Contingency, irony and solidarity*. Cambridge University Press.
Rorty, Richard (1999). *Philosophy and social hope*. Penguin.
Rosen, Gideon (2020). What is normative necessity? In Mircea Dumitru (Ed.), *Metaphysics, meaning, and modality: Themes from Kit Fine* (pp. 205–233). Oxford University Press.
Royce, Josiah (1913) [1968]. *The problem of Christianity*. University of Chicago Press.
Rozin, P. (2007). Food choice: An introduction. In L. Frewer & H. van Trijp (Eds.), *Understanding consumers of food products* (pp. 3–29). Woodhead.
Ryle, Gilbert (1945). Knowing how and knowing that. *Proceedings of the Aristotelian Society, New Series*, 46, 1–16.
Scanlon, T. M. (1998). *What we owe each other*. Harvard University Press.
Schopenhauer, Arthur (1818) [1958]. *The world as will and representation* (E. F. J. Payne, Trans.). (2 Vols). Dover.
Schroeder, Mark (2013). *Slaves of the passions*. Oxford University Press.
Seel, Norbert (2012). Problems: Definition, types, and evidence. In Norbert Seel (Ed.), *Encyclopedia of the sciences of learning* (pp. 2690–2693). Springer.
Sebeok, T. & Umiker-Sebeok, J. (1983). "You know my method": A juxtaposition of Charles Peirce and Sherlock Holmes. In Umberto. Eco & Thomas Sebeok (Eds.), *The sign of three* (pp. 11–54). Indiana University Press.
Shafer-Landau, Russ (2003). *Moral realism: A defence*. Oxford: Clarendon Press.
Shaughnessy, Haydn (2011, March 24). Solving the $190 billion annual fraud problem: More on Jumio. *Forbes Magazine*. https://www.forbes.com/sites/haydn-shaughnessy/2011/03/24/solving-the-190-billion-annual-fraud-scam-more-on-jumio/#c876eb0390e0.
Shook, John (2003). Introduction. In John Shook (Ed.), *Pragmatic naturalism and realism* (pp. 7–28). Prometheus books.
Shorey, Paul (1965). *What Plato said*. University of Chicago Press.
Singer, Peter (2000). *Writings on an ethical life*. HarperCollins.
Singer, Peter (2009). *The life you can save. Acting now to end world poverty*. Random House.
Skinner, B. F. (1966). An operant analysis of problem solving. In B. Kleinmuntz (Ed.), *Problem solving: Research, method and theory* (pp. 225–257). Wiley.

Smith, Michael (2000). Moral realism. In Hugh Lafollette (Ed.), *The Blackwell guide to ethical theory* (pp. 15–37). Blackwell.
Stanley, Jason (2011). *Know how.* Oxford University Press.
Sun, R., Merrill, E. & Peterson, T. (2001). A bottom-up model of skill learning. *Proceedings of the 20th Cognitive Science Society Conference* (pp. 1037–1042). Lawrence Erlbaum.
Talisse, Robert (2005). *Democracy after liberalism: Pragmatism and deliberative politics.* Routledge.
Taylor, A. E. (1957). *Plato: The man and his work.* Meridian.
Tiles, James (1998). Rationality beyond deduction: A guide for the perplexed and the disappointed. In Kenneth Westphal (Ed.), *Pragmatism, Reason and Norms* (pp. 265–292). Fordham University Press.
Turner, Stephen (1994). *The social theory of practices.* University of Chicago Press.
Velleman, J. David (2000). *The possibility of practical reason.* Clarendon Press.
Vlastos, Gregory (1956). Introduction. In Plato, *Protagoras* (Benjamin Jowett, Trans.). Bobbs-Merrill.
Vlastos, Gregory (1981). *Platonic studies* (2nd ed.). Princeton University Press.
Von Wilamowitz-Moellendorff, Ulrich (1919). *Platon.* Weidmann.
Wallace, James (2009). *Norms and practices.* Cornell University Press.
Walzer, Michael (1994). *Thick and thin: Moral argument at home and abroad.* Notre Dame University Press.
Weaver, Russell & Lively, Donald (2009). *Understanding the first amendment.* LexisNexis.
Wedgewood, R. (2007). *The nature of normativity.* Oxford University Press.
Welchman, Jennifer (1995). *Dewey's ethical thought.* Cornell University Press.
West, Cornel (1999). *The Cornel West reader.* Basic.
White, Daniel (2016, Feb. 24). Nearly 20% of Trump fans think freeing the slaves was a bad idea. *Time.* http://time.com/4236640/donald-trump-racist-supporters/.
White, Morton (1949). *Social thought in America: The revolt against formalism.* Viking.
Wigfield, Allan & Eccles, Jacquelynne S. (1992). The development of achievement task values: A theoretical analysis. *Developmental Review*, 12, 265–310.
Will, Frederick (1981). Reason, social practice and scientific realism. *Philosophy of Science*, 48 (1), 1–18.
Will, Frederick (1997). The rational governance of practice. In Kenneth Westphal (Ed.), *Pragmatism and realism* (pp. 63–84). Rowman and Littlefield.
Williams, Bernard (1985). *Ethics and the limits of philosophy.* Harvard University Press.
Williams, Bernard (1993). *Moral luck.* Cambridge University Press.
World Health Organization (2016). Top 10 causes of death. https://www.who.int/gho/mortality_burden_disease/causes_death/top_10/en/.
Xenophon (371 BCE) [1994]. *Memorabilia* (Amy Bonnette, Trans.). Cornell University Press.
Yale University (1905). *Bulletin of Yale University. President's report.* First Series (4). Yale University.

Index

abduction: in case law, 96–98; and detection, 96; Peirce on, 8, 39–40, 52, 102, 103, 124, 134–135, 146; and particularism, 8, 95–98; and practical knowledge, 95–98; and pragmatic rationality, 95–98; in scientific method, 102, 103, 124, 134–135, 146
Agre, Gene, 59
agrarian society. *See* hunter-gatherer society
Alexy, Robert, 123
Annas, Julia, 73, 84
Anscombe, G. E. M., 71
Apel, Karl-Otto, 11, 116, 122, 125, 126
Aquinas, Thomas, 86
altruism: types of, 148; failures, 12–13, 55, 148–150
Aristotle, 1, 6, 7, 17, 20, 22–23, 27, 73, 83, 84–87, 91, 92–94, 98, 109; on flourishing, 22–23, 109; on *phronesis*, 6, 7, 84–87, 92–94, 98
Audi, Robert, 70
Aydin, Ciano, 44–45

Babb, Genie, 96
Bain, Alexander, 33, 78–80
Barsalou, Lawrence, 76, 78

Belief: and assertion, 117–118; Bain on, 33–44; convergence of, 51–52; and desire-belief model of conduct, 5, 71–84; fallibilism of 88–89; Hume on, 71–81; in inquiry, 117–126; methods of fixing, 41–43, 120–121; Peirce on, 33–34; in practical reasoning, 70–71
Bell, David, 156–157
Benhabib, Seyla, 129
Bernays, Edward, 122–123
Bernstein, Richard, 25–26, 44, 47, 48, 49
Boisvert, Raymond, 23–24
Boyd, Kenneth, 116
Boyer, Eric, 54
Brandom, Robert, 5–6, 11, 69–70, 72, 75, 80–83, 116, 123, 126; on intention, 5–6, 80–84; on normative pragmatics, 5–6, 80–83; on practical reasoning, 5–6, 69–70, 80–83
Bratman, Michael, 80, 83
Burnet, John, 16

categorical imperatives, 75, 82
Ceruzzi, Paul, 161–163
Chadwick, G. A., 59
Cohen, Joshua, 126
Cohen, Mark, 140–141, 143

Colapietro, Vincent, 58
Collingwood, R. G., 142–143, 145, 147, 156
community of inquiry, 10–11, 115–137; end of, 116–119; means of, 119–120; Misak on, 11, 116–117, 120, 121–122, 125–126, 127; norms of, 10–11, 42–43, 120–126; Peirce on, 39–45, 46, 117–118, 119–122, 123, 128; virtues of, 42–43, 119–120. *See also* democracy; norms; virtues
Copp, David, 65–66, 105–106, 148–149; on governance of practices, 65–66; on normative naturalism, 105–106; on the problem of sociality, 148–149
Cornford, F. M., 16
cognitive dissonance, 125–126
convergence: strong, 152; weak, 152. *See also* truth
convergence theory of truth. *See* moral truth; truth

Dancy, Jonathan, 7–8, 93–95, 99
Davidson, Donald, 33, 71, 80
Davis, G. A., 59
declarative knowledge. *See* know-that
Deming, David, 103
democracy: and community of inquiry, 11, 43–48, 121–126, 167; Dewey on, 12, 27, 43–48, 50–51; Dewey-Lippmann debate about, 12, 128–134; and epistemarchy, 11, 126–130; governance of, 47, 122, 123–124, 131–132; norms of, 120–126; political idea of, 47, 122, 131–132; and science, 47–48, 50–51, 121, 167; social idea of, 11, 12, 29, 122, 124, 126, 131–132
desire: and desire-belief model of conduct, 71–84; endorsable, 12–14, 148–150, 154–155, 166; Hume on, 45–46, 71–72, 83; motivated, 75–76; Nagel on, 75–76; Peirce on, 76–79; Scanlon on, 76; unmotivated, 75–76. *See also* desire-belief theory of conduct; externalism; internalism
desire-belief model of conduct, 5, 33, 71–84; Bain on, 78–80; Hume on, 5, 45–46, 71–81, 83; Peirce on, 76–80; Schroeder on, 72–74. *See also* externalism; internalism
De Tocqueville, Alexis, 132, 133–134
Devitt, Michael, 100–101
Dewey, John, 2, 3, 4, 7, 10, 11, 21–28, 29, 38, 43–48, 48–51, 52–53, 54, 55, 56, 57, 58, 60, 65, 76–77, 87–90, 92, 93, 102, 104, 106, 109, 110, 112, 116, 121–122, 127, 128–134, 135, 148–149, 151, 155, 156–157, 167, 168; debate with Lippmann, 12, 128–134, 167; on democracy, 4, 43–48, 121–122, 127, 130–134, 151, 167; on growth, 38, 54; on ideals, 26–27; and meliorism, 24–28, 52–53, 110, 148–149; on the role of problems, 2–3, 24–28, 87–90, 148–149; on scientific ethics, 48–51, 92, 104, 112; and the tragic sense of life, 23–25
Diamond, Jared, 140–142, 144
discourse ethics: Alexy on, 123–125; Apel on, 11, 116, 122, 125–126; coming to agreement vs. strategic communication, 122–123; Habermas on, 11, 116, 122, 125–126; Misak on, 11, 125; norms of, 123–125
Dreyfus, Hubert: on Dreyfus model of know-how, 8, 98–99, 100–101
Dreyfus, Stuart, 100–101

DuPuis, E. Melanie, 62
Dykhuizen, George, 43
D'Zurilla, Thomas, 59

Eberhart, Russell, 25
Eccles, Jacquelynn, 79
Edel, Abraham, 50
ends: of community of inquiry, 11, 116–119; empirical warrant for, 109–111; endorsable, 12–14, 148–150, 154–155, 166; flourishing, 1, 22–23, 73–74; growth, 38, 54; in-view 76, 87, 89; and practical reason, 69–71; reasonableness, 27, 44–45, 51, 160; as set by problems, 87–90. *See also* desire; goodness; goods; ideals
epistemarchy, 11, 126–134; and Dewey-Lippmann debate, 12, 128–134; principle of, 127. *See also* democracy
equality: and democracy, 11, 122–123; as norm of inquiry, 11, 123; in speech practices, 122–123
Estlund, David, 11–12, 18, 128
ethics: as collective effort, 3, 4, 6–7, 10, 13, 14, 20, 29, 47, 55, 57, 64, 83–84, 95, 115, 117–118, 151, 166, 167; discourse, 122–125; and experiments of living, 3–4, 45, 48–51, 115, 151, 157, 166–167; function of, 4, 65–66, 105–106, 148; and instrumentalism, 69–70, 72, 74, 80; and normative naturalism, 6, 8–9, 104–113; as a normative science, 7–9, 45–47, 48–51, 91–114; and particularism, 7–8, 93–98; and pluralism, 3–4, 152–154; and practical reasoning, 44–46, 69–71; role of philosophers in, 3, 19–21, 48, 168–169; subjectivism in, 72, 74, 80, 83. *See also* norms; practices; pragmatist ethics; problem-based ethics
expanding the circle: as indicator of progress, 12–14, 149–150
experiments of living, 4, 20, 115, 151, 157, 166–167; and normative science of ethics, 45, 48–51; and practices, 39, 48, 115
externalism, 5, 74–75. *See also* desire-belief model of conduct

fallibilism, 88–89, 155
Feibleman, James, 44
Festinger, Leon, 125–126
flourishing: Annas on, 73–74; Aristotle on, 22–23, 109; as highest end, 1, 23, 73–74; Williams on, 73–74
Flower, Elizabeth, 50
Frega, Roberto, 65
Frensch, Peter, 58–59
Funke, Joachim, 58–59

Gauthier, David, 73
Glaude, Eddie, 167
Goldin, Ian, 156
Goldman, Alvin, 59, 71
goodness: functional concept of, 35–39; Hook on, 21–22; James on, 19–21, 35–39; Plato on, 16–19; problems as a proxy for, 1, 6, 9, 36, 87, 109, 165; truth as, 35–39. *See also* ends; norms
goods: conflict among, 21–24; endorsable, 12–14, 148–150, 154–155, 166; highest, 1, 17, 21, 22–23, 27, 44–45, 51, 73–74, 160; primary, 149. *See also* desire; ends
Gould, John, 16, 18
governance: Copp on, 65–66; in democracy, 11–12, 47, 122, 123–124, 131–132; in higher education, 135–137; of practices, 64–68,

governance *(continued)*
  134–138; as self-correction, 12, 27, 40 115–116, 139, 163; Will on, 56, 57, 63, 64–68, 134–138
growth: Dewey on, 4, 29, 38, 50, 54; and improvement, 54; James on, 26, 53–54; as moral end, 38, 54; Peirce on, 27, 38, 53–54; and principle of continuity, 54; as process, 53–54; and progress, 54; and self-correction, 51–52

Habermas, Jürgen, 11, 116, 117, 122, 125–126
Hanlon, Aaron, 156
Hare, R. M., 109
Harman, Gilbert, 106
Harrowitz, N., 96
Hayes, John, 59
Heid, Camilla, 103
Heney, Diana, 7, 10, 94–95
Hofmann, Wilhelm, 76
Holmes, John, 78
Hook, Sidney, 2, 21–26, 52, 88; on goodness, 21–22; on role of problems in ethics, 2, 24–26; on tragic sense of life, 21–24, 52
Hume, David, 5, 45–46, 71–81, 83, 104; on belief, 71–81; on desire, 45–64, 71–72, 83; on desire-belief model of conduct, 5, 45–46, 71–81, 83; and internalism, 5, 72
Hunt, Bruce, 34
hunter-gather society: vs. agrarian society, 140–142, 143–145; and progress, 140–142, 143–145
hypothetical imperative: and practical reasoning, 85; and pragmatic maxim, 7, 9, 33–34; as a prudential norm, 9, 85; as pragmatic imperative in Kant, 33–34
hypotheticalism, 74–75

ideals: of Enlightenment, 155–157; Plato on, 15–18; pragmatists' criticism of, 1–2, 20, 22–23, 26–28, 54, 139, 165
intention: Brandom on, 5–6, 80–84; Bratman on, 80, 83; as conduct-controlling, 5–6, 80–81; and practical reasoning, 80–84. *See also* desire-belief model of conduct
internalism, 5, 72–74, 83; Schroeder's defense of, 72–74. *See also* desire-belief model of conduct; hypotheticalism
instrumentalism: of practical reasoning, 69–70, 72, 74, 80; of science, 44

Jackson, Frank, 10, 55
James, William, 3–4, 12–13, 19–21, 22, 23, 26, 48, 53–54, 56, 105, 106, 109, 115, 128, 148, 150, 153, 168; on goodness, 4, 35–39, 105, 109; on meliorism, 26, 52–54; on progress, 52–54; on tragic sense of life, 21–23, 148, 150; on truth, 4, 29, 35–39
Jones, T. M., 62, 110, 159
Jonsen, Albert, 93–94

Kant, Immanuel, 33–34, 55, 62, 74, 75, 82, 85; on categorical imperatives, 75, 82; on hypothetical imperatives, 33–34, 71, 85; on pragmatic imperatives, 33–34, 71; on definition of practices, 55
Kennedy, James, 25
Kettner, Matthias, 64–65
Kitcher, Philip, 1, 3, 12–14, 55, 59, 88–89, 92, 126–128, 133, 139–142, 147–154, 158–159, 161; on altruism failures, 55, 147–150; on endorsable desires, 12–14, 148–150, 154–155, 166; on expanding

the circle, 12–14, 149–150; on moral truth, 88–89, 151–154; and pragmatic naturalism, 55; on pluralism, 152–154; on definition of problems, 59; on problem-solving effectiveness, 157–161; on progress, 1, 3, 12–14, 139–142, 147–151

know-how, 8, 98–101, 102, 135; Dreyfus model of, 8, 98–99, 100–101; as procedural knowledge, 100

know-that, 8, 98–101, 102, 135; as declarative knowledge, 100; Dreyfus on, 8, 98–99, 100–101

know-wh, 8, 101

Koopman, Colin, 1–2, 36, 53, 57–58, 139, 168

Korsgaard, Christine, 5, 71, 75

Kronfeldner, Maria, 169

Ladd-Franklin, Christine, 31

Laudan, Larry, 91, 106–108, 119, 143–147, 148, 150, 158, 159; on normative naturalism, 106–108; on problem-solving effectiveness, 13–14, 145–147, 148, 150, 158, 159; on progress, 143–147, 148, 150, 158, 159

Lippmann, Walter, 12, 59, 108–109, 128–134; on democracy, 12, 128–130; Dewey's debate with, 11–12, 130–134, 167

Lively, Donald, 97–98

Locke, Alaine, 153–154, 168; on ethical pluralism, 153–154

Machiavelli, Niccolo, 69, 85–86
MacIntyre, Alasdair, 55–56
Martin, Jay, 43
Mayer, Richard, 59
Mayeu-Olivares, Albert, 59
McGhee, Eric, 104

McLaughlin, Brian, 109
McPherson, Tristram, 109
means: empirical warrant for, 107, 111–112; of inquiry, 11, 118–121; as practical hypotheses, 70, 107–108; in practical knowledge, 85–87, 104; in practical reasoning, 66, 74, 85–87; and practices, 66, 69, 83, 85–87, 88; righteous, 6, 10, 11, 66, 69, 74, 83, 85–87, 88, 104, 107, 108–112

meliorism: Dewey on, 23–24, 52–54, 110; James on, 26, 53–54; Koopman on, 2–3, 53, 139, 168; Peirce on, 51–52, 110; Pinker on, 155; and problem-based ethics, 24, 166. *See also* growth; progress; self-correction; tragic sense of life

Merkl, Taryn, 109–110

Misak, Cheryl, 10, 11, 116–117, 120, 121–122, 123, 125–126, 127; on community of inquiry, 11, 116–117, 120, 121–122, 125–126, 127

Moore, G. E., 8–9, 104, 105–106

Moore, Gordon, 162

Moore's law, 162

moral intensity, 62–63, 158–159

moral truth: convergence theory of, 88–89, 151–153; as enduring norms in progressive changes, 151–152; Kitcher on, 88–89, 151–154. *See also* truth

Morrow, Glenn, 16, 18

Morse, Donald, 23–24

Murphey, Murray, 59–60

Nagel, Thomas, 5, 72, 75–76, 79–80; on desire, 75–76; on desire-belief model of conduct, 75–76, 79–80

naturalistic fallacy, the, 8–9, 107. *See also* normative naturalism

Nezu, Arthur, 59

Nickles, Thomas, 59
Nordgren, Loran, 76
noncoercion: as norm of inquiry, 124–125
non-exclusion: as norm of inquiry, 124–125
normative force, 3, 5, 72, 75, 106, 113, 165; as empirical warrant, 107–114; of good ends, 108–111; of normative claims, 106–107; of practices, 83, 125–126; of prudential norms, 9, 10, 111, 125; of righteous means, 111–113; and strong modal status, 72, 73, 75
normative naturalism, 7, 8–9, 92–93, 104–113; Copp on, 106; Jackson on, 105; Laudan on, 106–107. *See also* naturalistic fallacy
normative pragmatics, 5–6, 80–84
norms: of a community of inquiry, 10–11, 116–120; of democracy, 120–126; ethical vs. technical, 61–63; of good ends, 108–111; of *phronesis*, 6, 85–87; of practical knowledge, 85–87, 107–113; of practical reasoning, 6, 45–46, 69–71, 72, 74, 80; prudential, 6, 9, 10, 11, 71, 75, 85, 105, 107–112, 119–120, 125; of righteous means, 6, 10, 11, 66, 69, 74, 83, 85–87, 88, 104, 107, 108–112; strong modal status of, 72–73; warrant for, 10, 107–114. *See also* normative force
Nussbaum, Martha, 7, 93–94; and particularism, 7–8, 93–98; Wallace's criticism of, 7, 93–94

open question, the. *See* normative naturalism

Papies, Esther, 76, 78
Pappas, Gregory, 27

Parfit, Derek, 9, 74–75, 104–106
Particularism, moral, 7–8, 93–98
Peirce, Charles, 4, 8, 10, 11, 27, 29, 30–36, 38–46, 48–49, 51–52, 53, 56, 60, 65, 71, 76–79, 80, 85, 88–89, 92–93, 95–96 102–103, 106, 107, 110, 116–118, 119–122, 123, 124, 128, 134, 146, 151–153, 161; on abduction, 8, 39–40, 52, 102, 103, 124, 134–135, 146; on assertion, 116–117; on belief, 27, 33–34, 44–45, 51, 160; on community of inquiry, 39–45, 46, 117–118, 119–122, 123, 128; on convergence theory of truth, 35–36, 51–52, 88–89, 106, 151–153; on desire, 76–79; on evolutionary love, 110; on growth, 38, 53; on intention, 80; on meliorism, 52; on practical reasoning, 71; on the pragmatic maxim, 30–35, 102, 107; on reasonableness, 27, 44–45, 51, 160; on scientific ethics, 48–49, 92–93, 102–103
Phillips, Deborah, 103
phronesis: Aristotle on, 6, 7, 84–87, 92–94, 98; norms of, 6, 85–87; and particularism, 93–98; as practical knowledge, 85–86; and practical reasoning, 84; and scientific ethics, 7, 92–93; as skill, 98–101. *See also* practical knowledge
Pinker, Steven, 61–62, 154–157; on progress, 154–157
Plato, 3, 11, 15–20, 25, 27, 28, 127–128; and epistemarchy, 127–128, 130; failed mission to Syracuse, 15–16, 25; on the good, 16–19; on ideals, 15–18
pluralism; James on, 3–4; Kitcher on, 152–154; Locke on, 153–154
practical hypothesis, 7, 8, 70, 102–104; as means in practical

reasoning, 70, 107–108; and practical knowledge, 84–87, 102–104; and pragmatic maxims, 7, 30–34; transposed from theoretical hypothesis, 7, 32–35, 44, 102, 107; truth of, 7, 102–104, 107–108. *See also* practical reasoning

practical knowledge, 8, 70, 84–87, 101, 104, 107, 118, 127, 129, 135; norms of, 85–87, 107; and particularism, 93–98; as *phronesis*, 85–87; and practical hypotheses, 102–104; and skill, 98–101. See also *phronesis*; practical reasoning

practical reasoning, 4–5, 45–46, 69–71, 72, 74, 80, 84; explanatory character of, 70–72; generic form of, 70–71; instrumentalism of, 69–70, 72, 74, 80; norms of, 6, 45–46, 69–71, 72, 74, 80; vs. practical knowledge, 84–87; and pragmatic maxim, 32–34; predictive power of, 70–71; prudential norm of, 6, 9, 10, 11, 71, 75, 85, 105, 107–112, 119–120, 125; subjectivism in, 72, 74, 80, 83; types of, 81

practices: as collective, 6, 57–58, 95, 103, 166; as constituting practical life, 4, 55; definition of, 56–57; and experiments of living, 39, 48, 115; genealogy of, 58; governance of, 64–67, 134–137; and habits, 56, 58; of higher education, 135–137; of inquiry, 11, 115–127, 151; and knowing-that, 99–101; and knowing-how, 99–101; and moral guidance, 87–88, 168; normative character of, 4–5, 6–7, 10, 60–64, 66–67, 81–84, 86, 111, 166; and normative pragmatics, 81–84; and practical knowledge, 91–102; and practical reasoning, 4–5, 6, 7, 69–70, 86; as problem-solving, 3–5, 6, 12, 13, 14, 27, 57–58, 84, 103, 112, 115, 139, 147, 157–158, 162–163, 165; and progress, 149–151, 157–158, 162–163; Wallace on, 6, 55–58, 60–64, 66–67, 80, 82, 83, 84; Will on, 56–57, 64–67

pragmatic maxim: as hypothetical imperative, 7, 9, 33–34; and Gilded Age, 34–35, 44–45; and industrial revolution, 34–35, 44–45; and instrumentalism of science, 34–35, 44–45; in Kant, 33–34, 71; Peirce on, 30–35, 102, 107; and practical reasoning, 32–34; transposition of theory to practice in, 7, 32–35, 44, 102

pragmatic naturalism, 55

pragmatic rationality, 95–98; as abduction, 95–98. *See also* abduction

pragmatist ethics, 1–14, 24–54, 87–90, 134–136, 139, 165–169; overview of, 1–14, 165–169. *See also* ethics; problem-based ethics

problems: as basis of pragmatist ethic, 1–4, 13–14, 24–28, 165–169; definition of, 58–60; Dewey on, 2–3, 24–28, 87–90, 148–149; Hook on, 2, 24–26; James on, 53–54; as moral guidance, 1–2, 87–90; motivation to solve, 2–3, 14, 27; as normative claim, 109–110; as proxy for the good, 6–7, 87–88, 165; role in warrant for good ends and righteous means, 108–114; and supervenience, 9–10, 109–110. *See also* problem-solving effectiveness; problems, type of

problems, types of: altruism, 13, 55, 148–149; anomalous, 146, 160; base, 159; common, 159; conceptual, 146–147; difficult, 160; existential, 144, 159; of flow, 38–39; functional, 38–39; growth, problems, types of *(continued)* 38–39; imminent, 159; intractable, 160; maxima and minima, 3–4, 13, 47, 48, 53–54; scalar, 159–160; sociality, 4, 13, 41, 47, 65–66, 106, 148, 159, 167; systemic, 38–39; unsolved, 160

problem-based ethics, 1–14, 24–54, 87–90, 134–136, 139, 165–169; overview of, 1–14, 165–169; roots in pragmatism, 24–28, 29–54. *See also* ethics; pragmatist ethics

problem-solving effectiveness: in computer technology, 89, 161–163; efficacy in, 13, 146–147, 150–151, 158, 161–162; Kitcher on, 157–161; Laudan on, 11, 13–14, 145–147, 148, 150, 158, 159; as measure of progress, 2–3, 14, 52–53, 139, 145–148, 157–164, 167; and practical reasoning, 69; saliency in, 13, 144–145, 150, 158–161; and scaffolding, 140, 147, 151–152, 158, 161–163; and science, 116, 145–146; and solution rate, 158; and proportion of solved problems, 158, 161, 162

procedural knowledge. *See* know-how

progress: cumulative theory of, 142–145; and the Enlightenment, 23, 155–157; and expanding the circle, 149–152; and growth, 54; vs. improvement, 147; James on, 52–54; Kitcher on, 1–2, 3, 12–14, 139–142, 147–151; Laudan on, 13–14, 143–147, 148, 150, 158, 159; as measure of moral truth, 4, 88–89, 151–152; and meliorism, 2–3, 23–24, 51–54, 110, 139, 155, 168; vs. mere change, 140–142; moral, 1, 3, 12–14, 139–142, 147–151; originary vs. teleological, 139, 149; Pinker on, 154–157; pragmatic, 1, 149; as preference for a way of life, 139–142; as problem-solving effectiveness, 2–3, 14, 52–53, 139, 145–148, 150–151, 157–164, 167; in science, 13–14, 29, 41, 52, 53, 143–147, 148, 150, 158, 159

propaganda: and democratic norms, 122–123; and strategic communication, 122

prudential norm, 6, 9, 10, 11, 71, 75, 85, 105, 107–112, 119–120, 125. *See also* practical reasoning

Puma, Michael, 103

Putnam, Hilary, 24–25, 26, 47, 51, 121–122

Rawls, John, 126, 149

reasonableness: as highest end, 27, 44–45, 51, 160; as self-correction, 27, 51

Reber, A. S., 100

Richardson, Henry, 70, 84

Roberts, Debbie, 109

Rogers, Steve, 104

Rorty, Richard, 26, 168

Rosen, Gideon, 109

Royce, Josiah, 43–44

Rozin, P., 61, 22

Ryle, Gilbert, 8, 98–100, 102; on know-how, 8, 98–100, 102; on know-that, 8, 98–100, 102

Scanlon, T. M., 5, 76, 80; on desires, 76, 80

Schopenhauer, Arthur, 23

Schroeder, Mark, 5, 72–74, 83; on the desire-belief model of human conduct, 72–74, 83

science: instrumentalism of, 44–46; as model for community of inquiry, 46–48, 50–51, 121, 167; and

democracy, 46–48; progress in, 13–14, 29, 41, 52, 53, 143–147, 148, 150, 158, 159
scientific method, 41, 48–49, 118–119, 134, 167; and democracy, 47–48, 50; applied to ethics, 7–9, 45–47, 48–51, 91–114
Sebeok, Thomas, 96
Seel, Norbert, 59
Self-correction: and governance of practices, 12, 115–116, 139, 163; and growth, 51–52; in science, 40–41; and problem-solving effectiveness, 157–158, 167; and reasonableness, 27, 51
Shafer-Landau, Russ, 9, 106
Shaughnessy, Haydn, 111
Shook, John, 48
Shorey, Paul, 16
Singer, Peter, 112–113
Skinner, B. F., 59
Smith, Michael, 105
Sociality, problem of, 4, 13, 41, 47, 65–66, 106, 148, 159, 167; Copp on, 65–66, 106, 148; Kitcher on, 13, 148. *See also* altruism failures
Stanley, Jason, 8, 99–101; on know-how, 8, 99–101; on know-that, 8, 99–101; on know-wh, 8, 99–101
strong modal status, 72, 75. *See also* normative force
subjectivism, moral, 72, 74, 80, 83
supervenience, ethical: and normative naturalism, 9–10, 109; and problems, 109–110, 111

Talisse, Robert, 10, 11, 117–118, 119, 127–128; on epistemarchy, 11, 127–128; on virtues of inquiry, 119–120
Taylor, A. E., 16
Tiles, James, 95
Toulmin, Stephen, 93–94

tragic sense of life, 20–24, 27–29; Boisvert on Dewey on, 23–24; Dewey on, 21–24; Hook on, 21–24, 52; James on, 3, 20–21, 148, 150
truth: and community of inquiry, 39–43; convergence theory of, 51–52, 88, 121–122; as end of inquiry, 44, 51, 116–118, 120; and experiments of living, 48–49; functional account of, 35–39; James on, 29, 35–39; Peirce on, 35–36, 51–52, 88–89, 106, 151–153; of practical hypotheses, 34, 39, 49, 102, 107–108; and propaganda, 122–123; and self-correction, 44–45; as species of the good, 35–39. *See also* moral truth
Turner, Stephen, 56

Umiker-Sebeok, J., 96

Velleman, J. David, 74
virtues: of authority-based communities, 42, 120; of inquirers, 4, 10, 29, 41, 42, 46, 119–120, 167
Vlastos, Gregory, 16–17, 18
Von Wilamowitz-Moellendorff, Ulrich, 16, 18

Wallace, James, 4, 5–6, 7, 10, 55–58, 60–64, 66–67, 69–70, 80, 82, 83, 84–86, 87, 91, 93–94, 100, 111, 119, 127, 153; on practical hypotheses, 102–103; on practical knowledge, 84–86, 93–94, 100, 127; on practical reasoning, 69–70; on practices, 55–58, 60–64, 66–67, 80, 82, 83, 84, 87, 91, 111, 119
Walzer, Michael, 93–94, 153
warrant: for ends, 109–111; for means, 107, 111–112; for norms, 10, 107–114; for prudential norm,

warrant *(continued)*
    9, 10, 111, 125. *See also* normative force; strong modal status
Weaver, Russell, 97–98
Wedgewood, R., 106–107
Welchman, Jennifer, 48, 49, 106
West, Cornel, 36
White, Daniel, 140
White, Morton, 104

Wigfield, Allan, 79
Will, Frederick, 8, 56–57, 63, 64–67, 90, 95–98; on governance, 63, 64–67; on practices, 56–57, 64–67; on pragmatic rationality, 95–98
Williams, Bernard, 71–72, 73–74, 85

Xenophon, 16

www.ingramcontent.com/pod-product-compliance
Lightning Source LLC
Chambersburg PA
CBHW030654230426
43665CB00011B/1082